Slow Anthropology

Cornell University

Hjorleifur Jonsson

Slow Anthropology
Negotiating Difference
with the Iu Mien

SOUTHEAST ASIA PROGRAM PUBLICATIONS
Southeast Asia Program
Cornell University
Ithaca, New York
2014

Cornell Southeast Asia Program Publications
640 Stewart Avenue, Ithaca, NY 14850-3857

Studies on Southeast Asia Series No. 64

Printed in the United States of America

ISBN: hc 978-0-87727-794-1
ISBN: pb 978-0-87727-764-4

Cover designed by Kat Dalton
Cover photograph by Hjorleifur Jonsson, reprinted with permission.

TABLE OF CONTENTS

ACKNOWLEDGMENTS

This book is the outgrowth of the time I spent with Iu Mien peoples in Portland, Oregon, and in Redding and Oakland, California, as well as with mushroom pickers in a camp in the Oregon mountains. It also draws on my research in Thailand. Above all, I am deeply indebted to the many US Iu Mien who answered my queries, welcomed me to their events, trusted me with their histories, and otherwise offered me various kindness: Longsan Tzeo, Jiem Lao Chao, Kouichoy Saechao, Kao-Jiem Chao, Kuey Seng Chao, Longtsing Tzeo, Seng Fo Chao, Tsan Tsong and Liu Ta Chao, Wan Tso Pu and Muang Chao, Susan Lee, David Lee, Muong Song and Ton Khuon Lor, Fou Vang Tang, Kao Ta Tang, Seng Ue Tang and Seng Fu Tang, Khe and Wan Lin Chao, May Saechao, Kevin Saechao, and Chaosarn Chao. In Thailand, Rathasorn Srisombat and Kittisakr Ruttanakrajangsri were helpful in 2005 and yet again in 2012, and my connection with Kittisakr goes back to 1990.

If the book is any good, then all these Mien people deserve the recognition, and I owe them in the same way that I owe my parents and teachers. What they gave me is not for an ordinary person to ever repay, but I can make an effort to be mindful, careful, and creative regarding what I gained. I use the ethnic terms "Mien" and "Iu Mien" interchangeably, as do many Mien friends, and I now find reason to also wield "Man" and "Yao" as unproblematic ethnic references in some particular contexts.

To some degree, the project started by chance in late 2005 when anthropologist Anna L. Tsing invited me to visit her research site in the mountains of Oregon. She was with a diverse group of Matsutake-mushroom pickers, including quite a few Mien people. Later I spent a sabbatical semester in Portland, Oregon, in the fall of 2007, and I returned in the summer of 2008 in the good company of Sudarat Musikawong. Since then I have made visits, when possible, to Portland, Redding, and Oakland, but those trips are less frequent than I wish.

I have many people to thank for their comments and encouragement as I worked through issues in the manuscript, especially Sudarat Musikawong, Heather Montgomery, Davydd J. Greenwood, Anne Brydon, Herbert Purnell, Nicola Tannenbaum, Jaime Holthuysen, Dolma Roder, Miguel Rolland, Graham Fordham, Tim Forsyth, Masao Imamura, Yoko Hayami, Richard A. O'Connor, Jerry Sullivan, Holly High, F. K. Lehman, Jacob Hickman, Ward Keeler, Anne Hansen, and Ken George. Several Mien friends named above also offered various helpful reactions to my writing and saved me from many blunders. Since 2002, I have several times and in various ways benefited from the hospitality, generosity, interest, and collegiality of scholars at the Center for Southeast Asian Studies, Kyoto University. Finally, two anonymous readers engaged by the publisher, Cornell Southeast Asia Program Publications (SEAP), have my lasting gratitude for how seriously they took their task. I cannot repay them for the encouragement, challenges, corrections, suggestions, and critique they provided except with a book that I hope they accept as in some way worth their time and effort.

The Editorial Board gave me free rein to revise in whatever fashion I saw fit. That complete trust allowed me to write a different style of manuscript with a whole new tone. I tinkered to make it seem like I always knew what I was doing, and, finally, Deborah Homsher and Fred Conner, of the SEAP editorial office, helped me bring the project to completion. The maps were ably made by Lee Li Kheng of the Department of Geography, National University of Singapore.

• • •

This book responds to some academic traditions and to the animosities of the Cold War. I am slowly coming to a perspective on my ultimate task and on what tools and methods are called for. I wrote the book to slow down anthropology because I want to (but cannot) slow down the world. My concern is to avoid a fruitless academic fight and to change the ways we understand anthropology and ourselves and others, regarding Southeast Asia and more generally.

In places, the book draws on some of my already published materials that are recycled here with permission (and listed, in part, below). In general there was no way for any wholesale-import of a piece, and so, instead, I have dismantled and reassembled things and erased some of my earlier academic voice, since this book is quite different from my previous vehicles. The Introduction draws some material from the following:

> "Paths to Freedom: Political Prospecting in the Ethnographic Record," *Critique of Anthropology* 32,2 (2012): 158–72;

> "Above and Beyond: Zomia and the Ethnographic Challenge of/for Regional History," *History and Anthropology* 21,2 (2010): 191–212; and

> "Cracking up an Alligator: Ethnography, Juan Downey's Video, and Irony," *Journal of Surrealism and the Americas* 6,1 (2012): 61–86.

Chapter Two draws some material from:

> "War's Ontogeny: Militias and Ethnic Boundaries in Laos and Exile," *Southeast Asian Studies* 47,2 (2009): 125–49.

Some parts of Chapter Three are based on:

> "Mimetic Minorities: National Identity and Desire on Thailand's Fringe," *Identities: Global Studies in Culture and Power* 17,2 (2010): 108–30.

For the most part, I have learned my lessons in representation from settings where I could not have any control or authority, or claim any expertise. Art curator Heather Sealy Lineberry invited me to talk on indigenous people and ethnographic representation in connection with a museum exhibition of the works of Juan Downey. I was way beyond any zone of comfort or familiarity, but as Downey (1940–93) became something of a fellow-traveler through his films, I found some intersections and some ground on which to stand. His widow, Marilys Belt de Downey, has been very kind in offering corrections and sharing information. What Heather gave me was the chance to create and share something with people who could not care less about what I knew regarding Southeast Asia. The effort helped me to loosen up a bit.

More than twelve years ago I had the able help of Michael Glowacki in making an ethnographic documentary that he filmed and edited. Having sat for some time with four hours of raw footage, I was stumped but felt I owed the Mien people a film that could bring some attention to their modern issues and to the fun of their games. Michael and I met again two years after the initial filming, talked for a long evening, and then we compiled and edited the film long-distance over a few months because we lived far apart. I started the effort as an academic, with a dense, eighteen-page script that resembled an article for a journal. In the end, Michael got me to revise down to two pages of light narrative, and he found ways of matching words and visuals for the final fourteen-minute piece.[1] Somewhere among the raw footage, the Mien peoples and their issues, Michael's work, my own ideas, and a hypothetical audience, the work finally took some shape. These were small and slow steps into a whole new way with language and imagery.

I used to write for a scholarly audience, but my pieces on Mien-related things never found much of a following. During 2006–07, I wrote and rewrote applications for research grants that did not meet with any success. I learned quite a bit from that. My plan had been to continue work in Thailand, but instead I found myself in the United States. As I was making Mien connections in the United States, I gave some people copies of my previous book on the Mien in Thailand.[2] They read it and offered me some corrections, but it did not go much beyond that. They appreciated the effort, but the angle of that book was of no real interest to them. I was very curious about this, but could not find a way to ask. The problem was not with these Mien individuals and their biases, but, rather, that I had written the book for academics, and much of that in-group's preoccupations are neither accessible nor interesting to ordinary people.

Finally, three years ago, I had the pleasure and privilege of participating in an interdisciplinary conference on human diversity in mainland Southeast Asia. It was held in Siem Reap, Cambodia, and convened by Joyce White and N. J. Enfield. I was the only cultural anthropologist amid a diverse group that included, among others, linguists, archaeologists, physical anthropologists, and bioarchaeologists. I was not the conveners' first choice but the scholar they preferred was not free and suggested me instead. It was a great conference, but I found very few intersections, because cultural anthropology withdrew many decades ago from issues of historical reconstruction and any serious areal comparisons. I think I was a total flop at that conference.

My own amazement at how my discipline was completely lacking in certain tools and angles helped bring me to the things that fill and animate this book. I would have never realized certain things without having first felt like a total failure, at the conference and on some other fronts. But I knew this feeling already from my own fieldwork, and have come to accept lingering doubts about any academic convictions. I owe the spirit of the book to "my people" and things that have happened between and among us over time: my parents and siblings, my daughters Mána and Sóley, Sudarat Musikawong, and Mien East and West.

---

[1] Hjorleifur Jonsson and Michael Glowacki, *Mien Sports and Heritage, Thailand 2001*, video, 14 min. Initially distributed in VHS format by the Program for Southeast Asian Studies, Arizona State University, the film now streams over the Internet at a Southeast Asia-focused website hosted by Andrew Walker and Nicholas Farelly, at the Australian National University. See http://asiapacific.anu.edu.au/newmandala/2008/03/27/mien-sports-and-heritage/

[2] Hjorleifur Jonsson, *Mien Relations: Mountain People and State Control in Thailand* (Ithaca, NY: Cornell University Press, 2005).

A SENSE OF WHERE WE ARE

This book is set up as a journey of several interconnected legs that are sometimes also crossed. It is as an anthropologist and a specialist in Southeast Asia and the region's highland peoples that I take off to some curious and sometimes troubled times and lands. I am passing on and trying to offer, in my areas of academic specialization, some local answers to a question fielded by C. L. R. James some fifty years ago: "What do they know of cricket who only cricket know?"[1]

Anthropology has long produced understandings that have rested on colonial and national ideologies about people as races, nations, and ethnic groups in ways that flatly deny the history, reality, urgency, and even the possibility of political negotiation. The problem is still with us. I try to change the ways in which Asian peoples and places have been our objects of knowledge: Academic certainties may be viewed as refractions of how scholars participate (unwittingly, it seems) in how their home societies deny certain peoples the possibility of negotiating toward equality and justice. That is the plot of this book; the chapters are stories that play to a human interest in imaginary journeys, history, other peoples, dramatic episodes, war, music, scholarship, and self–other understandings.

In brief, the material flows in the following order: The Introduction is largely about the worlds of academia, representation, and appropriation. Chapter One is concerned with ancient China; Chapter Two with Laos; Three with Thailand; and Four with the United States. My primary concern is with things I have learned in relation to Mien peoples past and present, and in the Afterword I try to bring out some of the implications and to tie things together in relation to anthropology, theory, and the United States. I aim in part to surprise the reader, and try to be creative in responding to some pervasive problems in my line of academic work.

Time is a fundamental ingredient in this study. I have been involved in and exposed to representations of Southeast Asia and its highlanders since my graduate school days in the late 1980s. The case draws on research exposure in Southeast Asia that goes back to 1988 in Thailand, where I have continued my fieldwork intermittently and mostly with Mien peoples. I was in Cambodia for half a year in 1992, and have been to Vietnam for several periods between 1996 and 2005. Since 2005, I have had connections and conversations with Mien peoples in the United States who are refugees from the war in Laos and who left by 1975 and later. Learning with them and from them changed my view on anthropology, ethnography, and, gradually, on everything else. The book is a serious but virgin attempt to spell out what this may mean. The effort is personal but the point is meant to be more general.

There is an often-ignored legacy of negotiation across difference in Southeast Asia. I call attention to it in part to offer some perspective on our academic mode of production. Ignoring this legacy has gone on for long enough. If we learn to identify

---

[1] C. L. R. James, *Beyond a Boundary* (Durham, NC: Duke University Press, 1983 [1963]), p. xxi.

social situations in such a way that we have no problem with discrimination, violence, or harm, then we are incapable of recognizing that there is anything wrong with such scenarios. Only by seeing ourselves as somehow in the picture and implicated will we be motivated to change this. My own work is one of the sources for a recent, well-received study of Asian highlanders that I now disagree with; I cannot pretend any innocence in the field of academic production.

Anthropology and other sciences have benefited, and even profited, from studies of particular populations within and beyond Asia. The quest for prime samples has turned Australia, the Andaman Islands, Amazonia, Papua New Guinea, Northern Thailand, and Native American reservations into sites for extraction. Primitive religion, the evolution of kinship or of society, and various other topics have motivated such research. In 2000, scandal broke out on the borderlands of American anthropology and the popular media with a book by journalist Patrick Tierney that detailed how anthropological research had brought illness and suffering on the Yanomami peoples of Brazil and Venezuela.[2] Some of the strongest claims, particularly that anthropologist Napoleon Chagnon and geneticist James Neel had brought a measles epidemic upon the Yanomami or had done nothing to stop it— because it was scientifically interesting—turn out to have no basis. But the scandal triggered controversy and created rival points of view that allowed various peoples to position themselves in a big world of high stakes and extreme language.

Already in the 1980s, Brazilian anthropologists had contacted the American Anthropological Association with strong concerns about the ethics of Chagnon's research. But only after Tierney's book appeared was there any reaction. Mostly the response led to the formation of rival sides, with Chagnon claiming to speak with the voice of science against his anti-science detractors, and the critics asserting various ethical violations regarding the collection and storing of blood samples, Chagnon's aggressive way of collecting his data, and so on. Each side could be outraged at the other. While the issue stayed at the level of outrage, there was little inclination to explore the ordinariness of negotiating the ethics of research and the production of knowledge. In Chagnon's work, the Yanomamö (his spelling) are inherently a specimen for his scientific insight and prowess; they are "fierce," and among the Yanomamö the men who successfully kill others have more wives and children ("reproductive success" in this line of analysis) than do those who don't kill.

While people may debate the analysis, it is in my view more significant that other researchers have not arrived at any similar understandings of Yanomami in Venezuela or Brazil.[3] The obviousness of the Yanomamö case collapses once the

---

[2] Patrick Tierney, *Darkness in El Dorado: How Scientists and Journalists Devastated the Amazon* (New York, NY: Norton, 2000).

[3] Alcida Ramos, "Reflecting on the Yanomami: Ethnographic Images and the Pursuit of the Exotic," *Cultural Anthropology* 2,3 (1987): 284–304; Richard Borofsky, with Raymond Hames, Kim Hill, Leda Leitao Martins, John Peters, and Terence Turner, *Yanomami: The Fierce Controversy and What We Can Learn from It* (Berkeley, CA: University of California Press, 2005). For a glimpse of Chagnon in his element and on some other things about science and the recent controversy, see José Padilha's documentary film *Secrets of the Tribe* (Watertown, MA: Documentary Educational Resources, 2010). For a different angle from some works of artist Juan Downey, see Hjorleifur Jonsson, "Cracking Up an Alligator: Ethnography, Juan Downey's Videos, and Irony," *Journal of Surrealism and the Americas* 6,1 (2012): 61–86. On what there is to learn from the controversy, I suggest works by these committed neutralists: Stephen Nugent, "The Yanomami: Anthropological Discourse and Ethics," in *The Ethics of Anthropology: Debates and Dilemmas*, ed. Pat Caplan (New York, NY: Routledge, 2003), pp. 77–95; and Peter

attention is turned to the diversity and specificity of particular peoples, communities, and histories. Land encroachment for logging and mining has exposed Yanomami and other peoples of the Amazon to dispossession, deadly violence, and disease. There are various issues with Chagnon's work, but there is also the question of its popularity. When it was first published in 1968, it received considerable attention, and in part because of films made later with Timothy Asch, the Yanomami case became a staple of introductory college courses in anthropology. This was during the Vietnam War and civil rights protests in the United States, and for some reason everyone was captivated by the case of endemic violence among "our contemporary ancestors."[4]

Chagnon's *Yanomamö: The Fierce People* has sold several million copies over the last forty years. It seems by far the most popular ethnography ever published, and we are all implicated in perpetuating the stereotype of primitive violence. One important component of the triangular relationship among Chagnon, the Yanomami, and the world of representation (where we, the readers, as the audience, come into our knowledge) is the rise of indigenous movements and their global reception. During the 1980s and early 1990s, Davi Kopenawa Yanomami emerged as a spokesman for the Yanomami peoples to international audiences. In the Western scientific and popular media, Napoleon Chagnon lashed out at him as a fraud since he spoke in Portuguese and anchored his presentations to Western environmentalist values—unlike the ostensibly real Yanomamö, whom Chagnon exclusively mediated, who were squarely local, fierce men locked in conflicts (women only count as backdrop), and monolingual.[5] I do not dwell on the Yanomami, but some material from Amazonia comes up later in the text.

There are four main components to my book; the Mien people, who are one of the ethnic minority highland peoples of mainland Southeast Asia and southern China and also now refugee immigrants in the United States and elsewhere; anthropologists and related scholars in the United States and also from France, Japan, and other countries; Asian societies, particularly China, Laos, and Thailand; and myself. I make no attempt to be exhaustive or authoritative through endless citations or a literature review regarding the peoples of Southeast Asia or studies of them. I did some of that in a previous book,[6] and now I write instead to change our academic and other terms of engagement regarding self, other, and world.

My politics responds to some self-conscious efforts, by myself and other academics, to make advances in anthropology and Southeast Asian Studies, advances that have often involved a denial of our own diversity and specificity and

---

Pels, "'Where There Aren't No Ten Commandments': Redefining Ethics during the Darkness in El Dorado Scandal," in *Embedding Ethics*, ed. Lynn Meskell and Peter Pels (New York, NY: Berg, 2005), pp. 69–99. For a discussion of learning about science from a committed neutralist, see Ian Hacking, *The Social Construction of What?* (Cambridge, MA: Harvard University Press, 1999).

[4] That term is from Napoleon Chagnon, *Yanomamö: The Fierce People*, third ed. (Philadelphia, PA: Holt, Rinehart, & Winston, 1983), p. 214.

[5] Laura Graham, "How Should an Indian Speak? Amazonian Indians and the Symbolic Politics of Language in the Global Public Sphere," in *Indigenous Movements, Self-Representation, and the State in Latin America*, ed. Kay Warren and Jean Jackson (Austin, TX: University of Texas Press, 2002), pp. 183–205.

[6] Hjorleifur Jonsson, *Mien Relations: Mountain People and State Control in Thailand* (Ithaca, NY: Cornell University Press, 2005).

our duty to serve some peoples besides ourselves. I don't point a finger at any individual scholar or institution. When people consciously make the equivalent of "a giant leap for mankind," be it to the moon or in academics or the arts, many people are left with nothing and they may even—rather than profiting—have been robbed. Many celebrated schools of anthropology rest on the absolute denial of equality to or negotiation with certain peoples who are, instead, mined for material for the purpose of advancing science.[7]

Composure and some self–other help are the only way out; the negotiation of difference is and has been fundamental to humanity in all its forms. When it is denied and scholars fail to treat other people in ways that respect their human rights, needs, and desires, or in ways that leave them with something of value, then anthropology is a self-serving obfuscation. Sometimes the emperor has no clothes. Having once been a boy, I am in a position to express it in print. But no such statement needs to be made. Rather, people need to be brought back into a world that they have been denied for a long time; one where negotiation across difference is common and commonly rewarding. With that purpose, I set out to tell some distracting stories with adult content and suggestive language: My effort requires that I take the definition and treatment of adult content and suggestive language into my own hands, because of what world we share. While I write alone, the text shows some of my company and suggests the peoples and politics I wish to serve.

I am not native to anthropology, to the United States or Thailand, or to the worlds of Mien peoples. I am a guest on all these fronts and as such I do my best to treat sensitive and other matters with respect. As a nonnative speaker in all realms, I am fascinated by what I have learned and experienced regarding language, society, culture, and various combinations of seen and unseen worlds. Perhaps I have the strongest claim to insider status in the world of anthropology. On that front, I write in response to what seems to be our failure to reach out and offer general audiences some interesting and challenging intersections. We have more or less retreated from any constructive engagement with society and write mostly for our in-group of peers. My hope is to reach a more general audience without lecturing at people.

This may seem like vanity or pomposity on my part, but the effort is born out of dire necessity: If I write only for my peers, then I must become a participant in an academic fight, or be seen to plunder my Mien friends for material that would serve me academically as it might do disservice to them. I aim to avoid the fight and to reclaim Southeast Asia and Mien realities as something to engage with, not as somewhere "remote," but as a field for coming into knowledge and identity. I call attention to how much of ethnographic and related work is a refraction of ourselves, societies, debates, and denial of our own (academic and national) society's harmful ways. Offering the hypothetical reader an angry, frustrated, or self-important book that cannot point anywhere beyond the world of books is no solution to current troubles. So, instead, I aim to entertain and to assert some grounds for establishing a measure of trust, equality, and justice.

---

[7] I aim for no self-flagellation here, but suggest instead the need for some recognition, curiosity, and, perhaps, concern. For appropriation as fundamental to advances in genetics and health care, see Rebecca Skloot, *The Immortal Life of Henrietta Lacks* (New York, NY: Broadway, 2011); and for the relationship to the progression of art-styles (-isms) that are immortalized in important museums, see Carol Duncan, *Civilizing Rituals: Inside Public Art Museums* (New York, NY: Routledge, 1995), pp. 101–130.

This is a personal book created in an academic province. It seems that we scholars are generally rather clueless about our bodies of anthropological knowledge regarding Southeast Asia and elsewhere. But defining the problem in that way also suggested a possible solution: I thus borrow and translate inspiration and motivation from a group of women who forty years ago wrote a very different book together in order to establish some familiarity with and the grounds for safety, well-being, and pleasure regarding a very different body of knowledge, being, and interaction.[8]

---

[8] The Boston Women's Health Book Collective, *Our Bodies, Ourselves: A New Edition for a New Era* (New York, NY: Touchstone, 2005). The original *Our Bodies, Ourselves* was published in 1971.

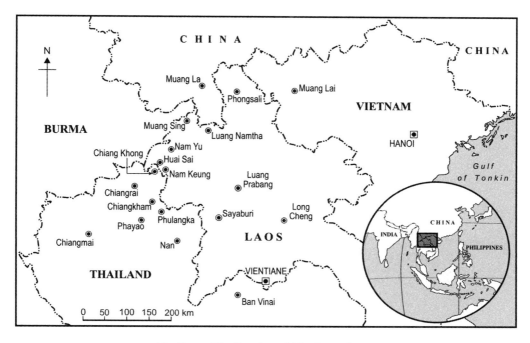

Northern Thailand and Northern Laos

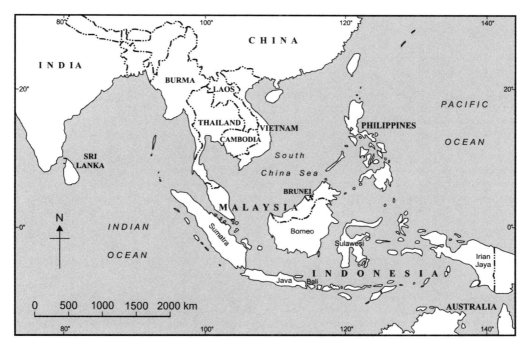

Greater Southeast Asia

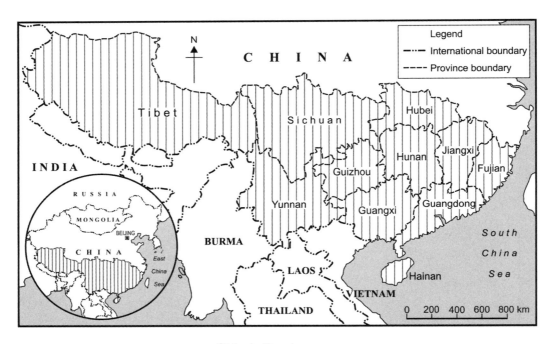

China's Provinces

INTRODUCTION

ZOMIA AND
THE WORLD OF BOOKS

James C. Scott's recent study, *The Art of Not Being Governed: An Anarchist History of Upland Southeast Asia*, argues regarding highland shifting cultivators (old anthropology's tribal peoples) that their various patterns of culture, social organization, agriculture, and religion cohered as adaptive strategies to stay outside the state's reach.[1] The book assumes a meta-history of human social evolution: With the evolution of agriculture came state structures, and with these came oppression; "the drudgery, subordination, and immobility of state subjects."[2] Scott prospects through the ruins of Southeast Asian ethnography for dramatic lessons about the world, on the assumption that states are oppressive and that this oppression's antithesis—freedom—lies in strategies of evading the state's grasp. These strategies have supposedly come to an end: The argument about highland people's strategies to evade the state "makes little sense for the period following the Second World War" because the modern nation state has the technologies "to bring nonstate peoples to heel."[3]

The label "Zomia" overrides considerable diversity of peoples, cultures, histories, and social conditions.[4] The term enables the analytical capture of all the highland regions together, in Burma, southern China, northern Thailand, Laos, Vietnam, Cambodia, and perhaps also Malaysia. Whatever diversity there has been within and among settlements, ethnic groups, subregions, societies, and different forms of economy and society are all swept away with the binary ethnology that defines highland peoples against the state. Through this analytical and descriptive strategy, history and identity emerge in a singular dynamic:

> The innumerable hill peoples of Zomia have been avoiding states for more than a millennium. It is perhaps because they have fought and fled under so many names, in so many locations, and against so many states, traditional, colonial, and modern, that their struggle lacked the single banner that would have easily identified it.[5]

[1] James C. Scott, *The Art of Not Being Governed: An Anarchist History of Upland Southeast Asia* (New Haven, CT: Yale University Press, 2009).

[2] Ibid., p. 10.

[3] Ibid., pp. xii, 78, 337.

[4] "Zomia" is derived from a self-designation by Zo or Chin peoples along the Burma–Bangladesh border. Scott drew the term from an article by geographer Willem van Schendel. Elsewhere, I show considerable difference in what world the label "Zomia" conveys, between Scott, van Schendel, and anthropologist F. K. Lehman's work on Chin (Zo); see Hjorleifur Jonsson, "Above and Beyond: Zomia and the Ethnographic Challenge of/for Regional Histories," *History and Anthropology* 21,2 (2010): 191–212.

[5] Scott, *The Art of Not Being Governed*, p. 245.

The term "Zomia" and the world it describes are two sides of the same paradigmatic coin. Highland shifting cultivation is "escape-agriculture," apparently non-hierarchical, and fluid social relations are "social structures of escape," and the alleged lack of literacy and of history typifying this group contribute to the absence of hierarchy and to an active disconnect from state structures, according to Scott. Religious prophets and "millenarian fervor [represent] an audacious poaching of the lowland ideological structure to [ward off or destroy] the states from which they are poached."[6]

This characterization is central to the mimetic productivity of the analysis, the ability to convey another reality that offers the readers a journey of discovery, through the tension between freedom and subjugation in the Southeast Asian past (on mimesis, see chapter Two):

> To stand back and take this all in, to wonder at the capacity of hill peoples to strike out, almost overnight, for new territory—socially, religiously, ethnically— is to appreciate the mind-boggling cosmopolitanism of relatively marginal and powerless people. Far from being a backward, traditional people in the presumptive grip of custom and habit, they seem positively protean (even Californian) in imagining themselves anew.[7]

Scott's analysis proceeds in the manner of adaptationist arguments to characterize apparently exotic practices in terms of effects that seem rational to Western readers.[8] The whole analysis hinges on two notions: the state is oppressive, and sedentism entails subjugation. Mobility, "the bedrock of popular freedom,"[9] accounts for the absence of revolt or other violent reaction to ostensibly pervasive oppression. This assumption lends sense to the data as it inspires its collection.

The highland people flee state contact, based on "ethnic and tribal identities [which] have been put in the service not merely of autonomy but statelessness"— ethnic labels are simply manifestations of the political project of avoiding the state. Ostensible Zomians had "a mixed portfolio of subsistence techniques [which yielded] a mixed portfolio of social structures that [could] easily be invoked for political and economic advantage."[10] Radically culturally-other Asian shifting cultivators of the past appear inherently familiar to educated Western readers once their alleged tradition and lack of progress have been redefined as strategies to gain and retain freedom from taxation and other sorts of oppression.

Zomia can be understood without any familiarity with Southeast Asian peoples, languages, places, or histories. Scott's analysis of the Southeast Asian hinterlands until about 1950 is a representation, one that allows the readers to come into a sense of self, other, and world in a single move. The effort is for the exclusive benefit of Scott's readers, who have come to rely on his books to situate themselves in the world through notions of peasants, moral economies, hegemony and resistance, weapons of the weak, state simplifications, and now state evasion. Books, on this front, may be for some people what clothes are for some others; they enable a person

---

[6] Ibid., pp. 190, 207, 220–27, 322.

[7] Ibid., p. 315.

[8] Marshall Sahlins, *Culture and Practical Reason* (Chicago, IL: University of Chicago Press, 1976).

[9] Scott, *The Art of Not Being Governed*, p. 33.

[10] Ibid., pp. 244, 238–82, 211.

to make an imaginary match and then declare that "this is *so me*" or "*so not me*." In my reading, the Zomia book offers no intersections for Southeast Asia and its peoples—the histories that produced freedom came to an end with the greater capacities for control that became available to states soon after the Second World War, so as readers we can forget the Asians in the picture except as relics.

Who and what we think are the highland peoples of mainland Southeast Asia has quite a lot to do with how we imagine ourselves and the world. Knowing the world or any part of it is always tied in part to an understanding of self, self–other differences and relations, and of the world that frames them. Thomas Kuhn's *Structure of Scientific Revolutions* centered on the key role of paradigmatic assumptions for the practice of science. Paradigms define key components of the universe and how one engages with them. To clarify his case, Kuhn draws the analogy of a child who first applies the term "mama" to "all humans [and then restricts it] to all females and then to his mother." The child:

> is not just learning what "mama" means or who his mother is. Simultaneously he is learning some of the differences between males and females as well as something about the ways in which all but one female will behave toward him. His reactions, expectations, and beliefs—indeed, much of his perceived world— change accordingly.[11]

The hypothetical boy's mama informs an understanding of the world through distinctions that are constitutive of relations, identities, and the meaning and composition of the universe. This happens all in a single move, as a person learns and acts and engages with the world—it refers not to an event but to the process of life. Concepts and relations influence and mark traffic between different realms. Paradigms imply the ontology of the world that is studied by science; theory and description are in all normal settings about the same thing. If paradigms imply not only fields of interaction but also traffic between different realms of reality, then attempting a definitive notion of paradigms may be counterproductive. As Johan Huizinga comments regarding another notion: "A technical term like *potlatch*, once accepted in scientific parlance, all too readily becomes a label for shelving an article as filed and finally accounted for."[12]

Thomas Kuhn allows considerable uncertainty regarding what world is implied in our understandings: "There is, I think, no theory-independent way to reconstruct phrases like 'really there'; the notion of a match between the ontology of a theory and its 'real' counterpart in nature now seems to me illusive in principle." Furthermore, "the normative and the descriptive are inextricably mixed. 'Is' and 'ought' are by no means always so separate as they have seemed."[13]

This analogy between learning a science and becoming a person by absorbing how concepts imply relations and categories, including those of gender, kinship, and generation, is quite similar to how anthropologists have characterized the dynamics of culture and enculturation. The world we know and describe or analyze is always

---

[11] Thomas Kuhn, *The Structure of Scientific Revolutions* (Chicago, IL: University of Chicago Press, 1970 [1962]), p. 128.

[12] Johan Huizinga, *Homo Ludens: A Study of the Play Element in Culture* (Boston, MA: Beacon Press, 1950), p. 62.

[13] Kuhn, *The Structure of Scientific Revolutions*, pp. 206–7.

tinged with where we are, what we can imagine, and things we wish for. But we in anthropology do not generally confess to desire and playfulness in our work. Vincent Crapanzano suggests that in cases when cultural anthropologists and other scholars have assumed an ironic analytical stance in recent decades, their posture has generally been "masked by a moralistic seriousness."[14]

Any answer to questions of who are the peoples of Southeast Asia and how we know, comes down to where a scholar situates herself, at home, away, and between them. The two basic choices are a) outside and in control, safe in one's expertise, and b) inside and implicated in interaction and negotiation, and answerable to whatever comes of the work. Within the former, subject–object distinctions are clear and a scholar–subject has an object of knowledge to mediate. In the latter, subject–object distinctions must be confused and exchanged to guard against appropriation. Instead of grasping an object of knowledge, the attention shifts to fields of interaction and the implications of different bases of knowledge—epistemes and the relations that surround them.

Anthropology has developed a curious relationship to its readers through its studies of the ethnic minority hinterland peoples of mainland Southeast Asia. For both anthropologists and the colonial administrators of French Indochina (Vietnam, Laos, and Cambodia), the idea of race provided an organizing principle for arranging a reality that was seen as somewhat disorderly. The French colonial-era ethnographer Henri Roux brings out some of the reality that colonials were up against:

> The Laotians use the derogatory term Khas ["slaves"] for all those who the Annamites [Vietnamese] call Moi ["savages"] or Nguoi Rung ["forest people"]. Because of this, different races, the Kha Khmus who resemble the Austronesian race and the Kha Ko who resemble the Chinese, are indistinguishably called Kha. This also extends to the Kha Lao who are Lao or Lu and are thus Thai and possess the language and clothing, but whom the Laotians refuse to recognize as their brothers for the simple reason that they have left the plains for the mountains and are also poor.[15]

Planetary consciousness, the lure of riches, and a deluded sense of their own grandeur brought the French to what they then called Indochina. This became a project for which they felt uniquely suited or even chosen. I refuse the moral high ground of the-French-did-x-and-I-will-assess-it. There is no such thing as "the-French"; the abstract term is illusory and should be turned around in a critical examination of how the colonial project informed a particular shaping of "the-French" at home as much as in Indochina and in scholarship. Comparing myself to the French with their classifications, I may (without notice) insert myself, with any definition, as the principle of the landscape—this I cannot really tell and obviously not prove, but the recognition makes me watch my steps in some new ways.

The notion of the-French was given both shape and substance through what people did and how their projects structured social life. The colonial project created

---

[14] Vincent Crapanzano, *Hermes' Dilemma and Hamlet's Desire* (Cambridge, MA: Harvard University Press, 1992), p. 317, note 1.

[15] Henri Roux, "Deux tribus de la region de Phongsaly," *Bulletin de l'Ecole Française d'Extrême Orient* 24 (1924): 373, my translation.

the intersection that made the French, in a way, rather than the French having had or run a colonial project: This was the yeast that leavened the baguette-dough and lent it particular energy and shape. Racial and ethnolinguistic classification facilitated a particular way of engagement and control; the theory enabled the production of the-French-and-their-others.[16] Henri Roux saw the divergence between social life and what he expected of groups marked (for him) by race and ethnicity, and he was certain that the locals just got things wrong: Racially related peoples should recognize their fraternity even if some were in the lowlands and others in the mountains. Given the French national identifiers of liberty, equality, and fraternity, it seems that Roux wanted the colony's natives to recognize their fraternity along racial lines, while as one of the-French he reserved liberty, equality, and perhaps elite fraternity for his own kind.

Many of the colonial-era expectations regarding races and their differences resurfaced in anthropological work that was based on notions of culture, social structure, kinship, and the like. This issue should be profoundly embarrassing. It is my intent to hold on to this discomfort in order to push for an anthropology that is more mindful of its steps. Practitioners should try to undo and counter some of the reckless appropriation of others' lives, stories, and identities for projects of scholarly achievements and factionalism that brush aside questions of the politics of producing knowledge through representations of social life.

Mary L. Pratt identifies and contextualizes the "planetary consciousness" that accompanied colonial-era scientific discoveries and exploration. Various expeditions and conquests drew on the reconfiguration of science, society, and transnational connections. Naming was claiming and dispossession in the same move. Scientific classification and discovery implied complete disconnect from any local names, signification, and relationships. Giving plants Latin names made this dynamic seem distinct from the rivalries among various European nations that competed for prominence and glory through their conquests-as-discoveries.[17]

The realm of nature belonged to science, while knowledge, science, and conquered domains belonged to particular nations; collaboration and any local significance systemically disappeared. There are various slippages between the universalism of a planetary consciousness and the exclusive ownership by colonial-era nation states. Pratt focuses on the complex context of literature (nature, travel, ethnography, etc.) about Latin America and Africa, and the dynamic of dispossession that she describes is analogous to what was played out on the overlapping zones of conquest, subjugation, science, discovery, and nation building in North America and in various parts of Asia.

In the accounts of colonial-era explorers from the northern parts of mainland Southeast Asia, there is frequent reference to the changing fortunes of different "races" over time, which explained the then-contemporary social landscape of colonial rule that was often not addressed. One example comes from Holt Hallett, a British explorer:

---

[16] This is a vast topic. For starters, see Daniel J. Sherman, "Peoples Ethnographic: Objects, Museums, and the Colonial Inheritance of French Ethnology," *French Historical Studies* 27,3 (Summer 2004): 669–703.

[17] Mary L. Pratt, *Imperial Eyes* (New York, NY: Routledge, 1992), pp. 15–37.

The Kha [highland peoples] are doubtless the aborigines of [the northern regions of Thailand and Laos]. They are supposed to have been ousted from the plains and driven into the hills by hoardes of Laos, an eastern branch of the Shans, migrating from [northern Vietnam] when it was conquered by the Chinese about BC 110.[18]

Colonials naturalized their presence through references to the long run of regional history, which they pictured as having been shaped by the uneven power of different races. This colonial inscription of history simultaneously wiped out any trace of the social and historical ruptures involved in the racial structuring of colonial encounters and routines. Colonial-era Western observers also commented on some local authorities they found unfit to rule. Examples include the missionary Lillian Johnson Curtis, who remarked that "the ruling class of [northern Thailand] have a dignity and refinement of manner that would be for them a passport into the elegant society of any capital city," but adds that "they are a selfish, self-seeking class and have not the interest of their people at heart … The parasitical life of the [rulers] is the cause of a state of stagnation."[19] This commentary on unworthy rulers—authorities who stood in the way of industriousness and profit—was written in the context of colonial takeovers of all of Siam's neighboring states: Vietnam, Laos, Cambodia (by France), Burma, and Malaya (by the British Empire). It was not simply Orientalist rhetoric. Rather, it was embedded in a hegemonic framework that combined violence, commerce, and ideas of modernity in a systemic delegitimation of previously common tributary schemes.

While colonial takeovers in the region were often violent, Western writers tended to depict colonial rule and capitalist economic relations as a blessing. One explicit example is Francis Garnier's account of the French exploration of the Mekong River in 1866–68, where he remarks that the local peoples in northern Thailand and Laos had experienced much warfare from the incursions of Burmese and Thai forces: "The locals deeply desired a less violent state of affairs, more regular and stable, and this aspiration, which was general, would be singularly favorable to the attempts of a European power, should it interest itself in the affairs of the region."[20] Within three decades of this account, French colonial authorities ruled all of Laos, Cambodia, and Vietnam. They made moves against Siam, too; it is not as if the French had any sense of restraint except when dealing with the British and the Dutch, who ruled the other colonies in the region.

Most likely these colonial-era authors were blissfully ignorant of how their expectations of inequality informed their characterizations, in the same way that "classical" anthropology later took for granted its definitions of ethnic groups, with their particular respective cultures, social structures, and so on. But what knowledge do we currently have of Southeast Asia, now that we are no longer seeking to find the remnants of traditional people, whose lives supposedly represent the opposite of our modernity?

---

[18] Holt Hallett, *A Thousand Miles on an Elephant in the Shan States* (London: William Blackwood & Sons, 1890), p. 21.

[19] Lillian Johnson Curtis, *The Laos of North Siam* (Bangkok: White Lotus, 1998 [1903]), pp. 122–23.

[20] Francis Garnier, *Further Travels in Laos and Yunnan, 1866–1868*, trans. and intro. Walter E. J. Tips (Bangkok: White Lotus, 1996), p. 56.

It is received knowledge that hinterland peoples are marginalized minorities. This notion replaced the "ethnic groups" of earlier anthropology, and allowed for Western academics to take a self-consciously critical stance through epistemology; whoever held up "marginalization" was on the side of the people and equality against the forces of oppression. The episteme—marginalized minority groups— offers conviction by category and by mimetic identification with one side of an antagonistic binary. My interest lies in offering an alternative, as the epistemology of Zomia (unwittingly) accepts particular state projects as descriptions of reality in order to offer critical credentials to readers who may know nothing of the languages, peoples, or histories of Southeast Asia.

The examples of highland peoples evading the state all come from situations where ordinary political relations across difference have broken down. One key scenario is contemporary Burma, which has been locked in an ethnicized civil war for decades. Scott calls attention to "hiding villages" of Karen peoples in the forests, where people try to escape notice from rival armies, as an effort that exemplifies the conditions of Southeast Asian highlanders for the last two millennia. In my view, this is a tenuous claim regarding historical continuity.[21] One parallel to the Burmese situation is Laos, where there were anti-government militias in hiding from 1975 and until very recently. In both settings, government forces were actively trying to capture and defeat rebel units.

I contend that these cases are not general and that the situation has little or no bearing on the long-term shape of Southeast Asian history or society. Vietnam supplies another scenario for checking the obviousness of the case for Zomia. Scott cites several campaigns from the 1950s and 1960s, such as the "Campaign to sedentarize the nomads" and "Clear the hills by torchlight," among others. Without any historical contextualization, these projects may indicate what the state is up to. But these were modernization campaigns that have no connection to earlier centuries, and instead drew some of their enthusiasm from an unfamiliarity and mistrust between the northern communist nationalists and lowland southern Vietnamese, on the one hand, and the ethnically diverse Central Highlanders on the other.[22]

These cases are not typical for Southeast Asia in the past, and draw instead on militarized nation building of the kind initiated in 1950. This issue is somewhat intriguing, as the whole case is pitched as if it were a valid image of the region up until 1950 and not thereafter. The credibility of the case for Zomia draws on how Scott's examples resonate with his readers' expectations of the state and history. If the state is expansionist and predatory, then the case holds; if not, then the case may fall apart. I suggest that Scott's case for Zomia normalizes politically pathological situations.

---

[21] For anyone wishing for a well-grounded understanding of modern Burma (Myanmar), see Mary P. Callahan, *Making Enemies* (Ithaca, NY: Cornell University Press, 2003).

[22] Scott's knowledge of this part of Vietnamese history draws on the important work of Patricia Pelley, *Postcolonial Vietnam: New Histories of the National Past* (Durham, NC: Duke University Press, 2002). Her concern was, in part, with the incongruities and misinformation in the official historical and ethnological record of postwar Vietnam. Indeed, Scott takes issue with the incongruities and misinformation of any and all states' historical and ethnological record, so to speak. Donning the public-spirited mantle of the London Underground railway system, I suggest that readers "mind the gap" between their own platform and different trains of thought.

It would be shortsighted and self-serving to argue against James Scott's book on the Asian hinterlands as if it were a singular case; the analytical tone of the work is widely shared, and he built his case on what other scholars had been writing over several decades. Our studies of what politics and identities are possible in Southeast Asia, which inhere in the ethnologies we construct for that region, imply what politics and identities we can imagine in our home societies and how we come to a sense of our selves. To a considerable degree, the resonance of the case for the readers rests on a shared epistemology or ontology regarding a fundamental antagonism between individuals and the state or "society":

> The man in the street still thinks in terms of a necessary antagonism between society and the individual. In large measure this is because in our [US American] civilization, the regulative activities are singled out, and we tend to identify society with the restrictions the law imposes on us. The law lays down the number of miles per hour that I may drive an automobile. If it takes this restriction away, I am by that much freer. The basis for a fundamental antagonism between society and the individual is naïve indeed when it is extended as a basic philosophical and political notion.[23]

My goal is to break the ethnological spell that the Zomia discovery offers, because it suggests nothing but subjugation for Southeast Asians as it celebrates bourgeois and academic privilege and disconnection at home in the West. Scott's book gives me somewhere to point, but I suggest that my own work and that of many other anthropologists, historians, and political scientists is involved. Thus the effort is not to wave at James Scott some yellow or red card as would a referee in response to a soccer player's transgression on the field. Rather, I take advantage of how his analysis exposes the priorities of anthropology about Southeast Asia and its hinterlands as aimed exclusively for Western scholars and their readers, and not in any way conceptualized for the benefit of anyone in Southeast Asia.

HISTORY'S META-FORCE/METAPHORS

As a key concept in a historical study, James Scott's Zomia may be placed alongside cases that Hayden White examined for nineteenth-century European history and historiography. White's monumental study draws its strength from the formalism of the analysis. History, White suggests, is variously plotted in romantic, tragic, comic, or satirical modes, the cases are argued in formist, mechanistic, organistic, or contextualist modes, and the ideological implications range among anarchist, radical, conservative, and liberal. White's study chases after tropes and literary styles, but it may not lead anywhere beyond the world of books. In his conclusions, White calls attention to diversity; that there are at least four equally plausible interpretive schemes for history, which are equally "consistent with the types of linguistic protocols sanctioned by the dominant tropes of ordinary speech."[24] Were I to fit James Scott's study in one or more of Hayden White's tropic boxes, the flagging of anarchism (Scott's subtitle is "an anarchist history") would present an interesting typification. According to White:

---

[23] Ruth Benedict, *Patterns of Culture* (Boston, MA: Houghton Mifflin, 1934), p. 252.

[24] Hayden White, *Metahistory* (Baltimore, MD: Johns Hopkins University Press, 1973), p. 28.

Anarchists are inclined to idealize a remote past of natural human innocence from which men have fallen into the corrupt "social" state in which they currently find themselves. They, in turn, project this utopia onto what is effectively a non-temporal plane, viewing it as a possibility of human achievement at any time, if men will only seize control of their own essential humanity, either by an act of will or by an act of consciousness which destroys the socially provided belief in the legitimacy of the current social establishment.[25]

The credibility of the case that defines the Southeast Asian highlands as "Zomia" draws on a sense of history that is common among educated Westerners. James Scott and many other scholars point to the work of Fernand Braudel as an inspiration for regional historical visions. French historian Braudel clearly asserts a particular metahistory, positing a historical dynamics fueled by a lowland and urban force field that is rendered visible in part by its absence from highland areas. His characterization of a "highland world" in the Mediterranean region is worth some examination:

> *Mountain freedom.* There can be no doubt that the lowland, urban civilization penetrated to the highland world very imperfectly and at a very slow rate. This was as true of other things as it was of Christianity. The feudal system as a political, economic, and social system, and as an instrument of justice failed to catch in its toils most of the mountain regions and those it did reach it only partially influenced. The resistance of the Corsican and Sardinian mountains to lowland influence has often been noted and further evidence could be found in Lunigiana ... This observation could be confirmed anywhere where the population is so inadequate, thinly distributed, and widely dispersed as to prevent the establishment of the state, dominant languages, and important civilizations ... It is only in the lowlands that one finds a close-knit, stifling society, a prebendal clergy, a haughty aristocracy, and an efficient system of justice. The hills were the refuge of liberty, democracy, and peasant "republics."[26]

The historian K. N. Chaudhuri applied the Braudelian structural perspective to Asia "before Europe." His rendering of the highland peoples engaged in shifting cultivation is worth noting, for it projects history's flows in a striking manner:

> The system of shifting cultivation was essentially a common response of man to a particular environment. Under the system of shifting tillage, the density of population must have remained very low. A situation of chronic underpopulation and an abundance of forest land justified the survival of swidden culture through the centuries.[27]

Chaudhuri projects a historically inert setting where no forces seem at work, and where a persistent lack of (population) pressure is coupled with an abundance of

---

[25] Ibid., p. 25.

[26] Fernand Braudel, *The Mediterranean and the Mediterranean World in the Age of King Philip II* (New York, NY: Harper & Row, 1972 [French orig. 1949]), pp. 38, 40.

[27] K. N. Chaudhuri, *Asia before Europe* (Cambridge: Cambridge University Press, 1990), p. 220.

basic (re-) productive resources: land. This formulation resembles that in Plato's *Laws* from two thousand years earlier, where the few and isolated mountain peoples, in their "[naïve simplicity,] weren't compelled by poverty to differ with one another."[28]

Anthony Reid's regional history of Southeast Asia on the eve of colonial encounters is much indebted to Braudel's perspective.[29] The work only mentions highland peoples in passing, suggesting that they are marginal to the historical dynamics of the region. Victor Lieberman's historical study of mainland Southeast Asia in comparison with Europe makes a few passing references to Southeast Asia's "hill peoples" with unfamiliarity and disinterest that should by now be recognizable:

> Between Shan valleys the mountain tracts inhabited by illiterate Chins, Kachins, Karens, Palaungs, and so forth escaped Burman political control entirely by virtue of their poverty, inaccessibility, and the fragility of their supra-village organizations. [In some cases, upland chiefs drew on lowland political and social models] to construct proto-statelets and to magnify internal stratification.[30]

It is a common notion in Southeast Asian scholarship that the highland regions only became integrated with the lowlands in the era of the modern nation state. Prior to that, states were not concerned with borders and "the tribal people wandering in the mountain forests were subjects of no power."[31] This and many similar notions reinforce an academic near-consensus on the nation state as territorial in ways that its precursors were not. Together, these studies project certain urban and state-biases into their ethnologies—the social landscape. History pertains to the lowlands, to rulers, armies, peasants, and traders. Thongchai Winichakul is not concerned with that history in his critical study of the role of mapping for the consolidation of modern Thailand. But as he depicts the growing tentacles of nation-state control against a historical backdrop, he reproduces the familiar imagery of highland people's fundamental isolation and separation from the region's dynamics of society and history.

Were highland peoples or settlements poor, inaccessible, socially inert, and remote, subjects of no (outside, lowland, political) power during the long run of Southeast Asian history, or freedom-seekers who were ultimately "brought to heel" (in Scott's terms) by the modern nation state? The notion of bringing somebody to heel—a phrase used by Scott, as noted above—suggests wild horses or other such creatures with whom no communication is possible. The imagery of highland remoteness and isolation does not describe highland conditions or the character of highland communities. Instead, it establishes a historical and social rupture that enables the readers to know the (nation-) state, Southeast Asia, politics, history, the world, and themselves, all in one move. Highland peoples, as Zomians or otherwise,

---

[28] Thomas L Pangle, trans., *The Laws of Plato* (New York, NY: Basic Books, 1980), p. 61.

[29] Anthony Reid, *Southeast Asia in the Age of Commerce, vol. 1: The Lands below the Winds* (New Haven, CT: Yale University Press, 1988); and Anthony Reid, *Southeast Asia in the Age of Commerce, vol. 2: Expansion and Crisis* (New Haven, CT: Yale University Press, 1993).

[30] Victor Lieberman, *Strange Parallels: Southeast Asia in Global Context, c. 800–1830, vol. 1: Integration on the Mainland* (Cambridge: Cambridge University Press, 2003), pp. 208–9.

[31] Thongchai Winichakul, *Siam Mapped: The History of the Geo-body of a Nation* (Honolulu, HI: University of Hawaii Press, 1994), pp. 73–74.

serve as a prop for establishing the coordinates of history, region, politics, and the world for particular educated Western selves.

This issue is common in relation to anthropology's marginal peoples. Adam Kuper's study of anthropology's many others, *The Invention of Primitive Society*, explored how notions of primitives played to Western speculations about its opposite, modern society, and how the notion informed nineteenth-century debates about society, family, and evolution:

> The idea of primitive society fed the common belief that societies were based either on blood or on soil, and that these principles of descent and territoriality may be equated with race and citizenship, the contrasting components of every imperialism and every nationalism. [But] while it could serve so many ideological purposes, it could at times also serve none.[32]

Kuper's work reads as if he were something of an Enlightenment rebel, and includes a promise to an academic in-group: "My aim has been to free us from some of our history by making one particular tradition explicit and demonstrating the way in which it has held us in its grip [as it went into the obscure realm of kinship theory]. If we liberate ourselves we may also be able to free others."[33] Kuper shows that the notion of primitive society was often used for ideological purposes but that this was not uniform. But such ethnologies enable readers to arrive at particular senses of the world, in ways that involve traffic among three often-distinct worlds: those of field sites whence observations or descriptions are derived; academia, the world of books and articles and their readers; and the home societies of the academics and their audiences.

The study of Zomia asserts a novel discovery—that Southeast Asia's highland peoples were freedom-seekers who held out as long as they could. What some of us had taken for traditional culture, social structure, religion, and agricultural methods was clouded in ideological illusions projected by agents of state control and assimilation. Until James Scott called attention to Zomia, none of us had realized that it was the quest for freedom that created the category of Asian highland peoples. In some oblique way, Scott is suggesting the same as what Adam Kuper declares: If by reading a particular book we liberate ourselves from particular Western academic or social illusions that draw on evolutionism and state projects, then perhaps we may become free and later this freedom may spread outside the narrow in-group enabled by the text.

In academic books as much as in tourism and elsewhere, Asian highland peoples sometimes serve as props for Western self-, other-, and world-realization. The ostensible Zomians are a case of retrospective prospecting, as the real ones are said to have expired at least sixty years ago. Thus we, the Western readers, come into our identity and political position through an imaginary composite character, the Zomian, who is killed (made extinct) for the purpose of our own animation. This is a representation and an invitation to play, while the aura of academic learning and the books in that realm tend to assume objectivism, moral seriousness, and the antithesis of play, desire, or fantasy:

---

[32] Adam Kuper, *The Invention of Primitive Society* (New York, NY: Routledge, 1988), p. 9.

[33] Ibid., p. 243.

The state was tyrannical, but episodically so. Physical flight, the bedrock of popular freedom, was the principal check on state power. [Subjects] who were sorely tried by conscription, forced labor, and taxes would typically move away to the hills or to a neighboring kingdom rather than revolt.[34]

This analytical and descriptive premise sets Southeast Asian history in motion and animates the ethnology—the account of what kinds of people there are in the region and what can happen to them through interaction. As a dramatic narrative, the story of Zomia sets history and ethnology in motion with a beginning (sedentism, oppression, and flight), middle (strategies of state avoidance), and an end (successful subjugation by the end of the Second World War), through which a reader can see herself in the world as the lessons from Zomia are transplanted.[35] The assumed equivalence between Southeast Asian pasts and the modern Western present enables the reach and relevance of the case. Perhaps more than half of those who read Scott's *The Art of Not Being Governed* are Western university students, who are assigned the book by their professors … that is, their lessons in freedom are learned if not under duress then certainly under constraints of time, inequality, and exams in institutional settings.

The Zomia case may refract a version of the hundred-year-old American Frontier hypothesis that is identified with Frederick Jackson Turner and asserts that "living in the wilderness fostered individualism, independence, and confidence in the common man that encouraged self-government. [Turner linked wilderness] in the minds of his countrymen with sacred American virtues."[36] Any such representation is never simply the work of an individual but is also of a historical moment and draws on complex traffic across cultural and other differences.[37] And as Hayden White's study of history and historiography suggests, any one book of history may offer a perspective that stands as an alternative to a range of equally plausible other works. Any such study can offer coordinates for identity-work among educated Westerners, where the identities of liberals, conservatives, radicals, anarchists, and so forth are all potential and may derive some of their attractiveness based on a person's choice to identify with or against each type.[38]

One of the sources for the dramatic plot in *The Art of Not Being Governed* is French anthropologist Pierre Clastres's book, *Society against the State*, about Latin America, particularly his "daring interpretation of state-evading and state-preventing native peoples."[39] This binary interpretation that pits the pure natives against the alien and oppressive state enables political identification across difference; the state is essentially the same anywhere, a machine of taxation and subjugation—anti-freedom. Regarding Scott's thesis, the contrast between Zomians and the state facilitates identity and distinctions in the educated West. It leads readers to focus on

---

[34] Scott, *The Art of Not Being Governed*, p. 33.

[35] Ibid., p. 324–37.

[36] Roderick Nash, *Wilderness and the American Mind*, third ed. (New Haven, CT: Yale University Press, 1982), p. 146.

[37] Peter J. Schmitt, *Back to Nature: The Archadian Myth in Urban America* (Baltimore, MD: Johns Hopkins University Press, 1969).

[38] White, *Metahistory*, pp. 22–29.

[39] Scott, *The Art of Not Being Governed*, p. xiii; and Pierre Clastres, *Society against the State* (New York, NY: Zone Books, 1989 [French orig. 1974]).

the evils of the state; from this exercise, they may apparently, possibly gain political rebirth. Ethnogenesis in opposition to the state is myth in British anthropologist Malinowski's sense of a charter for action and an ideal for aspiration.[40] It promises the readers that they, too, can be reborn politically—any trappings of previous identities and histories are erased once people come into new being through their opposition to the state. Zomians did it; so can modern anarchists.[41]

The notion of the state as oppressive, as a subjugating force, enables certain self-conscious anarchists to recognize those of alternative political or social persuasions as agents or dupes of the state: people who lack the political devotion to freedom. The plot may resemble that of the film *The Matrix* (1999, starring Keanu Reeves), with its "[central horrific] vision of nearly all humanity enclosed in pods, their vital energies serving as batteries fueling the artificial machine intelligence that dominates the world."[42] If so, then audience members can identify with the hero, Neo, who "always knew something was wrong." One of the dramatic tensions in the film is that "among the freedom fighters [who liberated Neo] is the slithery traitor Cypher, who wants back into the comforts of the matrix. He is weak, precisely because he desires the plug of dependence."[43] *The Art of Not Being Governed* implies that involvements with the state and sedentism are sources of pollution or weakness among considerable portions of humanity, and that this condition goes back to the origins of agriculture.[44]

Pierre Clastres's notion of state-avoidance, borrowed by Scott, may seem like a clear alternative to the notion of "primitivism" adopted by nineteenth-century anthropologists. But prior to his *Society against the State*, Clastres had written *Chronicles of the Guyaki Indians*. His characterization of the Indians in the earlier book is rather striking: "they and all the other tribes are condemned [to extinction]."[45] This approach to social life in Latin America was common in anthropology. In *Tristes Tropiques*, Frenchman Claude Lévi-Strauss brings up the "destruction" of the New World and European responsibility for the process. But in the same breath, the French anthropologist declares that we, the Western readers, "may even discover pristine freshness [in the human lessons learned from the poorest Amazonian tribe]."[46] In his *Chronicles of the Guayaki Indians*, the author Clastres argues in a similar vein, but his *Society against the State* brackets off the Indians not as pre-contact but as anti-contact; they ran away. Translation: Scholars take the liberty to signify peoples in the tribal zone to further their own debates about what world they inhabit and, perhaps, though it is often obscured, what world they share with others.

---

[40] Bronislaw Malinowski, *Argonauts of the Western Pacific* (Prospect Heights, IL: Waveland, 1922), p. 328.

[41] David Graeber, *Fragments of an Anarchist Anthropology* (Chicago, IL: Prickly Paradigm Press, 2004), pp. 43, 55; Peter Marshall, *Demanding the Impossible: A History of Anarchism* (Oakland, CA: PM Press, 2010), p. 704.

[42] Elisabeth F. S. Roberts, "American Death" (review essay), *Focaal: European Journal of Anthropology* 54 (2009), p. 114.

[43] Ibid.

[44] For anthropological studies that lay out such issues, see Mary Douglas, *Purity and Danger* (London: Routledge, 1966); and Emily Martin, *Flexible Bodies* (Boston, MA: Beacon Press, 1994).

[45] Pierre Clastres, *Chronicles of the Guyaki Indians* (New York, NY: Zone Books, 1998 [French orig. 1972]), p. 345.

[46] Claude Lévi-Strauss, *Tristes Tropiques,* trans. John and Doreen Weightman (New York, NY: Simon and Schuster, 1973 [French orig. 1955]), p. 448.

POETIC LICENSE

I cannot help seeing some equivalence between James Scott's Zomians and what Claude Lévi-Strauss implies are the pristine human lessons potentially offered by the poorest tribe for the benefit of educated Western readers—our chance "to appreciate the mind-boggling cosmopolitanism of relatively marginal and powerless people."[47] Speaking of and for humanity or a portion thereof is a political act, and in this there is no difference between media such as anthropology and poetry. The poet Nathaniel Tarn was once the anthropologist Michael Mendelson and did research in Guatemala and then Burma. He writes about his two selves as "Dr. Jekyll and Mr. Hyde," and there are various slippages between them.[48] Because of this tendency to have more than one perspective, Tarn does not take poetry for granted but can also see it as an anthropologist who knows that there may be people and particular relationships in the representations. He relates a meeting of anthropologists who were coming into poetry—perhaps around 1970—and appeared "unaware of how sharp the razor's edge can be between genuine love and appropriation." One of the attendees declared that:

> our poetry had "benefited from an immense blood transfusion" out of the poetries of the "primitive and archaic" worlds. I asked him in considerable horror how he could bear to use such words when so many human beings were being bled, in the flesh—bled in Brazil, in Guatemala, in South Africa, in Indonesia; bled for their lands, their forests, their lakes; their seas—so that we might continue to live in the style to which we had become accustomed.[49]

The tendency toward exploitation in this potentially global relationship is more noticeable and pervasive in World Music.[50] The seldom acknowledged parallel between anthropology and World Music lies in the dynamic of ethnic sampling for an appreciative audience, whereby the producer often gets the main credit and the material rewards.

Tarn writes as both a poet and an anthropologist about Pablo Neruda's ode to his American continent, *Canto General (de America)*. To its maker this was "a central poem that would bring together the historical events, the geographical situations, the life struggles of our peoples."[51] Neruda wrote this poem on his "return from the Spanish Civil War at the height of his commitment to the Communist Party of Chile." As Tarn reads the work, "Neruda can use an Indian object (Macchu Picchu) as a 'human root,' but Indian humanity itself is disregarded in its rich variety and subsumed under the category of the 'people' or lower classes." Tarn remarks that "for many, perhaps most, Latin American Marxists, Indians should be subsumed under proletariat. This is a Pan American problem: the revolution does not involve

---

[47] Scott, *The Art of Not Being Governed*, p. 315.

[48] Nathaniel Tarn, *The Embattled Lyric: Essays and Conversations in Poetics and Anthropology* (Stanford, CA: Stanford University Press, 2007), p. 14.

[49] Ibid., pp. 40–41.

[50] Steven Feld, "A Sweet Lullaby for World Music," in *Globalization*, ed. Arjun Appadurai (Durham, NC: Duke University Press, 2001), pp. 189–216.

[51] Tarn, *The Embattled Lyric*, p. 61.

continued Indianity when seen, that is, from a non-Indian point of view."[52] The anthropologist and poet Tarn continues:

> Neruda, perhaps, hardly even notices—when he says "I come to speak through your dead mouths"—that his enablement as a poet arises out of the enforced silence of the Indian, an enforcement in which he cannot help participating as a non-Indian. Indians have to have been oppressed, enslaved, and killed in order that he can speak. As with the rest of us, a useful Indian, alas, is a dead Indian. Or, perhaps, one who has disappeared into the faceless masses: if not genocide, then ethnocide. [It] is not because the non-Indian lives on an Indian continent that he can appropriate Indianity. [I] am not arguing here, need I say it, that not being an Indian makes one an Indian-killer [but] that we need to be perpetually on our guard in what we say about the Indian.[53]

Poems, like narratives and scientific accounts, are wholes that assume perspective and ontology in any of their parts. They present as real what they have classified while the artifice of their classification tends to disappear into the structure of its own making, leaving the representations with their semblance of reality that others then can encounter and engage with as particular things, peoples, identities, dramas, and such. As much as I may disagree with the case for Zomia, my own work supplied some ideas and lines for James Scott's book.

Reading the book, letting the case linger, and thinking about it against what I know about peoples and places and anthropology, I am left with a deep sense of discomfort and embarrassment. All of anthropology and history is implicated in the case; we have all been writing as if the highland people were isolated tribes, marginalized minorities, or otherwise cut off from the negotiation of difference except as victims of draconian state policies. Scott's notion that highland peoples were brought to heel by the 1950s draws on a combination of what Western scholarship declared, and on what has sometimes taken place in modern nation states.

The readers of Scott's case for Zomia are taken on a trip across time and space, where they learn something at the intersection of self, other, and world. This is how learning works through representation, play, and identification. Here I draw on Johan Huizinga's study of play, which he suggests is marked off in space and time: within it, people come into identities and interactions in terms of rules, relations, and rewards that have no deterministic relations to what happens in everyday life. A play is a pact that is often surrounded by secrecy, which enables the formation of an in-group. The awareness that play is pretense rather than reality is part of this, but "any game can at any time wholly run away with the players ... The inferiority of play is continually being offset by the corresponding superiority of its seriousness ... Play may rise to heights of beauty and sublimity that leave seriousness far beneath"[54] and "The *fun* of playing resists all analysis, all logical interpretation."[55]

---

[52] Ibid., p. 64.

[53] Ibid., p. 65. If the connection must be made explicit, then see Jonathan Marks, "Your Body, My Property: The Problem of Colonial Genetics in a Postcolonial World," in *Embedding Ethics*, ed. Lynn Meskell and Peter Pels (New York, NY: Berg, 2005), pp. 29–45.

[54] Huizinga, *Homo Ludens*, p. 3.

[55] Ibid., p. 8.

It is in such dynamics of play that I imagine the fun of Scott's book. Readers get to sojourn across Southeast Asian history and the landscapes of their own understandings of history, identity, politics, freedom, and the state. The book has dramatic tension, it delivers the readers from the trappings of primitivism by resignifying particular items as clever strategies to acquire freedom and egalitarianism, and ultimately the readers are brought back home. An escape from the state is not entirely possible in the contemporary world, but there are various inspiring lessons to be gleaned from unexpected quarters. Who would have thought that what looked so ethnic, traditional, un-modern, and Oriental (-ist) was, in fact, quite the opposite and anarchist ... strategies of acquiring the freedom and egalitarianism that we ourselves so value and desire in the Occident?

Any representation is an invitation to interactive and intersubjective journeys. Such journeys rest on the same basis as does play: a world is set in motion with a pact to share some discoveries and understandings in an interactive manner. As I understand it, this is also what Thomas Kuhn implied, that one's "reactions, expectations, and beliefs—indeed, much of [the] perceived world" take shape through interactions and items that refine our understanding of gender, generation, specific identities, and relations. While much of the self-image of academics insists that our work is logical and intellectual and independent of emotions, there is, in fact, no way clearly to separate emotions from these other dimensions. This issue may instead be ideological, one part of the distinction that academics assert as they mark their boundary from other ways of telling stories and enabling identities.

Previously I had no trouble with the notion of highland peoples and was instead invested in it. Nor was I bothered by signs of Thai chauvinism and somewhat racist disdain for highland peoples and societies. It now seems that some of my earlier work may have benefited from examples of Thai intolerance and racism that I found in the media, in museums, and in everyday life—this would boost the analytical charge of an article or a book chapter. For a junior academic wishing for notice and recognition, such a boost is a desired quality. This is reckless; we academics may benefit from cases of real or imagined harm as we identify vicariously with marginalized peoples and offer our readers such identification with all its seriousness and moral condescension.[56] Who and what we think are the highland peoples of mainland Southeast Asia has quite a lot to do with how we imagine ourselves and the world. We academics lend shape to Southeast Asia's highland peoples and places in terms of how we want to know ourselves and what world we want to offer our readers.

REALIZATIONS

Academic works are a form of play wherein readers can come to a sense of themselves and the world. Rather than try to call off such play, I contend that we are sometimes reckless and need to learn to play with more awareness of our ethnic sampling and other habitual ways. Is the ostensible Zomian a composite picture of Southeast Asia's highland peoples or is it something closer to home? If one allows for some unconscious desire in academic work and its reception, then it seems quite

---

[56] For a rare and compelling study of this issue of vicarious identification with suffering among anthropologists and related scholars, see Don Kulick, "Theory in Furs: Masochist Anthropology," *Current Anthropology* 47,6 (2006): 933–52.

possible that the Zomian character stands as an intersubjective Third (the term is from psychoanalysis) between self and other as "a guarantor of meaning that permits the play of desire."[57]

It is through the purported adventures of the Zomians in state-avoidance—in ethnicity, culture, agriculture, social organization, illiteracy, and millenarian fervor—that Scott and his readers unite on an intersubjective journey that defines the state as a force of subjugation and thus most likely as the focus of fear and dread. If the state is that which takes away our freedom, as the case for Zomia asserts, then engaging with the state or its agencies or attempting any political negotiation are ways toward the loss of freedom or, worse, the endorsement of one's own subjugation, extraction, and oppression. On this front, I view the dramatic tension in *The Art of Not Being Governed* as an invitation to political paralysis and a justification for such passivity.

Representation is intervention.[58] James Scott's Zomia belongs to a large corpus of Western metanarratives of modernity in the social sciences that assume a fundamental transition, a shift toward either fragmentation or increasing homogeneity, and, as a corollary, assume that the past was more coherent or cohesive than the present, or that it was more diverse and local. Either way, the key term and signifier is given meaning in terms of the characterization of the—assumed and projected—directional flow of history and society. It inheres in the category and becomes meaningful as it informs rival identifications variously for or against whatever modernity is made to stand for.[59]

Modernity and the state are notions for establishing the coordinates of history and identity and, for some, so is capitalism. Eric Wolf's *Europe and the People Without History* plots the last five hundred years of history as the ever widening spread of capitalism, a phenomenon that sweeps various peoples in its path and transforms them into its agents. Wolf challenged the ahistorical character of anthropology's ostensibly-isolated-and-separate peoples, but the manner of his challenge is also notable. He wielded a Marxian sense of economic relations as the structuring principle of society, which led him to a tripartite distinction among kin-based, tributary, and capitalist production regimes. The characterization was anchored to a global historical trajectory:

> [This is] the world to which capitalism has given rise [where for instance] the [Latin American] Mundurucú and the [Southeast Asian] Meo were drawn into the larger system to suffer its impact and become its agents. [Contemporary ethnicities are] not "primordial" social relationships. They are historical products of labor market segmentation under the capitalist mode.[60]

---

[57] Crapanzano, *Hermes' Dilemma and Hamlet's Desire*, p. 72.

[58] Ian Hacking, *Representing and Intervening: Introductory Topics in the Philosophy of Natural Science* (Cambridge: Cambridge University Press, 1983). For some lessons in academic contributions to political passivity, from sometimes-dubious but always-serious non-human-primate studies, see Donna Haraway, *Simians, Cyborgs, and Women: The Reinvention of Nature* (New York, NY: Routledge, 1981), pp. 81–108.

[59] One entry into this vast topic is Harri Englund and James Leach, "Ethnography and the Meta-narratives of Modernity," *Current Anthropology* 41,2 (2000): 225–48.

[60] Eric R. Wolf, *Europe and the People Without History* (Berkeley, CA: University of California Press, 1983), pp. 23, 281.

Wolf never explicitly declared the historical inertia of peoples not affected by global capitalist expansion, because he could not imagine the existence of such peoples. Over the last five hundred years, all the various supposedly isolated and traditional peoples who have fascinated ethnographers have not only suffered from the impact of capitalist expansion, but they have also become agents of furthering its process, according to Wolf. It is a particular theory of history that enables Wolf to assemble a range of materials to illustrate his big-picture view of capitalism's peoples. The theory lends sense to the data as it inspires its collection. Once Wolf had come up with his premise, the various peoples of ethnography were slipped into identities and narratives that manifested the plot structure that had, by then, disappeared into its own designs.

This anthropology, widely lauded as giving us a handle on history in our varied ethnographic fields, does symbolic violence. Depriving peoples such as the Meo (Hmong, Mong, Miao) of their own histories and identities in ways that enable us to get a grasp on the world over the last five hundred years is an act of dispossession. The theory behind this deprivation or dispossession removes Wolf and his appreciative readers from the act of symbolic violence; it is theory, history, ontology, and narrative in an inextricable bundle that pretends to convey to us the world as it is. The issue is not a question of Wolf's genius; he wrote his book by engaging with the works of other scholars, both those who agreed with him and welcomed his book and others whose work he disagreed with and wanted to challenge.

Wolf's Meo and his world-created-by-capitalism are equally artificial, but they acquire meaning as they come together in the readers' understanding of the world. Where representation begins or ends is profoundly ambiguous, as is the related boundary between what is real and what is not. It is not so simple to determine who the Meo are and what are their interests, politics, social organization, religion, and so on. The notion that the Meo are somehow inertly there to be picked up and analyzed (or dismissed) by science is not a neutral or obvious fact. It is instead a loaded assertion that can play to many conflicting political and academic views.

Europe and the People Without History expresses an interested engagement with the world that is, in part, a debate among colleagues and rivals regarding academic prominence. Such competition is part of the social context of academic production, reception, and relevance that needs to be a component of our sense of how anthropology relates to the world. But this is no simple matter. The content and argument of the book gives us Eric Wolf as a particular analyst, as it gives us a perspective on history, peoples, and the world, and may thus enable us to shape our selves through particular kinds of correspondence with knowledge and the world. The published book may thus be said to create or shape its author and its readers' identities insofar as the analysis is a successful effort—an intersubjective journey. "Writing and reading are forms of appropriation, but this is always accompanied by expropriation. Something is taken from [people] and reality which they have never possessed, namely complete coincidence with oneself."[61]

The underlying myth supporting Wolf's opus is that he is telling objective facts of the shared historical trajectory of the world's peoples—which, I note, deprives everyone except the abstract West and capitalism of their historicity. This may be

---

[61] Samuel Ijsseling, *Mimesis: On Appearing and Being* (Kampen, Netherlands: Kok Pharos, 1997), pp. 54–55; see also Michel Foucault, "What Is an Author?" *The Foucault Reader*, ed. Paul Rabinow (New York, NY: Pantheon, 1984), pp. 101–20.

analogous to the myth of another grand and foundational work of anthropology, James Frazer's *The Golden Bough*. A critic once remarked, "The one thing that is whole in *The Golden Bough* is the allegory itself," while the peoples, practices, and cultures behind its case are taken to pieces to fit the theme.[62] Cultural anthropology may wish to do better than just give the educated bourgeois Western readers of academic books some history and a place to stand by depriving others of theirs.

James Scott's *The Art of Not Being Governed*, Eric Wolf's *Europe and the People Without History*, and James Frazer's *The Golden Bough* are each a magisterial journey for their readers, guiding them through, respectively, political, economic, and religious terrains. Each establishes the coordinates of an object that an in-group of educated Western readers can identify against—the state, capitalism, and religion. Frazer does not describe Christianity, but his description of the components of "primitive religion" insinuates the parallel, and then he sends off the whole enterprise with his three-part evolutionary scenario: Magic and religion are sequential but pre-logical modes of engaging with the world, and they are doomed; ultimately they will be completely erased by science, the one true way of controlling nature and engaging with the world.[63]

The tone of James Scott's recent book is indicative of the spirit of our times. Many academics settle into studies that detail the sinister workings of governmentality that domesticates, subjugates, and deludes people. Such academic work explains how this happens through development projects, museums, health care and social services for refugee immigrants, urban planning, and much more.[64] The assertion that politics in Southeast Asia boils down to oppression and subjugation by states, and that throughout history the only alternative lay in running away to seek freedom in the remote hills, suggests the presence of a contemporary Western academic "freedometer."[65] Thus we come into our identity and analytical clarity about the world as we trivialize the damage done by discrimination and violent conflict. I wish to declare this state of academic affairs an emergency, and to take some steps against it. We have irresponsible fantasies of understanding other places, which have profound implications for how we make our own worlds

---

[62] James Boon, *Other Tribes, Other Scribes* (New York, NY: Cambridge University Press, 1982), p. 10; James G. Frazer, *The Golden Bough*, 2nd ed. (New York, NY: Macmillan, 1900).

[63] Mary Douglas, *Purity and Danger*; Robert Ackerman, "Anthropology and the Classics," in *A New History of Anthropology*, ed. Henrika Kuklick (Malden, MA: Blackwell, 2008), pp. 143–57; and Ivan Strenski, "The Spiritual Dimension," in *A New History of Anthropology*, pp. 113–27.

[64] James Ferguson, *The Anti-Politics Machine* (Cambridge: Cambridge University Press, 1990); Arturo Escobar, *Encountering Development* (Princeton, NJ: Princeton University Press, 1995); Tony Bennett, *The Birth of the Museum* (New York, NY: Routledge, 1995); Aihwa Ong, *Buddha Is Hiding* (Berkeley, CA: University of California Press, 2003); and James C. Scott, *Seeing Like a State* (New Haven, CT: Yale University Press, 1998). This focus comes full circle in anthropologist Carol Greenhouse's glowing praise for James Scott's *The Art of Not Being Governed*. Greenhouse writes that even if Scott's case is expressly limited to old Southeast Asia, it shines a fascinating light on contemporary dynamics of transnational migration, the modern liberal state, social movements and political mobilization, and the contracts and rule-making of large multinational firms. See Carol Greenhouse, "State, Power, Anarchism: A Discussion of *The Art of Not Being Governed: An Anarchist History of Upland Southeast Asia*," Review Symposium, *Perspectives on Politics* 9,1 (March 15, 2011): 88–92.

[65] The term "freedometer" (a play on speedometer) is my attempt to capture what Ruth Benedict, in *Patterns of Culture*, p. 252, suggested about commonsense US Americans' notions of freedom as being the absence of social restrictions, exemplified by an increasingly relaxed speed limits on roads.

comprehensible. If we recognize that dimension to our work—and don't run away in shock when faced with the pervasive lie regarding Western scientific objectivity—then there is some hope.

Because of this state of affairs, I mean to revisit a discarded project that is recognized by the gloss "the peoples of Southeast Asia." For the most part, anthropologists have taken for granted the ethnic divides that became entrenched during the colonial era. Our notion of culture or social structure as shared patterns that pertain to and distinguish ethnic groups from each other enabled academic specialization and productivity. These notions of ethnic groups sharing culture, kinship, adaptation to the environment, and the like often kept scholars from asking questions about the region and diversity. Instead, we generally accepted the colonial-era model of ethnolinguistic families with their branches. Mainland Southeast Asia is remarkably diverse in terms of ethnicity and culture, but underlying this diversity we share a sense of there being five ethnolinguistic families: Tai-Kadai, Sino-Tibetan, Hmong-Mien, Austoasiatic, and Austronesian. This model or representation imports a sense of history, as the aura of scientific objectivity obscures the political entanglements of this projection. This model is one current intersection of self, other, and world that academic specialists offer.

What does the model offer? In the colonial era, it suggested a general history formed by the migration and spread of races whose strength was uneven. Cultural anthropology took shape in reaction to that portrait, and anthropologists' specialization in individual ethnic groups, a common practice through much of the twentieth century, offered no general challenge to the racialized model that informed the contemporary nation states wherein much of the anthropological research was conducted. Thus we know that Mien are a minority group in Thailand, where the Thai are a majority.

As shorthand for an ethnographic situation, this model imports simultaneously a definition of who people are and what can happen between them, and through those definitions an audience can come into a sense of their world. Paul and Elaine Lewis's *Peoples of the Golden Triangle* is one example, a lavishly illustrated book about the traditional mental and material culture of the six tribes of the northern hills of Thailand, with a brief final chapter on "signs of change."[66] The book describes a timeless world that is just about to be profoundly undone by the forces of modernity. But people can still buy some delightful ethnic stuff in the souvenir shops now that they know from the book what stories that stuff tells. The two authors were missionaries, linguists, and practical anthropologists who tried to counter economic dispossession among ethnic minorities by establishing crafts training and a souvenir shop. They were trying to help people, working at an intersection of local livelihood and international tourism. Most recent scholars, though, have offered a different intersection among self, other, and world, with little sign of interest in producing knowledge that might offer practical or mutual benefits. The alternatives we have

---

[66] Paul and Elaine Lewis, *Peoples of the Golden Triangle* (London: Thames and Hudson, 1984). The book was translated into Spanish, French, German, Thai, and Japanese, and perhaps other languages as well. I once wrote the publisher to find out some sales figures, but never received an answer. The book reached a far greater audience than has any conventional anthropology book on the region.

come up with seem to declare that only marginalization and dispossession can happen in dealings between highlanders and lowland states.[67]

This current anthropological commonsense view is not an expression of Asian historical or ethnographic realities but rather that of Western and other scholarship in the process of epistemological collapse.[68] This may have to change, and we should perhaps revisit the intersection to see if it can offer other possibilities. I start with the idea of culture. Anthony F. C. Wallace defined culture as "turbulent, constantly oscillating between the ecstasies of revitalization and the agonies of decline [and shifting] in policy from generation to generation with kaleidoscopic variety." He insisted that culture was not the replication of uniformity but the organization of diversity. It was, he continued, "policy, tacitly and gradually concocted by groups of people for the furtherance of their interests, and contract, established by practice, between and among individuals to organize their strivings into mutually facilitating equivalence structures."[69]

---

[67] John McKinnon and Bernard Vienne, eds., *Hill Tribes Today: Problems in Change* (Bangkok: White Lotus and ORSTOM, 1989); Stevan Harrell, ed., *Cultural Encounters on China's Ethnic Frontiers* (Seattle, WA: University of Washington Press, 1995); Ralph Litzinger, *Other Chinas: The Yao and the Politics of National Belonging* (Durham, NC: Duke University Press, 2000); Jean Michaud, ed., *Turbulent Times and Enduring Peoples: Mountain Minorities in the Southeast Asian Massif* (Richmond, Surrey: Curzon, 2000); Loisa Schein, *Minority Rules: The Miao and the Feminine in China's Cultural Politics* (Durham, NC: Duke University Press, 2000); Cholthira Satyawadhna, ed., *Sithi Chumchon Thongthin: Chaokhao* [Local Community Rights: Mountain Peoples] (Bangkok: Nititham, 2003); Pinkaew Laungaramsri, ed., *Atalak, Chatphan, lae Khwam Pen Chaikhob* [Identity, Ethnicity, and Marginality] (Bangkok: Sirindhorn Anthropology Center, 2003); Oscar Salemink, *The Ethnography of Vietnam's Central Highlanders: A Historical Contextualization, 1850–1990* (Honolulu, HI: University of Hawaii Press, 2003); Khwanchewan Buadaeng, ed., *Wathakam Atalak* [Identity Discourse] (Bangkok: Sirindhorn Anthropology Center, 2004); Christopher Duncan, ed., *Civilizing the Margins: Southeast Asian Government Policies for the Development of Minorities* (Ithaca, NY: Cornell University Press, 2004); Neil Engelhart, "Resource Conflict and Ethnic Peace in Northern Thailand," *Asia Pacific Viewpoint* 49,1 (2008): 98–110; Chusak Wittayapak, "History and Geography of Identifications Related to Resource Conflicts and Ethnic Violence in Northern Thailand," *Asia Pacific Viewpoint* 49,1 (2008): 111–27; Prasit Leepreecha, Don McCaskill, and Khwanchewan Buadaeng, eds., *Challenging the Limits: Indigenous Peoples in the Mekong Region* (Chiangmai: Mekong Press, 2008); Frederic Bourdier, ed., *Development and Dominion: Indigenous Peoples of Cambodia, Vietnam, and Laos* (Bangkok: White Lotus, 2009); and Tim Forsyth and Jean Michaud, eds., *Moving Mountains: Ethnicity and Livelihoods in Highland China, Vietnam, and Laos* (Vancouver: University of British Columbia Press, 2011). This list includes many of my friends and colleagues in the field, and at one point I wrote in this vein. I have left out many references, but think it is clear that we have an embarrassment of riches on this gloomy front, and that we have not come up with many alternatives.

[68] I owe the term "epistemological collapse" to Viranjini Munasinghe, who writes on the Caribbean and Trinidad, and about Indians, Sri Lankans, and other East Indians (South Asians) in the West Indies. Her work brings out how Creole nation-making served to make the East Indians unthinkable as contemporaries and participants in modern Caribbean realities, and how scholarship has been complicit in making them unthinkable except as the carriers of language and culture derived from another time and place (the past, Asia). The dynamic is analogous to how I understand the unimaginable contemporary highland peoples of Southeast Asia in national and scholarly worlds. See Viranjini Munasinghe, "Rescuing Theory from the Nation," in *Knowing How to Know: Fieldwork and the Ethnographic Present*, ed. Narmala Halstead, Eric Hirsch, and Judith Okely (New York, NY: Berghahn, 2008), pp. 173–94.

[69] Anthony F. C. Wallace, *Culture and Personality*, 2nd ed. (New York, NY: Random House, 1970), pp. 22–24.

Wallace suggested that both individuals and groups were diverse, with many of them "in continuous and overt conflict in one subsystem and in active cooperation in another."[70] This shows none of the apolitical group-mind-characteristics for which the culture concept was critiqued and dismissed, and instead demonstrates something along the lines that Bruno Latour calls attention to in his discussion of continually shifting networks where no component or constellation can be taken for granted, and no politics can be known beforehand.[71] The culture concept is a representation that sets up coordinates for engagements with the world, establishing intersections among self, other, and world that may inform action.

So are other notions—people come into both identity and knowledge through representations. Southeast Asia, too, is a representation, as is history: There is no possible escape into a realm of objective facts that are not also representations that mediate self, other, and world. If culture is what can happen among people across difference, and not what distinguishes one group from another, then we have a whole new starting point. And it is not like the problem is new or has never been recognized regarding the hinterland peoples of mainland Southeast Asia:

> The observations of colonial administrators, missionaries, adventurers, and anthropologists were filtered through a grid of western preconceptions, assumptions, and expectations about "tribes," "social structures," "societies," and the like. The locus of the problem lies with the flaws of western theoretical and methodological preferences rather than in any intrinsic peculiarity of the upland peoples.[72]

In my view, after various conference panels and workshops and symposia, the whole Zomia thing was just a fuss. For a while I felt like the member of some Buddy Holly tribute band who now got gigs after years of laboring in obscurity, because the master had delivered another brilliant album and everybody was excited about the sound and some also wanted to know what they should make of it. "Tell me what you think of Scott's new book," was everyone's question or demand (and he has published at least two other books since, on other things). So, to explain myself: anybody curious should just read James Scott's book and make up his or her own mind. This is not really about Southeast Asia and getting it finally right. The issue concerns our knowledge and understanding of ourselves.[73] We get Southeast Asia wrong, systemically, because of certain things that are systemically wrong or mistaken elsewhere. That is what my book tries to address.

The case for Zomia is in many ways a very educated white bourgeois US American theory regarding what happens across difference. Later I will expand on that idea (see the Afterword), but this chapter closes on an oddball comparison: How

---

[70] Ibid., p. 24.

[71] Bruno Latour, *Reassembling the Social: An Introduction to Actor-Network-Theory* (Oxford: Oxford University Press, 2005).

[72] A. Thomas Kirsch, *Feasting and Social Oscillation* (Ithaca, NY: Cornell Southeast Asia Program, 1973), p. 35.

[73] This issue is more general regarding humanity and its evolution and boundaries; see Jonathan Marks, "Anthropological Taxonomy as Subject and Object: The Consequences of Descent From Darwin and Durkheim," *Anthropology Today* 23,4 (2007): 7–12; and Geoffrey A. Clark, "Neandertal Archaeology: Implications for Our Origins," *American Anthropologist* 104,1 (2002): 50–67.

do people overcome any difference, such as across species lines? In North America, the United States and Canada, there are several ways to do this. One is urban and bourgeois, and involves animals adopted as pets that receive our love and care and depend on us for food. Another is of the Frontier and appears at rodeos, where the aim is to battle and subjugate horses and cattle, which are absolute strangers to people. A third belongs to the (sub-) arctic regions and draws on Native American and First Nations traditions. It appears in sled-dog races that depend on mutual familiarity, collaboration, and trust between humans and dogs to navigate precarious terrain with a purpose that strikes a balance to accomplish what neither side could or would manage alone.[74]

I think that the three scenarios suggest a range of emotional and social registers: a) conditional love, familiarity, and dependency; b) mistrust, hostility, and forceful subjugation; and c) long-term familiarity and negotiation across lines of difference for mutual benefit. Zomia is in some ways a refraction of the US American admiration for Native Americans, an admiration that rests on the absolute denial of equality and fellow-humanity and instead appropriates Native Americans for the enhancement of identity among one faction of the US American bourgeoisie. That this shadow of Indians now crops up in images of Southeast Asians is quite intriguing, and has a lot to do with the long-distance fascination with Vietnam's Montagnards and the Hmong of Laos, who were military allies of the United States in wars in Asia. They were much admired, but this admiration has generally been anchored to an absolute denial of equality, specificity, or negotiation.

Because I have been around for a while, I could recognize in the Zomia notion that the state was an engine of oppression and extraction the echo of some other voices. This is what I had already seen in some Western missionary literature about how local animist religions of Southeast Asia were a machinery of exploitation; the hill tribe spirit mediums were deluding the people and sucking their resources away with expensive and repeated ceremonies against illnesses and such. Only by finding Jesus and casting away their old and ethnic ways could these miserable people ever come to any lasting relief.[75]

I never found this myself among the Mien, where instead I came to appreciate that their religious practices were particular relations across different realms that varied among households, kin-groups, and communities, but, when they worked, were always reciprocal and particular. The same was true for Mien relations with lowland kingdoms, officials, and traders; these are particular relations that are best viewed over time as an expression of contingent relations among a set of elements. The concept of the state as an enemy of the people is the same theory (an abstraction used to demonstrate how different elements can come together) as that behind

---

[74] Sharon Kemp, "Sled-dog Racing: The Celebration of Co-operation in a Competitive Sport," *Ethnology* 38,1 (1999): 81–95.

[75] I give no references. I have no intrinsic problem with missionaries and some are among my friends. The alarmist language is common in books and articles aimed at strangers, especially a Western audience that does not know the situation but can financially and otherwise help sustain the effort if their enthusiasm is drummed up in this manner. One example about not-yet-converted Mien in Thailand, published decades ago, mentioned their New Year activities as a "three-day demon worship" that, if I recall correctly, was run by "sorcerers." Many missionaries devote their lives to learning from and assisting other people, and they are as diverse as any other category of humans. Many become cultural hybrids. Their stories are in general very interesting and their worlds unstable. See James Clifford, *Person and Myth: Maurice Leenhardt in the Melanesian World* (Durham, NC: Duke University Press, 1992).

rodeo: this battle is between strangers, and it offers only hostile struggle that systemically hurts and harms one side. Negotiation and mutual reliance or benefit never emerge as options.

CHAPTER ONE

ASIAN ETHNIC FRONTIERS

At the intersections of Western academic disciplines such as anthropology, history, and political science, we all seem complicit in silencing the past, certain legacies of Southeast Asian history and society. The term "silencing the past" comes from Michel-Rolph Trouillot's scathing indictment of Western political thought and academic imaginations, how unthinkable it was that black slaves could successfully revolt and defeat French colonial rule in Haiti. The key terms of Western political thought, such as about "man" and "freedom," were shaped within societies that were anchored to colonial rule and slavery: "The Age of Enlightenment was an age in which the slave drivers of Nantes bought titles of nobility to better parade with philosophers, an age in which a freedom fighter such as Thomas Jefferson owned slaves without bursting under the weight of his intellectual and moral contradictions."[1]

In our studies of Southeast Asia, a different historical legacy has been silenced through much of our work. It seems unthinkable to many of us that cultures and societies of the region are shaped though interaction across difference, and that there is a long trail of political negotiation *within* as much as *between* or among hill and valley peoples. In our blindness, we reproduce the rhetorical framework not only of colonial rule, but also that of subsequent chauvinist nationalist authorities from within the region. In our passive endorsement of the impossibility of negotiated diversity or of equality in multi-ethnic settings, we make Southeast Asian highland peoples into scientific pin-ups for fantasies of our own political virtue and academic x-ray vision: we know that states are oppressive, and we believe we can see through the obfuscations of power.

There is a pervasive denial of internal diversity built into our academic notions of ethnic groups, and, equally, in our predominant notions of the state. Philip Abrams argues that "the state, like *the* town and *the* family, is a spurious object of sociological concern."[2] He argues against the practice of studying the state as if it had a thing-like quality, and instead advocates a study of the idea of the state, which would examine how the notion enables ideological and other control as it distracts from the recurring disunity and conflict within the political realm.[3] To shift the terms with which we relate to difference in Southeast Asia, I point to the academic rethinking of gender as a topic of history and social science.

---

[1] Michel-Rolph Trouillot, *Silencing the Past: Power and the Production of History* (Boston, MA: Beacon Press, 1995), p. 78.

[2] Philip Abrams, "Notes on the Difficulty of Studying the State," *Journal of Historical Sociology* 1,1 (1988): 63.

[3] Ibid., pp. 76–82. For a more contemporary look at the disjunctures between the images and realities of states, see Veena Das and Deborah Poole, "State and Its Margins: Comparative Ethnographies," in *Anthropology in the Margins of the State*, ed. Veena Das and Deborah Poole (Santa Fe, NM: School of American Research Press, 2004), pp. 3–33.

The historian Joan W. Scott argues that when scholars assume "that women have inherent characteristics and objective identities consistently and predictably different from men's, and that these generate definably female needs and interests, [they] imply that sexual difference is a natural rather than a social phenomenon."[4] Assuming Asian highlanders' society is fundamentally different from lowlanders' runs a similar risk, one that is simultaneously analytical, descriptive, and political. Scott's proposal for feminist history asserts that "the story is no longer about the things that have happened to women and men and how they have reacted to them; instead it is about how the subjective and collective meanings of women and men as categories of identity have been constructed."[5]

Scott's reaction to the universalistic claims of psychoanalytic theory regarding gender suggests one response to the antagonistic binary that inheres in the case for the Southeast Asian highlands as Zomia. Jacques Lacan's work suggested that gender systems were based on the fear of castration.[6] Letting the issue linger and thinking about it against the alleged fear of losing one's freedom—which James Scott suggests animated all the hinterland dynamics of culture, ethnicity, agriculture, language without literacy, and religion—I can only agree with Joan Scott's response: "the point of historical inquiry is denied."[7] The analytical certainty of James Scott's discovery of Zomia, discussed in the introduction, recycles what earlier tribal anthropology had declared—that the game must be over for the ethnic groups in the highlands because their authentic way of life is incompatible with modern national realities.

Was Southeast Asia shaped by expansive and extractive states progressively subjugating and incorporating more peoples, and is the region's ethnic and cultural diversity a marker of long successful strategies of state-avoidance? Anthropologists long cast the peoples of Southeast Asia and adjacent southern China in terms of their ethnically distinct culture, social structure, agriculture, and the like. There is little current interest in that analytical project.[8] But after most of us abandoned this project of examining distinct ethnic groups, James Scott took up what we had discarded and

---

[4] Joan W. Scott, *Gender and the Politics of History* (New York, NY: Columbia University Press, 1988), p. 4.

[5] Ibid., p. 6.

[6] The notion is from Sigmund Freud's work, while in Lacan's writings "the castration complex leaves behind all reference to anatomical reality." See: Gayle Rubin, "The Traffic in Women: Notes on the 'Political Economy' of Sex," in *Toward an Anthropology of Women*, ed. Rayna R. Reiter (New York, NY: Monthly Review Press, 1975), p. 190. Joan Scott draws her discussion from Gayle Rubin, who quotes from Jacques Lacan, *The Language of Self*, trans. Anthony Wilden (Baltimore, MD: Johns Hopkins University Press, 1968).

[7] Scott, *Gender and the Politics of History*, p. 44.

[8] See Alfred Kroeber, *The Peoples of the Philippines* (New York, NY: American Museum of Natural History, 1928); Frank LeBar, Gerald C. Hickey, and John Musgrave, eds., *Ethnic Groups of Mainland Southeast Asia* (New Haven, CT: Human Relations Area Files Press, 1964); Robbins Burling, *Hill Farms and Padi Fields: Life in Mainland Southeast Asia* (Englewood Cliffs, NJ: Prentice-Hall, 1965); and Victor King and William Wilder, *The Modern Anthropology of South-East Asia* (New York, NY: Routledge Curzon, 2003). A recent inventory of "peoples" has been compiled by Jean Michaud, *Historical Dictionary of the Peoples of the Southeast Asian Massif* (Lanham, MD: Scarecrow, 2006), and there is a study of traditional Akha culture and worldview by Deborah Tooker, *Space and the Production of Cultural Difference among the Akha Prior to Globalization: Channeling the Flow of Life* (Amsterdam: Amsterdam University Press, 2012).

turned it on its head by asserting that ethnicity was just a front for political strategy, of which there were two—subjugation and freedom.

The basic problem is that he was confined by how ethnologists had, over several generations, defined the object of study. We made the object in such a way that people's diversity, social entanglements, internal difference and inequality, and historically particular predicaments fell completely from view. We were, it seems, largely prospecting for distinct ethnic ways: an-other's autonomous past or present on which to build our scientific credibility and currency. Signs of national integration were read as the loss of ethnic culture and the like, and James Scott's recent book, *The Art of Not Being Governed*,[9] redraws this line for his readers and tells us that it indicates the loss of freedom in the highlands. "Game over" seems to be the conclusion of all our scholarship.

CHECKING THE SOURCES

Science tells stories through which its audiences can come to a sense of the world and of themselves. No such stories about identity and difference, such as of the character of intergroup relations, are politically innocent. Anthropologist Reo Fortune did research among Yao in southern China for two months in 1938, and his findings offer some perspective on the case for Zomia:

> No rice growers live voluntarily in the hills, where the poor land has to be terraced and irrigated foot by foot. In earlier history the present day highlanders were decisively conquered and driven into their present positions [by] the southward expansion of the Han, the Chinese proper. They gave ground, of necessity, but they gave little else, neither recognition, obedience, compliance, nor willingness to pay taxes, or to receive education or medicine. They kept their own national spirit and they paid for it in some disadvantages.[10]

The devotion to their "national spirit" explains the Yao's disconnect from the Chinese state. People were driven into the hills by expanding lowland society, and they stay in marginal areas because of who they are; they retreat into the ethnic past and won't back down in spite of the discomfort. In his article, Fortune made "practical proposals for effective work towards the assimilation and the civilizing of the Yao, [whom he declared] superstition-ridden to an excessive degree." He advocated for secular and medical education for Yao spirit mediums and anthropology training for Chinese government officials in minority areas, and urged that people with academic training in anthropology and government "should be encouraged to enter into the branches of the State service that are concerned with the assimilation of the non-assimilated races of China."[11]

The structural quality of Fortune's field influenced his depiction. He absorbed much from his Chinese colleagues and students about the apparent lack of assimilation being the result of stubbornness among various mountain peoples, but

---

[9] James C. Scott, *The Art of Not Being Governed: An Anarchist History of Upland Southeast Asia* (New Haven, CT: Yale University Press, 2009).

[10] Reo Fortune, "Introduction to Yao Culture," in "Yao Society: A Study of a Group of Primitives in China," ed. Reo F. Fortune, *Lingnan Science Journal* 18,3 (1939): 343–55.

[11] Ibid., pp. 353, 354.

the theory of Asian ethnic diversity also had various colonial-era roots. Fortune did not seek explanations for the apparent antagonism in harsh government policies and suppression campaigns from a few years earlier, and he took it for granted that the Chinese and the Yao were two separate entities whose interactions express and reproduce the ethnicities, their difference, and the character of their relations. In situating Fortune's study, my language borrows from Albert Einstein's theory of relativity: Time and space have no independent existence, there is instead only "the structural quality of the field."[12]

Fortune was employed by Lingnan University, an American university in Canton, and his writing on the Yao appeared with pieces written by the Chinese members of a research group—most were Fortune's students—in the *Lingnan Science Journal*.[13] Reo Fortune's generalization about mountain farmers drew on a range of sources. It was mediated by multiple Chinese interlocutors and the long Chinese history of signifying highland peoples. It is more important to note the historical background that Reo Fortune does not mention: A few years before Fortune's research, Chiang Kai-Shek's nationalist policies inspired the police to cut off the long braids of Yao women's hair and to demolish Yao village temples. "Anyone who resisted would be arrested, but only after being paraded through town."[14]

What Fortune characterized as their "national spirit" was not some timeless Yao trait but rather an ethnic consciousness that was triggered by deliberate policies of repression and abuse at a historically particular moment. What he declared for the Yao and their position on the landscape reflected how people had responded to government-sponsored discrimination, abuse, and destruction that was quite specific to time and place. It was only anthropology's expectation of some timeless quality in ethnic culture that made the situation seem an expression of the Yao "spirit."

In his dissertation on the Mong of Northern Thailand,[15] Howard Radley declared that "At the core of the culture is the idea that Mong have been oppressed and exploited over many generations by the Chinese. The visualization of space itself places the Mong in a small community of people who cooperate among themselves, but who are surrounded by the overwhelming power of the state."[16] Again, the highland's disconnect from the lowland is attributed to a shared and timeless culture. To understand the context of this analysis calls for some background on the situation in Thailand at the time.

For much of the twentieth century, most highland peoples had no official connections. They were frequently the subject of extortion by police and military, often because of their illegal opium cultivation. After one extended episode in early 1968, the Hmong retaliated by burning down a bridge leading to their village. In far-off Bangkok, the national capital, this was labeled a "Red [communist] Meo Revolt,"

---

[12] Albert Einstein, *Relativity* (New York, NY: Three Rivers Press, 1961), p. 176.

[13] On Fortune's life and work, see Caroline Thomas, "Rediscovering Reo: Reflections on the Life and Anthropological Career of Reo Franklin Fortune," *Pacific Studies* 32,2/3 (2009): 299–324.

[14] Ralph Litzinger, *Other Chinas: The Yao and the Politics of National Belonging* (Durham, NC: Duke University Press, 2000), p. 155.

[15] The spelling implies a subgroup difference between the Green Mong and the White Hmong.

[16] Howard Radley, "Economic Marginalization and the Ethnic Consciousness of the Green Mong (Moob Ntsuab) of Northwestern Thailand" (PhD dissertation, Corpus Christi College, Oxford University, 1986), p. 78.

and it triggered massive military violence against highland settlements that was disproportionately centered on the Hmong. Over a decade later, the violence still occurred (but was abating), and the Hmong sense of discrimination and alienation within Thai society remained evident. But I contest the understanding of ethnic culture; what some Mong people reported to Radley was their position in a hostile situation that was, again, quite specific to time, place, and particular government policies of intolerance; it did not express some inherent Mong nature.

The case for Zomia draws in many ways on the contemporary situation in Burma, where there is an entrenched sense of the ethnic and political frontier. Since the military's takeover of the country in 1962, the national government has taken ethnic difference as a threat to national unity and waged a sporadic war against the Shan, Karen, Kachin, and other ethnic groups. Political scientist Mary Callahan, a Burma-specialist, offers the following description:

> Throughout most of the ethnic states, there is a widely held consensus about the image of the central, or national, state as predatory. This image of the state as oppressor has a particularly strong hold among populations who have lived in war zones. In areas of ongoing or previous combat, "Burma" and the national government are synonymous with [the national military] and its brutal counterinsurgency tactics, some of which included forced displacement and forced labor, confiscation of food and other resources, burning of villages, and many other human rights abuses.[17]

How we draw on difference for the work of signification depends on what we may know, as much as on where we want to take this knowledge. Our knowledge of the peoples of Southeast Asia has often been an uncritical reflection of the ethnicized social types within the region that have been routinized by colonial rule, subsequent nationalisms, and the professionalization of anthropology as the study of ethnic types. This is the fundamental problem: Our objects of knowledge, minorities and the state, bring with them a sense of what they are, how they can relate, and the consequences of their interactions. Unless we rethink difference, we are stuck with this epistemology. We may need another perspective on history, power, and ethnic and political frontiers.

Drawing on fieldwork and conversations with Mien people in Thailand, and with people from Laos in the United States, I suggest a different characterization of the structural quality of mainland Southeast Asia as a field. Starting with Mien culture and cosmology, I call attention to how people situate themselves through contracts. Culture is not transmitted through replication; it is continually being constructed and reconstructed along various social and cognitive causal chains.[18] When people establish a household at marriage, they make an initial contract with ancestor spirits that then has to be maintained with annual offerings. The same happens when a leader forms a village; he establishes a contract with the spirit of the most powerful lowland official, for the people's well-being. A multi-village unit,

---

[17] Mary P. Callahan, *Political Authority in Burma's Ethnic Minority States* (Washington, DC: East-West Center Press, 2007), pp. 18–19.

[18] Tim Ingold, "Why a Deep Understanding of Cultural Evolution Is Incompatible with Shallow Psychology," in *Roots of Human Sociality*, ed. N. J. Enfield and Stephen Levinson (New York, NY: Berg, 2006), pp. 431–49.

such as the one whose descendants I worked with in Thailand, can become a ritual unit if the leader establishes a relationship with a royal spirit. In the case I know, this ritual relationship was matched with a political and economic relationship. The leader received a title from the lowland king and his people were allowed to settle.

Learning about the chant to this king's spirit, I arrived at a list of lowland kingdoms with which this group had had formal relations, in Laos, Vietnam, and China. In the 1990s, the list of kings ended with the current king of Thailand. If this is some indication of how highland peoples have viewed their situation within the region, it suggests particular relationships and contracts, and the expectation that people make such agreements in specific situations. A householder does not form a personal relationship with the spirit of a lowland official; that is only done at the village level. There is a considerable match between how Mien people have related to the realms of spirits and governments. If there is a contract, then there is an obligation of exchanges as long as it lasts. If there is no relationship, then interactions are effectively conducted among strangers, which can be dangerous or violent.[19]

Lowland valley kings, such as the king of Nan, the area where this group had settled, had a framework for such relationships. The Mien leader and the Tai king had never before met, but they had a notion of each other and a framework for establishing relations of mutual benefit. The relationship was initiated with a payment of silver and either an elephant tusk or rhinoceros horns, and it was continued through visits and the payment of tribute and then taxes. The population received official recognition of their villages in the early twentieth century, and five villages were officially licensed to grow and sell opium to a royal monopoly. These events happened around the time of national integration, when Bangkok authorities subjugated various formerly independent kingdoms and turned them into provinces. With the shaping of the modern nation state, most officials came from Bangkok and many were completely disinclined to cultivate relationships with highland peoples.[20]

While my material draws on the history of a particular group of Mien people from the 1860s to the 1990s, the implications are much more general for the region, including the southern parts of China. There are multiple reasons for our ignorance (of extensive and pervasive networks of interethnic relations that people actively made and maintained), and for the lack of regional and historical imagination and awareness that might have brought this out. One is that kingdoms were not simply political and economic ventures, but also social projects. The archives of these kingdoms do not often detail whatever intimacies or relations their representatives had across ethnic lines in the hinterlands. The chronicles of Buddhist lowland kingdoms were often efforts to enshrine legacies of Buddhist virtue and the like. Some of the chronicles would also detail how the Buddhist lowland peoples came into their position by driving out the non-Buddhist savages. When I first worked through such materials, I found a rather clear match to contemporary nationalist chauvinism and was led to assert that an upland–lowland divide was foundational to the shaping of the region. Now, instead, I think that the chronicles are using

---

[19] Jonsson, *Mien Relations: Mountain People and State Control in Thailand* (Ithaca, NY: Cornell University Press, 2005), pp. 73–98.

[20] For some exceptions to this political trend at the time, see Jane R. Hanks and Lucien M. Hanks, *Tribes of the North Thailand Frontier* (New Haven, CT: Yale Southeast Asia Studies, 2001).

rhetoric that expresses social boundaries, a form of strategic essentialism that should be questioned both theoretically and empirically.[21]

The Mien are one of many so-called Yao peoples that I once took as having come into their group identity expressly as outsiders to Chinese rule. After decades of research concerning southern China, however, historian David Faure found no regularity in the position of Yao as a people inside or beyond the state, upland or lowland; Yao–state relations were in each case a matter of various local arrangements and histories, and there is no commonality among Guilin, Hunan, and Yunnan Provinces.[22] As soon as one abandons certain confidence in the categories "the Chinese" and "the state," the obviousness of categories defining highlanders or the Yao dissolves, too. But Faure's intimate knowledge of the archives, and of Chinese personalities and issues, revealed how the state could be activated against the Yao in particular cases. So-called Yao Wars in the fifteenth and sixteenth centuries resulted from deadly intra-elite rivalries in Guangxi, connections to eunuchs at the Beijing court, and the ability to amass a force of thirty thousand imperial soldiers and 160 thousand soldiers from within Guangxi. Nearly eight hundred people were arrested and 3,200 were beheaded.

Such violent suppression campaigns were based on trumped-up charges of banditry that served to establish the credibility and prominence of particular local ruling families and bring them to the attention of rulers in Beijing. The fear of local uprisings, if conveyed through influential-enough sources, brought "some of the most trusted military officials of the realm" to a faraway province, and thus brought imperial attention to individuals who might otherwise never attract any attention from the innermost circle of the imperial elite.[23] Faure describes the careless slaughter of thousands of people as an act that eased a faraway province's local official's access to the central court as it entrenched his local power. Such stories, that may take decades of scholarly devotion to figure out, may not be easily accessible to the average educated Western reader who is not inherently interested in some fifteenth-century particulars concerning lineage–state tensions in the Pearl River Delta.

Eli Alberts's recent archival research on historical and literary sources indicates that when *Man* ("barbarians of the south") and Yao became objects of Chinese awareness and attention, their strangeness was noted but in ways that had no policy implications.[24] Richard Cushman's dissertation, focused on Chinese-language sources on the Yao, finds a pervasive duality between the images of Yao as outsider-rebels and as curious strangers. There is considerable difficulty in drawing lines around the ethnic group Yao. Still, Cushman's research reveals various important issues. One is that in Guangxi province, the *t'u kuan* and *t'u szu* officials, whom we generally assume to have been the arm of the Chinese state that subjugated and

---

[21] Jonsson, *Mien Relations*, pp. 16–43. For a discussion of this issue in the Mediterranean region and regarding the ostensibly clear boundaries of Greek identity, see Michael Herzfeld, *Cultural Intimacy: Social Poetics in the Nation State*, 2nd edition (New York, NY: Routledge, 2005), pp. 73–91.

[22] David Faure, *Emperor and Ancestor: State and Lineage in South China* (Stanford, CA: Stanford University Press, 2007), pp. 46–47.

[23] David Faure, "The Yao Wars in the Mid-Ming and Their Impact on Yao Ethnicity," in *Empire at the Margins: Culture, Ethnicity, and Frontier in Early Modern China*, ed. Pamela Crossley, Helen Siu, and Donald Sutton (Berkeley, CA: University of California Press, 2005), p. 181.

[24] Eli Alberts, *A History of Daoism and the Yao People of South China* (Youngstown, NY: Cambria Press, 2006), pp. 49–73.

ruled the ethnic minorities through co-opted minority leaders, were Chinese people who ruled only in areas of Chinese settlements. Further, in Guangxi, "there was no formal system of tribal administration in the province at all."[25] Ideas of a collective Chinese past dissolve rather fast; this is true, for instance, of ideas regarding differences in how the *t'u kuan* and *t'u szu* played out in Gueichow and Yunnan provinces compared with what happened in Guangxi. In Guangxi, the four *t'u kuan* each ruled over their own peoples, and they were primarily in competition with one another rather than engaged in extending the (imagined) arm of the state. Cushman suggests that "part of the power of [each of the four] *t'u kuan* was undoubtedly due to the good relations which they managed to establish with the local tribal groups."[26]

Our general expectations of the state, or the Chinese state, tend to ignore matters of diversity, specificity, and the contradictions that may exist between ideals and practice. David Faure and Ho Ts'ui-p'ing note some fundamental problems:

> First, the imperial Chinese state was built on a loose structure that presumed much greater political unity than its institutions could deliver … Second, over the last millennium, what became known as Chinese culture was only gradually taking shape … Third, although it is true that at times—and maybe quite often— the imperial government acted as though it wanted to impose its will on local society, it is an error in the reading of centralized records to accept the fiction that local society accepted the imposition without negotiation.[27]

People established relations through exchanges. One nineteenth-century national gazetteer notes tribute from a particular region: "five kinds of incense, namely sandalwood, laka-wood, mangosteen, orange bark, and rattan, all coming out of Yao settlements."[28] Other records indicate that Yao peoples come with "deerskins, mushrooms, and laka-wood incense" to trade at certain markets.[29] Cushman suggests that Yao people and lowland rulers often made alliances and maintained relations in part as insurance against banditry that might equally threaten both groups. But Cushman notes also that for those Yao who had no recognition or relations, the so-called "raw" barbarians, "there was no means for settling grievances with the Chinese outside of the threat or use of force."[30] Unless strangers become familiars, one can expect hostility in situations of inequality.

David Faure suggests that our sense of the imposition of Chinese command over minority areas in the south needs revision, that most of this authority only took hold during the Ming and Qing eras, and that the process of *gaitu guiliu* ("replacing the

---

[25] Richard Cushman, "Rebel Haunts and Lotus Huts: Problems in the Ethnohistory of the Yao" (PhD dissertation, Cornell University, 1970), p. 201.

[26] Ibid., p. 205.

[27] David Faure and Ho Ts'ui-p'ing, "Preface," in *Chieftains into Ancestors: Imperial Expansion and Indigenous Society in Southwest China,* ed. David Faure and Ho Ts'ui-p'ing (Vancouver, BC: University of British Columbia Press, 2013), pp. xi–xii.

[28] Cushman, "Rebel Haunts and Lotus Huts," p. 34.

[29] Ibid., p. 45. The general point may motivate a revisiting of F. L. Dunn's analysis of Malaya as not about that place in particular but as suggestive of the whole region. See F. L. Dunn, *Rainforest Collectors and Traders: A Study of Resource Utilization in Modern and Ancient Malaya* (Kuala Lumpur: Monographs of the Malaysian Branch of the Royal Asiatic Society, No. 5, 1975).

[30] Cushman, "Rebel Haunts and Lotus Huts," p. 232.

native official with a circulating official") was quite varied.[31] But even in the nineteenth century, Yao people and local authorities in Guangxi were maintaining relations through exchanges of goodwill and goods, apparently for mutual benefit:

> At the beginning of each year the [Yao] headman [*ch'iu chang*] heads up a hundred of the men under his command who carry bamboo baskets [filled] with tailed deer, stags, roebucks, foxes, ringed pheasants, and rabbits, to present to the mandarin; this is called *pai nien* [lit. "to pay New Year calls"]. When they meet the mandarin they prostrate themselves and do not dare look up … They are presented with savory food, wine, and cakes. They drink their fill and leave, carrying the left-over cakes in their sleeves.[32]

Such material from the historical record may be difficult for us to credit for two reasons. One is the expectation that any interaction between Chinese or other officials and peoples we now think of as terminal minorities has to be one of oppression, subjugation, and unfair extraction. It is here that the insights of feminist scholarship can make a crucial difference by its insistence that one must examine how particular subject positions, identities, and perspectives are produced through patterns of relations over time. The other reason for our collective obliviousness regarding the ethnographic and historical record as one that describes ongoing negotiation across difference concerns our modern view of so-called pre-capitalist exchanges, such as tribute, which we view as a one-way process of extraction, assuming that only the authorities or the supposed state would stand to benefit from such arrangements. Thus, in the case for Zomia, taxation and tribute can only appear as the means of fueling the oppressive state. This is an expression of a particular contemporary Western view that considers social relations and obligations of any kind as a threat to the autonomy of the individual.

Mien people have "always" expected relations and exchanges with spirits, people, and officials to come at a cost, and, when all goes well, to lead to things of mutual benefit. All relations are subject to assessment, renewal, renegotiation, or rejection. There is nothing regarding the Mien that supports the idea that highland peoples' identities and ambitions concerned a search for freedom or autonomy outside networks of political, economic, and other exchanges and negotiations. Instead, there is everything to support the understanding that Zomian isolationism was the product of political breakdown and entrenched hostilities at specific moments, and does not accurately represent highland peoples by granting them some abstract and historically transcendent identity or subject position.

Chinese ethnology was part of Chinese rule; the classification of peoples was about gaining command over the landscape and its forces. One example of stately ethnology is the *Man Shu: Book of the Southern Barbarians*, attributed to Fan Chuo in about 860–872 CE. At one point I might have mined it for materials on different *Man* peoples, but now I think it is only useful as a source regarding the production of ethnological knowledge in the absence of political or other relations. The work describes the Chinese borderlands near Vietnam and some parts of Yunnan Province. The following extract gives some of the work's tone:

---

[31] David Faure, "Introduction," in *Chieftains into Ancestors*, pp. 2–3.
[32] Cushman, "Rebel Haunts and Lotus Huts," pp. 207–8.

> Going 350 *li* southeast of Chiung-pu one reaches the Wu-teng tribes. It is the land of the Great Devil-Lord Meng-Chung, a thousand *li* in extent. In Chiung-pu one clan is Pai-Man (White *Man*) and five clans Wu-Man (Black *Man*). At first there were only five clans. In between Chiung-pu and T'ai-teng they are all Wu-Man. The women make their clothes of black silk. They are so long that they trail along the ground.
>
> Internally, the White *Man* of Pei-ku accept favors and presents from the Emperor but externally they have secret dealings with the Tibetans.[33]

Such views are rather easily found in the archives. They project a unity to the Middle Kingdom (China) that sometimes motivated projects of discrimination, oppression, and the like, and make it seem that China can only appear as an oppressive power when viewed from the ethnic frontier.[34] But they do not describe the long run of history in the minority areas of southern China. Such views allow for rather easy stereotyping through a binary of the strong state and the weak margins that can have many permutations. This idea may offer some peculiar delights to Westerners feeling themselves modern, democratic, and enlightened relative to the backdrop of the brutalities and oppression carried out by Western colonialism and ancient China:

> The soldiers who kept the T'ang [Chinese] yoke on the necks of the indigenes were by no means all Hua-men [the ostensible Chinese ethnic majority]. Many of them were the native neighbors and natural allies of the peoples held in subjection. As Cortes used the Totonac people against the Aztec in Mexico, so did the Chinese employ some of the aboriginal subjects to bring others into subjection.[35]

One may take the state for an entity and assume with Reo Fortune that it is a benevolent civilizing force, or with James Scott that it is a malevolent subjugating force. The alternative, following Joan Scott and David Faure, is to suggest nothing of the sort and rather examine in each particular case how difference is produced, how it brings people into relations, whether it regularly produces inequality, and how an understanding of the production of relations can lead to situations of greater equality and practical benefit.

If a state is not the structure of social control and oppression but rather whatever particular arrangements people arrive at through negotiation as much as a sense of differences or opposition, it is no longer so easily known or characterized, and the analytical or descriptive separation of national communities and minorities is no longer predictable. This might undo some of our complicity in naturalizing contemporary social boundaries. Our understanding of the state expresses not what is there but what politics we can imagine, through representation and other means.

---

[33] Fan Chuo, *Man Shu: Book of the Southern Barbarians* [860–873], trans. Gordon H. Luce and ed. Giok Po Oey (Ithaca, NY: Cornell University Southeast Asia Program, 1961), p. 12. The original burned to ashes, along with a whole library and much more, during a World War II bombing raid on Rangoon, Burma.

[34] For case studies, see *Cultural Encounters on China's Ethnic Frontiers*, ed. Stevan Harrell (Seattle, WA: University of Washington Press, 1995).

[35] Edward H. Schafer, *The Vermilion Bird* (Berkeley, CA: University of California Press, 1967), p. 69.

Our knowledge of the state also expresses the limits of what we can know through engagements on the ground—in fieldwork, in the archives, and at home.

If the "state" is whatever distribution of benefits people can negotiate among themselves across difference,[36] then we may wish to recognize scholarship as already a political act and an engagement with possible futures in parallel universes. Culture and the state have no independent existence: There is only the structural quality of the field. This must in each particular case be figured out through what interactions happen, by examining their elements, patterns, and consequences, and by reflecting on our position inside that field. This calls for an areal anthropology that is historical and comparative and is reflexively alert to how some of our common understandings may reflect national or other modern biases that make negotiation across difference seem unthinkable.

BACK TO SOUTHEAST ASIAN BASICS

The problem regarding the peoples of Southeast Asia is not specific to cultural anthropology and its ethnological orientations. The problem is much more general across the fields of history, political science, linguistics, archaeology, and other academic disciplines. We do not seem to expect that social life is shaped in and through negotiation across difference, and we expect ethnicity to rest on some common core that is rooted in the past. Conventional archaeological approaches to Southeast Asia are very often national in focus, and the areal views we are commonly given rest on unexamined notions of the evolution of technology. In this scheme, the invention of agriculture is a major watershed, one that is anchored to the spread of ethnolinguistic groups. Implicit in this model is a nineteenth-century notion of races of equal strength, some more advanced than others (or at least we can say there is nothing in the mainstream approaches within linguistics and archaeology to challenge such a scheme).

Scientific and vernacular notions of ethnic groups as bounded, biological units reproduce the "tautologies of race, ethnicity, and culture [that characterize contemporary] nation-hood."[37] Richard A. O'Connor asserts, regarding ethnic shifts and agricultural change in the past, that there is "no direct evidence that an actual influx of immigrants ever displaced earlier peoples … Awaiting evidence that may never come is unrealistic and leaving racial waves unchallenged is irresponsible."[38] But some recent work in archaeology and linguistics has created fundamentally new perspectives on matters of diversity in the Southeast Asian region. From the work of linguist N. J. Enfield and that of archaeologist Joyce White, the shaping of the region is coming into a different light.

Enfield advocates a shift from taking language and community for granted as units of analysis, toward a focus on "individual speakers and individual linguistic

---

[36] Anthony F. C. Wallace, *Culture and Personality*, 2nd ed. (New York, NY: Random House, 1970), pp. 22–24, defines "culture" in this way.

[37] Richard A. O'Connor, "A Regional Explanation of the Tai Muang as a City-state," in *A Comparative Study of Thirty City-States*, ed. Mogens Herman Hansen (Copenhagen: The Royal Danish Academy of Sciences and Letters, 2000), p. 441.

[38] Richard A. O'Connor, "Agricultural Change and Ethnic Succession in Southeast Asian States: A Case for Regional Anthropology," *Journal of Asian Studies* 54,4 (1995): 987.

items."[39] He shows that if one examines vowels, the unrelated languages of Khmer, Cham, and Lao turn out to have more in common with one another than any of these languages do with their supposed and separate relatives. In terms of language family trees, Cham is an Austronesian language, Khmer is Mon–Khmer (Austroasiatic), and Lao is a Tai language. Extensive interactions among the speakers of these particular languages have created similarities over time, and the areal focus brings out aspects of how these three languages have taken shape. The more common genealogical focus on the branching of languages within language families, with its assumption of an origin point and subsequent divergence, systemically misses this regional, interactive, and situation-specific character: "Scholars of language need to work through the implications of the view that 'the language' and 'the community' are incoherent as units of analysis for causal processes in the historical and areal trajectories of language diffusion and change."[40]

Various and primarily national ideologies preclude recognition of commonalities. Khmer (Cambodian) and Vietnamese are linguistically related but marked by various surface differences that concern engagements with separate spheres of cultural references over a period of at least a thousand years—Sinitic in the case of Vietnam and Indianized in the case of Cambodia. The relationship between the peoples of the two countries is marked, since the colonial era at least, by animosity. Thai and Khmer languages have various surface similarities while the languages are not related (in ethnolinguistic terms). Historically, many Siamese (Central Thai) and Khmer were bilingual in these two languages; they are not the distinct populations that contemporary and biologized national sentiments assume[41] —an oppositional identification that in recent years has produced recurring episodes of military and other violence.

Enfield shifts the analytical focus from expectations regarding origins, ethnolinguistic essence, and ethnic separateness and toward complexity and the production of patterns—patterns of similarity as much as of difference—through interactions. This does not imply any theory of what changes take place over time; there is no inherent directionality to actions, interactions, differences, or similarities. Enfield's approach is supported by the compelling example that shows Khmer, Cham, and Lao languages becoming similar through contact, while remaining distinct, a case in which there was no reason to expect influences.

No one had thought to even look for these relationships among languages, and our categorical certainties kept us from ever having any curiosity or imagination. Enfield's approach completely undermines any anxieties regarding an analyst's use of ethnic and linguistic categories, because there is no assumption that the languages have any predictable character. It pushes for a regional approach while not taking the character of a region for granted; the region is simply an adequate field for examining complex interactions in varied settings over time, where comparisons may even suggest themselves once we have some familiarity and fluency. The focus is on individual speakers and individual linguistic items, and on the ways things relate and differ over time.

---

[39] N. J. Enfield, "Areal Linguistics and Mainland Southeast Asia," *Annual Reviews in Anthropology* 34,1 (2005): 181.

[40] Ibid., p. 198.

[41] Ibid., pp. 191–92.

Regarding the historical continuity of languages and communities, Enfield gives, tongue-in-cheek, the example of a "fifty-year-old axe which has had three new blades and four new handles [to make the point that] an *idea* has endured, transcending the facts of continuity."[42] From linguistic comparisons, Enfield notes that there is no ambiguity about the five language families of mainland Southeast Asia, but that multilingualism is common, and, most strikingly, languages of separate families show remarkable structural similarity and typological convergence. Hmong and Khmu, which belong to separate families, measure at about the same rate of similarity as do German and English, which are quite related. Polish and Russian are similar to roughly the same extent as are Thai and Vietnamese and Thai and Khmer, which are not related.[43] Enfield suggests that the structural similarity of unrelated Mainland Southeast Asian (MSEA) languages derives

> from a historical context in which adults widely learn and use the languages of neighboring groups, yet while keeping sufficient distance from those groups so that children are not heavily embedded in multilingual learning settings. This kind of social context may be called ethnic pluralism, as it requires the co-presence and interaction of a plurality of ethnic groups, yet where the distinctness of their respective identities is maintained as a matter of common preference.[44]

Risking redundancy, I call attention again to Anthony Wallace's notion of culture as the organization of diversity, frameworks of policy and contract that may enable the structuring of interactions for mutual benefit. Mainland Southeast Asia in all its apparent diversity was produced through such patterns of interaction that aimed for engagements across difference.

Archaeologist Joyce C. White distinguishes between two approaches to the archeological record. View One, global in scope and rooted in high-level theory, promotes an evolutionary model that is anchored to ruptures, progressive stages of tool traditions, the invention of agriculture, and the evolution of political society from bands to chiefdoms to states, in relation to separate language families. One aspect of this is the so-called Farming/Language Dispersal Hypothesis.[45] Against this perspective, White offers View Two, which "sees MSEA diversity as a fundamentally autochthonous process and a byproduct of tropical subsistence systems, both generally and with some aspects peculiar to the Southeast Asian geographic region."[46] She sees the roots of cultural diversity beginning among Pleistocene hunter-gatherers who attuned their sophisticated technologies to the resources of local habitats. In contrast to expectations of "immediate return hunter-gatherer societies at the smallest scale," she points out that archeological findings from Niah

---

[42] N. J. Enfield, *Linguistic Epidemiology: Semantics and Grammar of Language Contact in Mainland Southeast Asia* (New York, NY: RoutledgeCurzon, 2003), p. 4.

[43] N. J. Enfield, "Linguistic Diversity in Mainland Southeast Asia," in *Dynamics of Human Diversity*, ed. N. J. Enfield (Canberra: Pacific Linguistics, 2011), p. 66.

[44] Ibid., p. 71.

[45] Peter Bellwood and Colin Renfrew, *Examining the Farming/Language Dispersal Hypothesis* (Cambridge: McDonald Institute for Archaeological Research, 2003).

[46] Joyce C. White, "Cultural Diversity in Mainland Southeast Asia: A View from Prehistory," in *Dynamics of Human Diversity*, p. 10.

Cave on Borneo, from between twenty-four and fifty-nine thousand years ago, show plants that required advanced planning and promised only delayed results: "forward planning and resource processing over the course of days to weeks."[47] This counters and undermines all the evolutionary premises of the conventional model.

White calls attention to climate changes and considerable micro-regional ecological diversity in ways that undo the credibility of models that feature a population with a particular technology gradually taking over the landscape. Such notions of racial migrations are common, and cultural anthropology has no answer to them since we completely retreated from historical reconstruction and evolutionary questions in the wake of the professionalization of the discipline around concepts such as culture, social structure, and individual ethnic groups.[48] White shows that so-called Hoabinhian stone-tool technology is not associated with any single subsistence orientation or social regime dating from the terminal Pleistocene or early Holocene. "In other words, there is no reason to infer that users of Hoabinhian tools belonged to a single 'culture' or had a single cultural configuration."[49]

Exploring the tools in relation to social, subsistence, and environmental diversity, White is led to argue that their focus was the exploitation of bamboo. As with Enfield's findings about similarities across linguistic divides, this is an area where no one had previously thought to look. Bamboo can be used for food and building-construction materials, and for making rafts or other floatation devices, containers, traps, musical instruments, and hand tools (including weapons). Vegetation maps show that mainland Southeast Asia is home to an enormous range of bamboo species, more than anywhere else in the world. "Regular exploitation of bamboo likely entailed horticultural and other delayed-return behaviors," with no material traces that scholars regularly associate with agriculture. In her conclusions, White suggests that "Because the material properties of bamboo species vary, it is plausible that investment in particular basketry technologies and styles would lead to increased investment in particular geographic areas in order to maintain access to preferred species." She relates this to specializations in food and other resources for exchange, noting that Thailand's archeological record reveals similar technologies pertaining to distinct resources such as millet, rice, and marine resources during 3000–1500 BCE.[50]

In another publication, White illustrates the marked cultural and technological diversity during the metal age of Thailand among societies that were clearly interacting. These interactions did not result in progressive homogeneity. Rather, diversity appears to have been maintained over two thousand years, presumably deliberately, in concert with the sharing of things like metal technologies.[51]

---

[47] Ibid., p. 20.

[48] A rare exception is Edmund R. Leach, who shows how the idea of Aryan invasions into India took hold in nineteenth-century European scholarship while nothing of the sort had happened historically. See Edmund R. Leach, "Aryan Invasions over Four Millennia," in *Culture through Time: Anthropological Approaches*, ed. Emiko Ohnuki-Tierney (Stanford, CA: Stanford University Press, 1990), pp. 227–45.

[49] White, "Cultural Diversity in Mainland Southeast Asia," p. 27.

[50] Ibid., pp. 28, 30, 37.

[51] Joyce C. White and Chureekamol Onsuwan Eyre, "Residential Burial and the Metal Age of Thailand," *Archeological Papers of the American Anthropological Association* 22,1 (2011): 59–78.

I cannot do justice to the complexity of this recent work by White or Enfield, but it suggests that mainland Southeast Asia took shape socially, culturally, and in other ways over the last ten thousand years or longer through networks across difference that were maintained through exchanges of locally particular resources and technologies—the transmission of technologies emphasized in-group dynamics, while exchange emphasized group boundaries and differences. In White's View Two of the archeological record, the invention of rice cultivation most likely was gradual and far from group specific, and perhaps was never an event. It stands as a compelling challenge to the prevailing model that posits racial migrations anchored to technological advances, a proposed scenario that replicates the colonial-era model of ethnolinguistic families that index socially and politically distinct populations of unequal strength. In my reading of White's work, technology explains nothing; people were continually shaped through adaptations to particular environments that varied widely across the region, and in each setting there is considerable indication of localized traditions and patterns of extended interactions across difference.

In this rethinking of the archaeological and linguistic record, there is a radical alternative to our established ways of representing mainland Southeast Asia. Group identities were actively produced, through language, technology, livelihood, and more, but it now seems that these differences among groups were at least partly driven by attempts to harness diversity for projects of mutual benefit.[52] Identity and difference have been shaped in place and through interaction, and there need not be any particular continuity within an ethnic group across time and space. Any analytical expectation of ethnic patterns independent of particular situations becomes untenable. Areal, historical, and comparative work can change the prevalent understandings of the shaping of Southeast Asia, shifting it away from the model that offers a majority and minorities, the strong state with its arm enforcing subjugation and extraction. This expectation lends a particular shape to history, culture, and region, and it should be replaced with questions regarding how diversity related to everyday dynamics of political negotiation.

The peoples of Southeast Asia, then, are the ever-shifting product of relations and negotiations across difference. They should be understood in local and regional contexts of networks of interaction. This is a statement about ethnology, and it is also a political statement about the world that we make available to our students and readers. Some recent scholarship in linguistics, biology, and agriculture suggests on lexical grounds that Mien–Hmong speakers were the first to cultivate rice, and others believe that the honor goes to Austroasiatic speakers or that the two language families are associated with separate rice-origins, while some Chinese scholarship issues a flat denial to such ideas on the grounds that all important things in these southern regions clearly originated with the Chinese from the north.[53]

---

[52] For one contemporary example from the region, see Masaru Nishitani and Nathan Badenoch, "Why Periodic Markets are Held: Considering Products, People, and Place in the Yunnan–Vietnam Border Area," *Southeast Asian Studies* 2,1 (2013): 171–92.

[53] Martha Ratliff, "Vocabulary of Environment and Subsistence in the Hmong–Mien Protolanguage," in *Hmong/Miao in Asia*, ed. Nicholas Tapp, Jean Michaud, Christian Culas, and Gary Yia Lee (Chiangmai: Silkworm Books, 2004), pp. 147–65; Martha Ratliff, *Hmong–Mien Language History* (Canberra: Pacific Linguistics, 2010); George van Driem, "Rice and the Austroasiatic and Hmong–Mien Homelands," in *Dynamics of Human Diversity*, pp. 361–90; and Zhijun Zhao, "New Archaeobotanic Data for the Study of the Origins of Agriculture in China," *Current Anthropology* 52, supplement 4 (2011): S295–S306.

This and other work in related fields asserts that ethnic groups are biologically, linguistically, and culturally distinct and uniform. In a curious revival of colonial-era imagery, all these studies present tree diagrams (two-dimensional) and network trees (three-dimensional) showing ethnic groups as individual nodes, and usually tied to notions of homeland and dispersal.[54] If the linguistic diversity that characterizes mainland Southeast Asia was produced in the last ten to fifteen thousand years, across southern China and mainland Southeast Asia, through interactions across difference that accentuated language as an ethnic marker at the same time as people were engaging across language and thus ethnic boundaries in a sustained fashion, then any notion of historically continuous ethnic uniformity and distinctness is suspect.

In some ways, colonial and nation states produced a political breakdown of long-standing and localized networks of relations. Because cultural anthropology did not ask evolutionary and comparative questions on this front, we anthropologists have offered no challenge to the revamping of colonial-era imagery of distinct racial groups in our sister disciplines. Our retreat, first into functional studies of ethnic groups and then into accounts of marginalization, indicates political paralysis that was often of academic benefit but which isolated our work from any relevance for social life in Southeast Asia or in our home societies. Our scholarship needs to be examined in a comparative light, as an engagement with our audiences at specific moments and in particular contexts.

It was the work of anthropologists including myself that set up James Scott to arrive at his notion of highland dynamics. All of us were carried away by a game that never insisted on the necessity or even the possibility of political negotiation. Instead, we sought out "pure" or "authentic" ethnic or marginal communities, which meant places where boundaries seemed clear and where engagements across difference were not much in evidence. The idea of the ethnic group, like the idea of the state, gives us a handle on history and society in ways that are academically productive and rewarding for ourselves. Viewing the broad situation from that angle, we see that Southeast Asia contains various lessons about the intersections of scholarship, diversity, and negotiation that expose our political paralysis and the passivity that we transmit to our students and readers in the name of our expertise regarding ethnic and political landscapes.

THE ART OF LOOKING THE OTHER WAY

French anthropologist Charles Archaimbault was a long-time resident and researcher in Laos. He relates how the upland–lowland division of peoples was regularly reenacted, in a manner that played out the Laotian cosmogony explaining how the Lao peoples and the upland Kha peoples came to be and to differ.[55] His analysis makes the separation an issue not of unequal power or intelligence that established a permanent ranking of different "races," the theory that had been predominant among his colonial precursors. Instead, as he sees it, the separation

---

[54] Roger Blench, "The Role of Agriculture in the Evolution of Mainland Southeast Asian Language Phyla," *Dynamics of Human Diversity*, pp. 125–52; Laurence Sagart, "The Austroasiatics: East to West or West to East?" in *Dynamics of Human Diversity*, pp. 345–59; and Van Driem, "Rice and the Austroasiatic and Hmong–Mien Homelands."

[55] Charles Archaimbault, "Religious Structures in Laos," trans. Jane R. Hanks, *Journal of the Siam Society* 52,1 (1964): 57–74.

expresses a mythically inspired division in which upland peoples were complicit. He notes their participation in rituals—hockey games and feasts that involved three days of social and sexual intermingling, otherwise frowned upon, and that concluded with a return to the spatial and social division between uplanders and lowlanders on day four. In this analysis, the difference between upland swidden farmers (shifting cultivators) and the wet rice farmers of the lowland states prompted the repeated reenactment of the myth of the origin of the Lao world.

The study thus involved an ethnological move from a world of unequal power and intelligence, a conception that colonial-era ethnography had naturalized, to the "cultural" world of professional anthropology, where myths shaped social orientations and ethnic difference. In some ways, Archaimbault was conjuring something similar to what Claude Lévi-Strauss and other French scholars were after in Amazonia—authentic pre-contact societies—though with one important difference. Archaimbault's brand of cultural relativism implied social unity across a fundamental ethnic divide, a perspective that may be taken as pro-Laos. It contrasts sharply with what anthropologist Oscar Salemink has described for Vietnam, a case for which Western ethnographers' cultural relativism insisted on the radical separation of upland peoples from their lowland neighbors and an incipient national society.[56]

It was Archaimbault's aim to find the "original T'ai substratum [of] cosmogony"[57] pertaining to Lao, Black Thai, Phuan, and other Tai speakers. As such, this project has some similarity to Claude Lévi-Strauss's work on American Indian cultures and their myths and masks.[58] The focus on Lao–Kha relations may reflect the French quest for a means of holding the colony together. Highland–lowland interactions are carried out across various divisions and are continually open to negotiation and subject to the various internal politics of elites, upland villages, traders, and other parties. Any definition of the shape and direction of such relations invites the introduction of political or ethical ideals regarding who people are and what can happen through their interactions.

Charles Archaimbault found a place for the Kha peoples in the Lao worldview; his study does not chase after what the various hinterland peoples made of the relationship or how they might differ from one another. But the French anthropologist was also very likely looking away from the reality of ethnic interactions and social conflict concerning the colonial era and its aftermath. In the introduction to a much later publication on buffalo-sacrifice rituals in Xieng Khwang, Archaimbault relates how the world of Lao ritual was destroyed by the war of 1958–75 and the communist victory. He mentions that the princes of Champassak and Xieng Khwang had become exiles in Perpignon, France, after 1975. They had opposed the Japanese occupation during World War II, and kept alive the memory of their kinsman Chao Anu who, in the 1820s, had marched to attack Bangkok. But

---

[56] Oscar Salemink, *The Ethnography of Vietnam's Central Highlanders: A Historical Contextualization, 1850–1990* (Honolulu, HI: University of Hawaii Press, 2003), pp. 129–210.

[57] Archaimbault, "Religious Structures in Laos," p. 56.

[58] Claude Lévi-Strauss, *The Way of the Masks* (Seattle, WA: University of Washington Press, 1988).

there is little on how the Lao related to the French aside from a mention of the great friendship between certain Lao princes and some French scholars.[59]

The work of Archaimbault is deeply nostalgic for a pre-colonial Lao world, and it appears strikingly out of touch with the unequal and violent relations that sometimes prevailed between Lao lowland rulers and the Mon–Khmer speaking highlanders. Nothing about the running of the French colony went along the mythical lines that Archaimbault found in the old Lao texts, where Lao–Kha relations were characterized by some measure of peaceful coexistence and mutual recognition. I am as fond of the idea as was the French scholar in his time. But pointing to an ideal order as found in some old texts is not a way to understand Laos then and there; such an approach completely brushes aside various concrete problems of interethnic prejudice and abuse.

I do not mean to dismiss this study by recognizing it as a particularly French act of engagement. Rather, I mean to insist that science consists partly of stories that make the world meaningful for particular people in specific times. Japanese scholars have come to Southeast Asia with questions quite different from those that have animated French scholars, for instance. In the 1950s to 1970s, Southeast Asia and southern China offered, through field research and work in the archives, sites for prospecting about Japanese national identity and evolution. In some ways the scholarly work pursued by Japanese academics may be considered an aspect of national reconstruction after the devastation of the Second World War.

One major Japanese study of Yao (Mien) manuscripts and histories in Thailand around 1970 was led by Yoshiro Shiratori, and it "yielded a collection of almost two thousand items of ethnological material, tens of thousands of photographs, as well as many copies of ancient Yao documents." One motive behind the research effort was the possibility that "the actual origins of the non-Chinese tribes in Central and South China and Southeast Asia [and the shift from dry-rice to wet-rice cultivation would help to solve] directly or indirectly the origins of the Wajin, and the formative process of Japanese culture."[60]

The various ramifications of rice and rice cultivation were important for Japanese scholarship and national self-image,[61] and Shiratori's research project in Thailand during 1967–68 had a precursor in a project concerning rice culture in Southeast Asia that studied Vietnam, Cambodia, and Laos in 1957–58 and encompassed some villages of the Yao in Laos. The idea that scientists could crack the code of Japanese national identity through their research on rice cultivation in Southeast Asia and adjacent southern China offered a way to boost the creative and productive promise of Japanese international scholarship; here was an investment that the Japanese government could enthusiastically support.[62]

---

[59] Charles Archaimbault, *Le Sacrifice du Buffle a S'ieng Khwang (Laos)* (Paris: École Français d'Extrême Orient, 1991), pp. v–ix.

[60] Namio Egami, "Preface," in *Ethnography of the Hill Tribes of Southeast Asia* (*Tonan ajia sanchi mizokushi: Yao to sono rinsetsu shoshuzoku*), ed. Yoshiro Shiratori (Tokyo: Sophia University, 1978), p. 281.

[61] Emiko Ohnuki–Tierney, *Rice as Self: Japanese Identities through Time* (Princeton, NJ: Princeton University Press, 1993).

[62] Keiji Iwata, "Minority Groups in Northern Laos, Especially the Yao," trans. H. Sakomoto, ed. Joel Halpern (Laos Project, Paper No. 16, University of California–Los Angeles, Department of Anthropology, 1961). For discussion and historicization, see Yoko Hayami, "Within and beyond the Boundaries: Anthropological Studies of Mainland Southeast Asia since the 1950s,"

The Art of Not Being Governed by James Scott is a scientific story, a representation through which people can come into knowledge of self, other, and world.[63] It is not, in my view, a good story. The book rests on fatalism about ethnic frontiers, politics, and history, and declares that what is interesting about ethnic diversity in Southeast Asia are strategies of state-avoidance, a story that allegedly came to an end by 1950. The case rests on an acceptance of the ethnic chauvinism of some modern nation states as a legacy of two thousand years of history. History, then, serves to demarcate a field for creating knowledge, similar to how the idea of nature operates in primatology.[64] The story of Zomia is one of gradual conquest, and the case rests on conviction regarding the impossibility of negotiating across ethnic difference in Southeast Asia. To respond to it with other than argument or dismissal, I suggest that the evidence can be traced to particular situations of political breakdown, and then one can ask what it means to have our examples only or primarily from such settings.

The case for Zomia makes completely trivial how United States involvement and wars in Laos, Vietnam, and Cambodia destroyed these countries and did considerable damage to the social and academic imaginations of US Americans at home. In Vietnam, US Special Forces and CIA operatives actively sought out ethnic minority leaders as allies and potential guerrilla leaders. The notion of highland people's commitment to freedom was important to bolster the United States' identity and its global position as one that supported freedom and resisted oppression. In Laos, US agents established, trained, equipped, and funded militias in the cosmic struggle for freedom and against (communist) oppression, with Hmong, Mien, Khmu, Lahu, Akha, and other highland peoples playing a significant role along with many Lao and others.

What disappears completely from the many surfaces of Zomia is the US contribution to obliterating the possibility of peaceful, multi-ethnic accommodation in Southeast Asia, and, at the same time, paving the way for subsequent authoritarianism in Laos, Vietnam, and Cambodia. We get to enjoy and appreciate the freedom-seeking highlanders of the past, and to identify with their struggle to avoid the trappings of oppression. Through an imaginary Zomia, Southeast Asia offers a foil for coming into particular US American identities and origin stories that deny any contemporary reality to many people's need for negotiation toward recognition or equality in the United States or elsewhere.

If I failed to implicate my own self and work I would be pretending immunity, suggesting that I can somehow see through what others have been doing while I am outside the picture, wearing an analytical HazMat suit—an outfit protecting me as a scholar from contamination by hazardous materials. Claude Lévi-Strauss's notion that Western readers "may even discover pristine freshness [in the human lessons learned from the poorest tribe]"[65] is an indication of how some academic sojourns

---

Japanese Review of Cultural Anthropology 2 (2001): 66–69. On the role of archaeology in Japanese national prospecting, see Clare Fawcett, "Nationalism and Postwar Japanese Archaeology," in *Nationalism, Politics, and the Practice of Archaeology,* ed. Philip Kohl and Clare Fawcett (Cambridge: Cambridge University Press, 1995), pp. 232–46.

[63] James C. Scott, *The Art of Not Being Governed*.

[64] Donna Haraway, *Primate Visions* (New York, NY: Rouledge, 1989).

[65] Claude Lévi-Strauss, *Tristes Tropiques,* trans. John and Doreen Weightman (New York, NY: Simon and Schuster, 1973 [French orig. 1955]), p. 448.

perpetuate the art of looking the other way thanks to the way our work "samples" certain peoples identities, lives, stories, or fate. One need not declare any of these efforts to constitute the cynical manipulation of ethnic others. An alternative is offered by Johan Huizinga, that people may not be particularly aware of some dimensions of their play or of its implications:

> Even [musical composers] Bach and Mozart could hardly have been aware that they were pursuing anything more than the noblest of pastimes, pure recreation. And was it not this sublime naïveté that enabled them to soar to the heights of perfection?[66]

Perhaps all representation, including the narratives of science, is an invitation to discover things through journeys on the borderlands of self, other, and world. It is through representation and intersubjective play, in which roles can be reversed, that even pre-lingual infants come to be and learn.[67] Recent research in psychology emphasizes the social aspects of cognition, including false-belief understandings that require an understanding of the knowledge in other people's minds. The development of false-belief understandings, which generally occurs around age three,

> marks a transition to higher-level metarepresentational abilities. With this ability, children are able to represent another representation and, instead of simply understanding that people have different viewpoints, they can now represent a belief, assess whether it is true or false, and use the representation to predict human behavior. [The role of false-belief understanding] in adult social interaction is not fully understood.[68]

The case for Zomia is a possible site for exploring these dynamics. The analysis rests on a plot that has a fundamental reversal built into it regarding the place of highland peoples on the landscapes of history and politics in Southeast Asia, and, more generally, elsewhere. The people we had been told were traditional, ignorant, and backward (and whatever other deficiency comes to mind) were, in fact, clever freedom-seekers whose apparent deficiencies were clever disguises for the strategies that we ourselves admire and with which we identify. Evolutionism, state rhetoric, and other forms of obfuscation muddied our thinking for a time, but with the help of this recent book we can now see through the deception and reassess history's marginalized peoples. The knowledge of what forces benefited from this deception adds to the allure and value of the de-masking. A community of understanding is thus enabled through a shared disbelief in certain kinds of classifications and narratives.

But the modern nation state is not the culmination of a history of several millennia. The militarized chauvinism of contemporary Burma is quite unprecedented, as was the anti-hill-tribe ideology of Thai nationalism that was most

---

[66] Johan Huizinga, *Homo Ludens: A Study of the Play Element in Culture* (Boston, MA: Beacon Press, 1950), p. 189.

[67] Michael Tomasello, "Why Don't Apes Point?" in *Roots of Human Sociality*, pp. 506–24.

[68] Jennie E. Peters, "Constructing the Social Mind: Language and False-belief Understanding," in *Roots of Human Sociality*, pp. 208, 224.

pronounced from the 1950s to 1980s. Taking such particular structures of intolerance, discrimination, abuse, and violence to be the shape of Southeast Asian history for the last two thousand years is the ultimate concession to the racialized inequalities that sometimes take hold in modern nation states, and to the self-serving rhetoric of some national elites. A reader of *The Art of Not Being Governed* cannot register any surprise at situations that I would call tragic and politically pathological, violent episodes that can tear apart whole societies, which in some ways is the story of the war in Laos that is the focus of the next chapter.

Dismissing ethnicity as socially constructed refuses any recognition of the interethnic or other identity-based violence, abuse, and discrimination that does take place in contemporary Southeast Asia as well as elsewhere. It disables any critique that might claim equality and recognition for ethnically or otherwise diverse subjects, at home, away, and between them. Meanwhile, the conviction that the state or the national majority is hostile to difference and that any political negotiation is harmful (subjugating) to minority subjects accentuates how scholarship can induce epistemological and political collapse. It discourages the search for solutions to problems in diverse and democratic societies, and it tends to find peculiar comfort in the critique of hegemonic nationalism. My sense of peculiar comfort derives from the fact that that scholars generally refuse to attack the truism of such ideologies by showing how unrepresentative they may be of the peoples and societies ostensibly behind them—the Thai, Chinese, Lao, or whomever. Insisting on diversity in Southeast Asia past and present is not a celebration of some apolitical multiculturalism but an insistence on the need for, and long history of, negotiation across difference.

Charles Archaimbault may have known of the diversity of Lao and other Tai groups, but his insistence on a binary Lao–Kha ethnic frontier is an obstacle to understanding. It should be removed with reference to social life and history, and through some indication that the state and ethnic categories are abstractions. Prior to French colonial rule, there were various Lao kingdoms, and they had multiple kinds of relations with highland neighbors who were generally glossed as Kha. Prior to colonial-era road projects in the 1930s, lowland Lao were dependent on highland farmers for their rice, for instance, and there was active trade that balanced intersecting needs between the two kinds of environments. But in 1879 all of this came to a halt, and many Khmu and other so-called Kha peoples left for wage work in logging on the Thai side of the border. The king in Luang Prabang had maintained relations with various Kha peoples, but there is every indication that those relations were strained. The Khmu rebelled at one point, and that was the end of whatever contract there was with the king. The king then issued a pardon, and the relations were reinstated.[69]

---

[69] I summarize, as the material is complicated and the fine (and gory) detail does not make or break my case. My understanding draws on reading started many years ago when I wanted to understand what landscape Mien peoples had moved through in the late nineteenth century. My main sources are: "Report on a Journey in the Me-Kong Valley," by W. J. Archer (first assistant in Her Majesty's Consular Service in Siam), *Parliamentary Papers 1892–93, Accounts and Papers*, vol. 32 (London: United Kingdom, House of Commons, 1892–93); Holt Hallett, *A Thousand Miles on an Elephant in the Shan States* (London: William Blackwood & Sons, 1890); James McCarthy, *Surveying and Exploring in Siam* (London: John Murray, 1900); James McCarthy (anonymously), *An Englishman's Siamese Journals* (undated reprint of the 1895 original, Bangkok: Siam Media International, ca. 1985); and H. Warington Smyth, *Five Years in Siam, from 1891 to 1896* (New York, NY: Charles Schribner's Sons, 1898). The complexity of pre-

But apparently the king and the viceroy were at odds about many things. While the king was away in Bangkok, the viceroy's people were supervising work by the highlanders, and the viceroy's son was injured in an accident attributed to the Kha. People came to blows, and then a full-scale fight erupted, and the Lao fled. Later, the viceroy summoned about one hundred Kha headmen to the capital in Luang Prabang. They held up the white flags of pardon that the king had issued, but the viceroy was intent on revenge, ready to use violence and deception, and he had each of the highland leaders executed. Somewhere between five and twenty-five thousand Khmu left for northern Thailand, and the ones who remained in Lao domains did not get incorporated in any high positions within the kingdoms. Instead, Lao rulers made or took offers of relations with Mien, Hmong, and Lanten peoples, giving their leaders titles such as *Phaya* and *Saen*.

The viceroy–Kha example is meant to offer an alternative to expectations of disconnect and to ideas that political and other relations across difference are unproblematic. Such relations are always subject to review or failure; politics and society may be inherently volatile. But there is no predetermined character to relations on the ethnic frontier, and the long run of regional history offers many and often-ignored cases of peaceful accommodation. No such network is in the abstract, and in this case concerning northern Laos one of the components was regional markets for cattle, forest products, and labor that were somewhat specific to time and place.

Anthropology has helped make us blind to this world. Swedish anthropologist Karl Gustav Izikowitz did field research among Lamet (Rmeet) in 1936–37. He suggests that Khmu fit the model of Kha groups that paid tribute to lowland courts, while Lamet had been more independent. He notes that Lamet had earlier paid tax to Yuan rulers in Chiang Khong, but, as that domain fell or faded away, they came to trade rice to Luang Prabang for salt and metal, while Khmu contributed forest products. In this light, we can see that it is unlikely that Lamet as such were any more intrinsically independent than Khmu.[70]

The difference between Lamet and Khmu had been anchored to separate courts, and once they dealt with the same court the difference was reproduced in terms of separate goods and the divergent options of trade. But given how Izikowitz characterized the ethnic difference, it seems plain that he considered the Lamet a

---

twentieth-century "Lao" kingdoms is slowly emerging, such as through the work of Volker Grabowsky and Renoo Wichasin, *Chronicles of Chiang Khaeng: A Tai Lue Principality of the Upper Mekong* (Honolulu, HI: Center for Southeast Asian Studies, University of Hawaii, 2008). It is possible, say, that the Khmu troubles drew on the Luang Prabang king's attempt to deny the power of many other kings, and that we do not ask the right questions regarding such situations because we take the one-capital nation-state for granted. Some recent work suggests that the Khmu ethnic label imports expectations of ethnic sameness, whereas social life is shaped by subgroups and divergent histories; see Olivier Evrard, *Chroniques des Cendres: Anthropologies des sociétés Khmmu et dynamiques interethniques du Nord-Laos* (Paris: Institute for Development Research [IRD], 2006). This recent work may help situate the reality conveyed by Edmund Leach, *Political Systems of Highland Burma* (Boston, MA: Beacon Press, 1954) as squarely of the British-ruled 1930s. His study was done fifty years after the British takeover, and the British had quickly dismantled whatever local political arrangements there were. And Leach and the Kachin were involved in war—the Kachin label is very much of the British era, but it later became entrenched because of how the ethnicized civil war has played out.

[70] Karl Gustav Izikowitz, *Lamet: Hill Peasants of French Indochina* (Gothenburg, Sweden: Etnografiska Museet, 1951), pp. 28, 346, 311.

purer sample of highland peoples, less sullied by extensive contact with the Lao and other lowlanders. There is much to learn from the work of Izikowitz, but the expectation of ethnic patterns and the quest for non-contact peoples as the "pure" samples for ethnography is one of the legacies that helped inspire the search for and discovery of Zomia.

It was not the state that was out to get the Khmu. Instead, the court was a potential party to a relationship that at one point turned increasingly hostile and had various tragic and other consequences. And the court was the site of various internal politics—in his orchestrated violence, the viceroy undid the political alliances that his rival, the king, maintained with the hinterlands. To remove any doubt about my trust in analytical categories, I suggest that "viceroys" is about as useful as "the state"—without specifics, the category can be made to mean anything, which is to say, also, that it means nothing.

The examples of networks across ethnic frontiers may contribute to a different sense of Southeast Asia as a region. For decades, historian Ronald D. Renard has been conducting research about Karen peoples in relation to Thai states. Few paid much attention to his work, it seems, which I now see as a manifestation of how academic orientations helped silence the past of negotiation and contracts across ethnic lines.[71] One historian of Sumatra, Indonesia, "found a situation where two coastal rulers each commanded distinct lines of loyalty with different sections of the [hinterland] Batak population." In one part of Sulawesi, Indonesia, separate clusters of upland and coastal communities sometimes "act[ed] in concert [against armed Bugis incursions, but at other times] looked upon one another with suspicion. Above all, these polities were consumed with their own internal rivalries and power struggles [before they collapsed in 1872]."[72]

Here I resist giving a long list of counter examples, which has been one reaction to the case for Zomia: "[Nothing is] scientifically proven by the endless multiplication of examples, except that anthropology can be boring."[73] But sometimes an additional example is more than just another case. Oona Paredes's work on Lumad in Mindanao in the colonial-era Philippines shows how a people everyone thought of as isolated highlanders who avoided contact into the lowlands have, in fact, a very different past. From archival research she draws out their multiple relations and friendships with Spanish (Basque, to be more specific) Catholic priests. This was not subjugation to the colonial state. Instead, people came

---

[71] Ronald D. Renard, "Kariang: History of Karen–T'ai Relations from the Beginnings to 1923" (PhD dissertation, University of Hawaii, 1980); Ronald D. Renard, "The Integration of Karens in Northern Thai Political Life during the Nineteenth Century," in *Anuson Walter Vella*, ed. Ronald D. Renard (Honolulu, HI: Center for Asian and Pacific Studies, University of Hawaii at Manoa, 1986), pp. 229–48; Ronald D. Renard, "On the Possibility of Early Karen Settlement in the Chiangmai Valley," in *Inter-ethnic Relations in the Making of Southeast Asia and Southwest China*, ed. Yukio Hayashi and Aroonrut Wichienkeeo (Bangkok: Amarin, 2002), pp. 59–84.

[72] Jane Drakard, *A Malay Frontier: Unity and Duality in a Sumatran Kingdom* (Ithaca, NY: Cornell Southeast Asia Program, 1990), p. 46; Kenneth M. George, "Headhunting, History, and Exchange in Upland Sulawesi," *Journal of Asian Studies* 50,3 (1991): 548.

[73] Marshall Sahlins, *Stone Age Economics* (London: Tavistock, 1972), p. 73. Two historians of Burma have responded to James Scott's case: Victor Lieberman offers an extensive fifteen-page refutation with seventy-six footnote references: "A Zone of Refuge in Southeast Asia: Reconsidering Interior Spaces," *Journal of Global History* 5 (2010): 333–48; while Michael Aung-Thwin offers the same in five pages with no references: "Debate on Zomia," *Bijdragen tot de Taal-, Land- en Volkenkunde* 167,1 (2011): 95–99.

into particular relations across differences for mutual benefit that can and must be historicized in considerable detail.[74] In this case as elsewhere, identities and difference were negotiated in place, among particular partners, and rested on some equivalence. The contemporary look and outlook of their descendants shows no signs of these earlier relations, which again is a reminder that cultures and identities are continually being reproduced with new coordinates.

The expectation of ethnic frontiers and their match with political position and ideology is profoundly wrong for Southeast Asia. And what scholars call "the state" is usually a composite image that serves to misconstrue the complexity, particularity, and urgency of political life in any actual setting. Our categories offer analytical shortcuts toward representations of history, politics, kinship, and whatever else drives our academic work. The Zomia case obliterates the complex and varied histories of Southeast Asia's peoples and places. It participates in the academic and political silencing of certain people's claims to recognition and equality within modern nation states. They become unthinkable as long-time participants in negotiation across difference.

Scholars sell products on the academic market—tribes, social structure, culture, marginalization, escape strategies—all of this reproducing expectations about peoples as distinct, disconnected, and, sometimes, antagonistic. In the next three chapters, I situate the Mien historically in Laos, Thailand, and the United States. On the basis of the three scenarios, I expand, in the afterword, on the complex reality that is involved in the making, selling, consumption, and recycling of academic products such as Southeast Asian highland peoples, "traditional peoples," and negotiation across lines of difference.

Taking a clue from Karl Marx's discussion of commodities, which gets a brief mention in Chapter Three but would otherwise be a distraction, I point to some of the things that we may learn from our own scholarly products if we can suspend our naïve empiricism and political posturing. The case rests on ethnography and comparisons, but I am also telling stories through or with ethnography: "Some fictions are closer to 'real' life than others, and our [anthropological] task must be to seek those out in preference to those that are less so."[75]

---

[74] Oona Paredes, *A Mountain of Difference: The Lumad in Early Colonial Mindanao* (Ithaca, NY: Cornell Southeast Asia Program Publications, 2013).

[75] A. Thomas Kirsch, *Feasting and Social Oscillation* (Ithaca, NY: Cornell Southeast Asia Program, 1973), p. 35.

CHAPTER TWO

IU MIEN AND THE WAR IN LAOS

In his *Poetics*, philosopher Aristotle focuses on representation and theatrical drama. He is an individual voice and not the representation of any larger identity or collective project, such as "Greek philosophy." Aristotle distinguishes tragedy from comedy and remarks that the historical trajectories of the two are unevenly known: "Now, while the stages of tragedy's development, and those responsible for them, have been preserved, comedy's have not been, because it was not originally given serious attention."[1]

The impulse to write dramatic histories is generally attuned to weighty matters such as war and death, while peaceful or playful interaction across difference is passively or actively ignored to the point that there may be no trace of it in archives or other histories. A focus on hostility or other clear binaries offers easily translated drama. There is little doubt that educated Western readers of works influenced by the case for Zomia see some of themselves in these mind-boggling cosmopolitans who for centuries or millennia held onto freedom and resisted subjugation despite the odds. Binary drama has "contrasting outcomes for good and bad characters. It is the weakness of audiences which produces the view of this type's superiority; poets are led to give the spectators what they want."[2]

Poetic dramas in Aristotle's time were written in response to contests for prizes and attendance, and he suggests that to win accolades the poets would flatter the audience with easy opportunities of identification with good characters. While the war in Laos never received the amount of attention as did the US–Vietnam War, the little there has been published tends to play up such moral binaries, particularly regarding the Hmong who are depicted—for those who identify with the US war and its allies—as noble and heroic freedom fighters, and, in one academic case, with deep traces of "white" identity. For those who identify against the US war and its allies, the Hmong are described as sinister mercenaries and drug traffickers.[3]

Such works play to readers' wish for a perspective on US wars abroad in terms of emotional identification with the attractive Other or against its repulsive counterpart. I discuss such characterizations at the end of this chapter, once I have provided some sense of Mien experiences and the impact of war on Mien identity and social life. The Mien people have never been a symbolically overcharged object of American identification, for or against. This leaves me with some leeway for

---

[1] Stephen Halliwell, *The Poetics of Aristotle: Translation and Commentary* (Chapel Hill, NC: The University of North Carolina Press, and London: Duckworth, 1987), p. 36 (*Poetics*, Ch. 5).

[2] Ibid., p. 45 (*Poetics*, Ch. 13).

[3] "Hmong" and "Mien" are ethnic labels for peoples best known as highland farmers. The labels demarcate "peoples" as the object of anthropological expertise, ethnic tourism, and more. This chapter is meant to offer a sense of the contingency of any particular understanding of a people, equally a matter of historical conditions and of self- and other-prospecting.

exploring diversity, historical specificity, and the contingencies of Mien involvement in Lao worlds and beyond.

Mien leadership was anchored to valley kingdoms that offered trade relations, titles, and other benefits of regional networks before the 1940s. This reality had faded away by the time anthropologists became interested in the group. Scholarly generalizations about the highlands belong to the era of nation states and particular forms of ethnic divides and prejudice that may have no historical precursor. That is, the "highland world" of relatively egalitarian ethnic communities that formed the scaffolding of the argument for Zomia may only have emerged in the twentieth century, and may also be somewhat specific to Thailand. The Mien case suggests not only that people settled into relations with lowland kings, but that chiefs dealt with these political connections and ordinary people were in relationship with their chief. The upland–lowland divide that I at one point focused on is not a historically transcendent condition. Instead, it is clearly shaped by modern nation states and their colonial precursors. Predating this upland–lowland divide were various regional networks across difference, similar to what Joyce C. White shows for the archaeological record. While ethnicity has long been important, it does not with any regularity imply antagonism or separate worlds. Instead, it establishes one aspect of relational networks that are themselves always particular to place and time.

In a recent historical study of Luang Namtha in northern Laos, Nathan Badenoch and Shinsuke Tomita point to how Lanten, Sida, and Bit peoples settled the area in the 1800s, paid tribute to Luang Prabang and Nan, and then invited a group of Nyuan ("northern Thai") lowlanders to move from Nan in order to clear the lowlands and make wet-rice fields. From the uplanders' perspective, they made the polity possible by inviting some lowlanders to play particular roles in a complex relationship.[4] This runs counter to predominant lowland narratives featuring royal agency and to the expectation that upland peoples were motivated to run away from states. In lowland court narratives of history, entanglements with upland peoples are usually little commented on. It may simply be that the self-image of Buddhist lowland rulers could not easily admit to intimacies with non-Buddhist Others. As with the unknown history of early Greek comedies, the issue may never have been taken seriously by the scribes of royal chronicles. One may view the royal scribes as having been carried away by a particular game about lowland kingdoms, whose serious concerns were often their rivalries with similar entities.

The regional networks that included various upland–lowland relations were primarily among neighbors. With the establishment of modern nation states that have a single capital, innumerable valley kingdoms were erased and with them went most of the localized regional networks. But in Laos and Thailand, some highland areas became integrated into opium monopolies that created new networks and leadership opportunities. In Thailand, these went exclusively to Mien people, but in Laos they went to both Hmong and Mien. Khmu and Rmeet peoples had previously been the main parties to upland connections in northern Laos, but these relationships were varied and subject to the uneven fortune of individual kingdoms that came and went.[5]

---

[4] Nathan Badenoch and Shinsuke Tomita, "Mountain People in the Muang: Creation and Governance of a Tai Polity in Northern Laos," *Southeast Asian Studies* 2,1 (2013): 29–67.

[5] Guido Sprenger, "Political Periphery, Cosmological Center: The Reproduction of Rmeet Sociocosmic Order and the Laos–Thailand Border," in *Centering the Margin: Agency and Narrative in Southeast Asian Borderlands*, ed. Alexander Horstman and Reed Wadley (New

Lanten are a Yao people, like the Mien, but they are in some ways distinct from the Mien. While Mien leaders had *phaya* titles, the Lanten leader had the lower-ranking title of *saen*. The Lanten people grew poppy, but they were not brought into the opium trade: "We never knew how to sell it."[6] This is some indication that highland peoples' experiences were quite varied and differentiated, and their interactions could shift from one lowland regime to another. I take the Lanten gloss of "knowing how to sell [some product]" in the context of Joyce White's discussion of localized networks of mutually interdependent specialization for trade; ignorance of market protocols indicates that a group is being excluded from particular networks.

My focus in this chapter is on Lao Iu Mien experiences and perspectives over a century, from the 1870s to the 1970s. I show that Mien settled into relations with valley kingdoms through their leaders. Their farming was quite differentiated between leaders who could claim a whole mountain for their fields and the commoners who were migratory swidden farmers. I offer a description of one such large upland farm to counter the image of highlanders as uniformly small-scale farmers in rather egalitarian settlements. Recollections from a range of Iu Mien reveal varied perspectives on the past; commoners assess their experiences in terms of the ability to farm and hold onto their resources and their children, which some were forced to sell off to adoptive families to afford a steep tax. People in wealthy households and those in leadership positions could benefit from valley kingdoms, French rule, or the opportunities provided by the CIA-sponsored militia.

Once the US-Vietnam war became entrenched, the militia had considerable command over their Mien affiliates and could demand that young men serve as soldiers. Hmong and Mien militia leaders worked toward multiethnic accommodation, against considerable national prejudice—their national context was quite different from the previous networks of interaction surrounding particular valley kingdoms. For some time during and after the war, between the battlegrounds in Laos and the refugee camps in Thailand, there emerged a three-way division of Mien as Northern, Central, and Southern. The geographic distinctions were shaped by different relations to the main militias, and by how the camps created ethnic constituencies that played to militia leaders after the war was supposedly over.

The war and the refugee camps involved many intersecting regional dynamics, and I draw on a range of conversations and interviews to suggest some of the particularities that distinguished how people experienced this time. Rituals that venerate soldier-spirits became very important during the war, as did other means of acquiring invulnerability. As an ethnographer, I offer the material as a complement and counter to village-based studies that often have a very shallow time span. I am also working against the temptation of easy identifications for or against particular people caught up in some US-related war in a faraway country. As far as possible, my account strives for neutrality regarding the motives of Mien militia leaders Chao Mai and Chao La. My Mien acquaintances, who related to those leaders in a range of

---

York, NY: Berghahn, 2006), pp. 67–86; Volker Grabowsky and Renoo Wichasin, *Chronicles of Chiang Khaeng: A Tai Lue Principality of the Upper Mekong* (Honolulu, HI: Center for Southeast Asian Studies, University of Hawaii, 2008); Olivier Evrard, "Oral Histories of Livelihoods and Migration under Socialism and Post-Socialism among the Khmu of Northern Laos," in *Moving Mountains: Ethnicity and Livelihoods in Highland China, Vietnam, and Laos,* ed. Tim Forsyth and Jean Michaud (Vancouver: University of British Columbia Press, 2011), pp. 76–99.

[6] Badenoch and Tomita, "Mountain People in the Muang," p. 54.

ways, vary in their assessment of them. If I am playing politics with this account of Mien in wartime, it is explicitly against easy moral binaries from afar (e.g., common perceptions that the Hmong are admirable freedom fighters, or that the Hmong are repulsive drug traffickers and CIA mercenaries).

In Aristotle's discussion of different kinds of drama, he claimed that comedy depicted people as laughable and that the experience of watching a comedy offered no means of identification with the characters but instead merely evoked indifference toward people who were inferior and laughable. The poetic mode that he declared the best was one that played up human fallibility through reversal, which might bring us (the audience) to recognize the risk of all social interaction when we don't know our relations. This does not offer any flattering sense of self through an "other," but rather heightens the sense that we are all at risk of doing one another harm because of mistaken identifications.[7]

Poets, the writers of dramatic theater, are makers of *mythos*, plot structures wherein the cast of characters and the outcome of their interactions cohere in a single move.[8] I cannot offer such artistic coherence, but want to push for recognition of how our characterizations of the Asian hinterlands have generally made political negotiation across difference seem neither possible nor rewarding. The Mien are not a singular subject, and negotiation across difference does not inherently involve some Mien–Other configuration. There is considerable negotiation within the Mien category as well as beyond it. Culture, in Anthony Wallace's understanding, is both policy and contract that enables some mutually beneficial interaction. In contemporary academic language, it can be compared to the "common ground" that is fashioned through language and interaction and is always particular to specific networks as much as it is general for the human condition.[9]

The chapter aims to chart what common ground Mien people engaged with before, during, and after the war in Laos (1954–75). When I first presented some of this material at a conference of the American Anthropological Association in San Francisco in 2008, a colleague who had some familiarity with the Mien in the United States responded quite critically, "You are fundamentally wrong in putting all this emphasis on the militia, Chao La, and the war in Laos. Iu Mien culture and identity are about the twelve lineages, about ancestor worship, wedding customs, and ritual ordinations." I could only nod and smile and thank the scholar for the correction. But when I told some Mien people in nearby Oakland about that interchange, they were adamant about the impact of the war and the militia leadership on their experiences and identity.

At war's end, the Mien fled across the border into Thailand, and they could not return to Laos for fear of extreme punishment. The common ground that I describe was not stable, nor was there any one shared Mien perspective on Laos and the wartime. There is nothing inevitable or predictable about how the war and its aftermath played out. Through citing descriptions of episodes, experiences, and recollections regarding social life in the hinterlands of Southeast Asia, I want to challenge some prevailing categorical convictions about our "others" and the selves we recognize from them.

---

[7] Halliwell, *The Poetics of Aristotle*, pp. 36, 43 (*Poetics*, Ch. 5, 11).

[8] Ibid., p. 40 (*Poetics*, Ch. 8).

[9] N. J. Enfield, "Social Consequences of Common Ground," in *Roots of Human Sociality*, ed. N. J. Enfield and Stephen Levinson (New York, NY: Berg, 2006), pp. 399–430.

The issues concern the world of representation, what Aristotle called *mimesis*. The term is best left untranslated, because its ambiguity and promise are useful attributes. I have learned most about these issues from the translations and commentary of Stephen Halliwell, who identifies pervasive problems with the common translation of "mimesis" as "imitation" (from the Latin *imitatio*). Mimesis is usually nothing of the sort, but rather suggests representation, rendering, enactment, expression, and the translation of something from one realm into another. Mimesis, suggests Aristotle, is fundamental to humanity and to human understanding, language, music, dance, and much else. All humans are equally dependent on it. Representation and understanding are their own sources of pleasure for people.[10]

One of the terms in the *Poetics* that has made for enormous distraction (spilled ink and imagination) among Western scholars and others is *katharsis*. This is generally taken to mean the purging of some undesirable emotion. In Halliwell's rendering, the issue is different and simpler; some representations lead people to new understandings of self, other, and world by triggering a realignment of emotion, reason, and experience. That is all.[11] In revisiting some aspects of the war in Laos and the peoples in that picture, I am deliberately serving up some materials that may, if people are so inclined, lead to one such realignment of identity, understanding, emotion, reason, and the world, but I cannot make up anyone else's mind.

BACKGROUND

From one angle, the war in Laos was an elaborate family fight, starting with the rivalry among Princes Petsarath, Souvanna Phuma, and Suphanuvong and King Sisavang Vong. With backing and intervention from North Vietnam and the United States, the king's and princes' different ideas about the future of Laos—after it had been ruled by the French and then the Japanese—tore the country apart, with the help of ostensible neutralist Kong Le, who had staged a military takeover in 1960 (and who remained active for a long time, as he was still trying to raise funds in 1990). There were members of any and all ethnic groups on any side of the conflict. The country, the Lao people, and the Hmong and other highland and lowland ethnic groups all suffered extensive damage. Among the first refugees to cross the Mekong River in 1975 were Tai Dam, Nung, Tai-Tho, Tai-So, and Tai-Han. They crossed into Thailand toward Nong Khai, while the Mien who also left at this time went toward Chiang Khong.[12]

---

[10] Stephen Halliwell, *Aristotle's Poetics* (Chicago, IL: University of Chicago Press, 1998); and Halliwell, *The Poetics of Aristotle*. See also Amelie Oksenberg Rorty, ed., *Essays on Aristotle's Poetics* (Princeton, NJ: Princeton University Press, 1992).

[11] Claude Lévi-Strauss claims something of this sort as his discovery regarding what South American Indians' "magico–religious" cure and Western psychoanalysis have in common; see Claude Lévi-Strauss, *Structural Anthropology* (New York, NY: Penguin, 1963), pp. 186–205.

[12] See: Nina Adams and Alfred McCoy, eds., *Laos: War and Revolution* (New York, NY: Harper, 1970); Timothy Castle, *At War in the Shadow of Vietnam: US Military Aid to the Royal Lao Government 1955–1975* (New York, NY: Columbia University Press, 1993); Martin Stuart-Fox, *Buddhist Kingdom, Marxist State: The Making of Modern Laos* (Bangkok: White Lotus, 1996); Martin Stuart-Fox, *A History of Laos* (Cambridge: Cambridge University Press, 1997); and Bernard Van-es-Beeck, "Refugees from Laos, 1975–1979," in *Contemporary Laos*, ed. Martin Stuart-Fox (St. Lucia: University of Queensland Press, 1982), pp. 324–35.

Compared to the Lao and the Hmong, these are largely unknown and unnoticed peoples; the various small Tai groups had left Northern Vietnam for Laos in 1954 because they had been on the side that lost. The trail of refugees may stretch back as far as one cares to look, but it is also important not to get carried away by the categorical certainty that we can identify all these people on the move as "refugees," or, in the newer terminology, "Internally Displaced Persons." These are people who are always particular, who differ from their own compatriots, and may also share long histories of interactions across shifting fields of relations.[13]

The war in Laos was a contest full of deceptions. After a temporary truce among rival political factions in 1962, "foreign ministers of fourteen nations signed a Declaration and Protocol on the Neutrality of Laos."[14] This agreement committed the United States to withdraw all forces from Laos. Thailand, too, had extensive military engagements in Laos, as did North Vietnam, which also had considerable logistical and equipment support from the Soviet Union. Each of these governments lied and deceived their antagonists and the whole world about their intentions and role in slowly destroying Laos. No one much noticed Laos; the world was preoccupied with events in Vietnam.

From the perspective of US leaders, whose military involvement in Southeast Asia replaced French colonial management and repression, the spread of communism was viewed as the outbreak of a dangerous contamination that would poison the global political body and endanger the United States. This set in motion the equivalent of an immune-system response, to rid the body of the threat. As anthropologist Emily Martin describes the social imagery in her study of American notions of immunity, only some cells have VIP status and recognition, such as "T4 cells [that] have a masculinity composed of intellect, strategic planning ability, and propensity for corporate team participation, powers well suited for the world of global corporations."[15]

The enormity of the war in Laos is not a topic for me to tackle. Instead, I attempt to describe some aspects of how the war became a particular reality for the Iu Mien people, who were swept up in it alongside the ethnic militia that was formed. I will not attempt a national history, but note that, after a coalition government was formed in 1957, the two sides still did not trust each other and the US-backed side used hardline tactics and marginalization that drove the North Vietnamese-backed side (Pathet Lao) to "illegality" and armed confrontations.[16] It is impossible to separate internal from external factors in this case, unless one means to take sides. The internal inability to arrive at some mutually beneficial compromise invited the external intervention that involved resources well beyond local means, which then tore the country apart.

From stories and histories about particular people and encounters, I try to convey a field of relations over time through various interactions where the character

---

[13] Lorraine Aragon, "Reconsidering Displacement and Internally Displaced Persons from Poso," in *Conflict, Violence, and Displacement in Indonesia*, ed. Eva-Lotta Hedman (Ithaca, NY: Cornell Southeast Asia Program Publications, 2008), pp. 173–205.

[14] Castle, *At War in the Shadow of Vietnam*, p. 46.

[15] Emily Martin, *Flexible Bodies* (Boston, MA: Beacon Press, 1994), p. 59.

[16] Oliver Tappe, "The Escape from Phonkheng Prison: Revolutionary Historiography in the Lao PDR," in *Multidisciplinary Perspectives on Lao Studies*, ed. Karen Adams and Thomas Hudak (Tempe, AZ: Arizona State University, Center for Asian Research, 2010), pp. 237–41.

of the Mien or anything else cannot be predetermined, but must be established from how things play out. I am concerned with a complex and interactive process and not a simple and causal event; the war was not an outside thing or a process that affected the Mien. Rather, it was one historical context that has lent particular shapes to Mien social and cultural forms as much as to individual lives, as people engaged with the various components of their social interactions from uneven and particular vantage points. They were already in various relations and identities before the war became a reality—the process of change over time goes back as far as one can trace it. There is no single origin point, but continuous and sometimes hazardous movement as people engage with their worlds and live out their lives.

Mien people vary in their recollections of those time periods when Laos was ruled or controlled by the French, the Japanese (during World War II), and the United States. Some memories are favorable:

> At the beginning, Mien served under the French, then under the Lao, and then under the CIA. *Thahan ban* [village soldiers] served only at the village level; they did not have to go to war. My father was under the French army [in a village militia]. Mien people felt very protected under the French commanders, who would take the heat of fighting and shelter the Mien soldiers.[17]

This recollection, that things were easy under the French, makes sense in the context of the subsequent war and exile. Mien had not actively fought during the French colonial era; the multiple traumas of death, fighting, resettlement, refugee status, and exile related to the Second Indochina War turn the days of French influence into good times.

Those with unfavorable recollections of the French colonial presence express positive feelings about the arrival of Japanese soldiers, who did not tax people. I learned of one regiment that a Mien man had accompanied. The Japanese soldiers had *faatv* (magical protection) against bullets and swords, and they subsequently defeated a French regiment:

> When the French fired their guns at the Japanese, the bullets fell like little bee babies in front of the Japanese commander's sword, which he had stuck in the ground. He just sat there [on the opposite bank of the river from where the French were shooting], having told his soldiers to take shelter and get some rest. Later, the Japanese soldiers used magic to take the French by surprise across the river, and they cut off their [French soldiers'] heads the way we chop banana stalks.[18]

This I learned from someone whose father had been caned by French soldiers for insubordination, and the man seemed positively delighted at recounting the episode as a case of revenge by proxy.

---

[17] Personal interview, Portland, Oregon, December 11, 2007. The recollections that I draw from in this chapter come from various conversations with Mien people in California and Oregon, from 2005 to 2012. I only provide people's names when they have expressly stated that I may identify them.

[18] Personal interview, Portland, OR, March 3, 2008.

Other recollections suggest that the French oppressed people with their tax collection, to the point that some poor families had to sell off their children for adoption in order to afford the tax. One old woman said that, according to her parents, "there is always fighting here [in Laos]; it is the Lao and the French and the Japanese, outsiders [*jan,* any non-Mien group; M. *janx*] are always coming here to fight, this country is not a good place to live."[19] This family crossed the Mekong River and settled in Thailand in the early 1960s, but they became refugees in the 1980s when the UN forces collected Mien people in certain parts of Thailand in response to Thai authorities' complaint that many Lao Mien were living outside the designated refugee camps. Many Mien people living on the Thai side had no identification papers, and Thai highlanders had come under considerable military attacks and been subject to social animosity; becoming a refugee may have seemed no worse an option than was daily life.

The historical recollections from Laos are rooted in family or household-specific orientations, though some do refer to ethnic allegiances or divisions. In the case noted above, my interlocutor's bad memories of the French, and his related delight in how the Japanese defeated one French regiment, were fueled by the memory of his father's humiliation and physical punishment by French soldiers. The more positive memory of the French came from a man whose father had been promoted to a village militia and not sent to fight a war. That recollection also rested on a comparison with the US-influenced period when Mien had to take up arms and leave their home area to be resettled, and when many died. Opposing recollections are from people whose parents or grandparents were well off and had claims to local prominence, but who differed in their relationships with the colonial administration. The third kind of recollections are those from farmers who had no stake in connections to armies or the Lao authorities—ordinary people.

SETTLEMENT IN LAO DOMAINS, CHIEFS, AND DIFFERENTIATED FARMING

One of many origins of Mien entanglements with the war goes back a century before, to roughly the 1860s, when a large group of people migrated from Guangxi Province, China, to the northern part of Vietnam, then to Yunnan and later to Laos. To these migrants, the region was a continuous terrain of mountains, valleys, and political domains; the country references provide us with the illusive sense that members of the group moved between separate containers and give us somewhere to point on a map, but these boundaries meant nothing to the travelers. I knew of this migration from working with Mien people in Thailand, and at the time thought that it only pertained to the Mien people I knew in Phayao Province.[20] It turns out that many more people were involved with this migration; they certainly numbered in the thousands, including the Iu Mien who eventually settled in Muang La in Yunnan, China, and in the northern part of Laos adjacent to Yunnan. The areas of northern Laos are known to my Mien friends as Sam Sao, Muang Sing, and Nam Tha. In those areas, each core village was about a day's walk from the next closest one(s).

---

[19] Personal interview, Portland, OR, October 12, 2007.

[20] Hjorleifur Jonsson, *Mien Relations: Mountain People and State Control in Thailand* (Ithaca, NY: Cornell University Press, 2005), pp. 73–98.

In each of those highland regions, there was one dominant village where lived a prominent man with a large household. Some of the men were chiefs who had a title, Phya Long or Phaya Luang, from a lowland king. The kings were all speakers of Tai languages: Yuan (Northern Thai), Tai Khoen, Tai Dam, Tai Neua, and so on. To the north, in Muang La, of Yunnan, lived a Mien leader who had the title Phya Long Wang, or Great Royal Chief; his title sounds more genial than does the Lao nickname for the main Mien chief on the Laos side who lived in Sam Sao and was called Phya Long Hai, or Great Cruel Chief. These chiefs, in villages ranging from northern Thailand to southern China, were all in competition with one another, and their competition centered on the acquisition of royal titles that conferred trade benefits for their followers, and the maintenance of a large household numbering a hundred people, so big it would outshine the others. The chiefs' rivalry was over issues that were completely out of reach for ordinary householders, and while it drew on political and economic connections that spilled over into lowland domains, it was very much about Mien issues and on Mien terms.

I had known about the Mien highland chief in Nan, Thailand, who received the title Phaya Inthakhiri and the family name Srisombat from the king of Nan in the late nineteenth and early twentieth centuries. More recently I learned that the chief in Sam Sao had received the title Phya Khuen Kham, and the family name Srisongfa. The two chiefs—Phaya Inthakhiri Srisombat and Phya Khuenkham Srisongfa—seem to have been trying to outshine one another. There is considerable resemblance between the two names, and I have no way of determining which came first and stirred the other into reaction. Recollections about the old leader on the Laos side were mixed. One man said:

> Tzeo Wuen Tsoi Lin, who had the title Phya Long Hai, was good at doing things, and at talking. He would humiliate whoever was against him. He was a cruel ruler. He had the title Phya Long, and told [Mien] people, "I am far beyond that [Phya Long]; you must call me Phya Long Hai Khuen Kham Meuang Srisongfa."[21]

While still a student, I had come across Peter Kandre's description of Tzeo (Zeuz) Wuen Tsoi Lin ("Uen Tsoe"), whom he learned about in Phale village, Chiangrai Province, in the 1960s. The Mien in Phale had left Laos for Thailand in the 1940s. Kandre was left with a favorable impression of this leader, but it was tinged with a fear of the rich and powerful: "According to Iu Mien standards, one has to be rich to get away with murder without extremely serious consequences for oneself. This is one reason why rich men are feared."[22] One account that I heard in recent years reported that Wuen Tsoi Lin had a habit of going around his village at daybreak and wielding a large stick, with which he would beat anyone who was not already up and about. He himself did not physically engage in any farm work.

There were many rich and powerful Mien village leaders in Laos in the early twentieth century, during French colonial times, and much of their prowess was tied to the ability to gain wealth from farming and trade, particularly involving opium.

---

[21] Personal interview, Portland, OR, December 8, 2007.

[22] Peter Kandre, "Autonomy and Integration of Social Systems: The Iu Mien Mountain Population and Their Neighbors," in *Southeast Asian Tribes, Minorities, and Nations*, vol. 2, ed. Peter Kunstadter (Princeton, NJ: Princeton University Press, 1967), p. 604.

Men came to prowess by running a big household. Among the Lao Mien a century ago, big leaders aimed for a household of one hundred people. At the beginning of the twentieth century, Tang Tsan Khwoen, who was Phaya Khiri Srisombat and a leader in Nan, Thailand, lived in an elevated house, which was next to the ground-level house of his sons, that contained eighty-nine people. When I first worked with this material, I thought that if the father's and sons' physical structures are separate, then these would not be considered the same household. But from various conversations with Iu Mien from Laos, I now think that this is not so plain. If people make rituals at the same altar, they form a single household.

Chaosarn Chao, grandson of Wuen Tsoi Lin, offered this recollection to me in 2007: The old chief and his wife had two sons themselves and also ten more whom they had adopted. It was about a hundred-person house. But yet it was "always ninety-nine people"—someone got married and moved out, or someone died. Something always happened when Wuen Tsoi Lin attempted to reach a household of a hundred people. I asked Chaosarn Chao if he had heard of Tsan Khwoen, the leader who went to Nan. He had, and explained: When the group settled in Laos, his grandfather, Wuen Tsoi Lin, stayed, and Tsan Khwoen went off toward Nan to hunt elephants, and never came back.[23] When I first heard of the migration towards Nan, it was from people who saw Nan as a destination and everything before it as a journey. But from the perspective of people who settled earlier, northern Laos was the real destination and the people who eventually settled in Thailand had gone off on an errand one day and somehow gotten lost or fallen off the map.

These Mien leaders settled into tributary relations with lowland kings that benefited their followers in various ways. Their leadership was forged in conditions of warfare as they moved through southern China and the adjacent areas of Southeast Asia. Phya Long Wang, in the Muang La region of Yunnan, is not known for military prowess. Fouchoy Sio Chao, who now lives near Salem, Oregon, told me of his grandfather who had lived in Yunnan for some time before moving within Lao orbits; his name was Tzeo Wuen Wa. He had been a *tao mien* (Chinese, *t'o yin*), or *fai laang tsio*, "small-village ruler." He was under a bigger leader named Wan Yun, who had the tit*le phya long.* The latter had three wives, and the Lao called him *phya sam mia*, "three-wives chief." He was also known as *phya sam mong*, "three-domains chief." He died before 1963, which was the year when the communists took over the north of Laos and the villagers left for Nam Dui and Nam Nyu.[24]

Tzeo Wuen Tsoi Lin had risen to prominence not because he was the only leader, but because he was motivated to overshadow his Mien peers through tax collection and military suppression campaigns for the benefit of French colonial authorities. His two sons later rose to prominence in the context of war and American support. The entry of an Iu Mien militia into the Second Indochina War was both a break with the past and the perpetuation and enhancement of certain leadership positions against rival claimants. War is never just war; it is always equally the shaping of social life while any social life also brings its own particular elements into play that influence the dynamics of a war.[25]

---

[23] Personal interview, San Fancisco, CA, December 18, 2007.

[24] Personal interview, Salem, OR, November 15, 2007.

[25] Stephen Lubkemann, *Culture in Chaos: An Anthropology of the Social Condition of War* (Chicago, IL: University of Chicago Press, 2008); and Chris Coulter, *Bush Wives and Girl Soldiers: Women's Lives through War and Peace in Sierra Leone* (Ithaca, NY: Cornell University Press, 2009).

The old leaders' prowess stabilized during the relatively peaceful conditions of the early twentieth century, when the articulations of a chief's prominence shifted from military leadership to success in farming and trade. The region was no longer on a war footing, but the French in Laos brought Mien into militias that people refer to with the Lao term *thahan ban*, "village militia." Wuen Tsoi Lin's two sons had been given the princely Lao titles of Chao Mai and Chao La, "new prince" and "last prince." The older had become a district ruler, *tasseng*, and he was in that position when American special agents were looking for ethnic leaders in order to form militias in the late 1950s and early 1960s against the growing tide of anticolonial nationalism in Laos and Vietnam that they viewed as a communist threat.

I end this section with recollections from Longsan Tzeo, who ended up living in Portland, Oregon. He was born in about 1951, and thus was about twelve years old when people moved to Nam Dui and Nam Keung. I asked him about households and farming in an attempt to understand the practice of extended households. What Longsan described was typical for prominent families that could claim a whole mountainside or more for their fields. Those of ordinary means farmed small fields and moved about frequently. The stability of big farms is somewhat similar to what was the case in northern Thailand among the very few settlements that had formal deals regarding the legalized cultivation of poppy in the first half of the twentieth century.[26]

I re-present Longsan's description in part because such large households with extensive fields and a large pool of laborers have not been part of our knowledge about the social and other dynamics in the Asian hinterlands. The large households belong to a particular historical moment when some men's chiefly ambitions intersected with the ability to make privileged political and trade connections with nearby valley kingdoms, during a period of opium monopolies (between roughly 1880 and 1940). Ethnology's descriptions of highland opium farmers have generally featured small households and egalitarian social relations. What we generalized for ethnic groups appears, in retrospect, to hold only for the period after tributary relations and opium monopolies had been erased by new national regimes, when upland leaders' chiefly ambitions no longer had resonance among lowland rulers. There are multiple parts to this configuration. One is that modern nation states and their colonial precursors systemically erased the autonomy of multiple valley kingdoms that were often in internal competition and maintained links with a range of settlements. The scaffolding for James Scott's Zomia came from anthropologists who generalized about ethnic groups and highlanders based on observations from the remote villages where they found what they were looking for in ethnic social life. Writing as a one-time participant in the fashioning of the highlander-as-object for an academic audience, I now think that our object was shaped by regional and national conditions that only pertain to twentieth-century national contexts. The point relates equally to N. J. Enfield's remark about the idea of continuity for languages and communities, and Joyce White's emphasis on micro-adaptations within networks of relations across difference that have to be figured out on a case-by-case basis.

Longsan Tzeo described households and farming:

> There was one big household in Sam Sao, where Chao Mai and Chao La were from. In Ta Fang village, near Longsan *laang* [village] in Muong Xing, there

---

[26] Jonsson, *Mien Relations*, pp. 82–94.

was one big house [I had heard of Ta Fang village from friends; Longsan *laang* is named after his grandfather; the family is of the Palong sub-lineage of the Tzeo or Chao lineage; Tsan- and Long- are generation names]. In Longsan *laang*, grandfather [Tsan Fin Long] and two brothers had an extended household. Tsan Fin had three of his four or five sons there, Tsan Tsoi had three sons, Tsan Fu had two sons, for each of the brothers some of their sons lived in their big house. Only one of Tsan Tsoi's sons joined him—it was quite uneven whether a man had all his grown sons with him in a large household.

Tsan Fin Long was village chief for a long time, he had the biggest house. As chief, he had three or four deputies. One was Yao Fong, who was Tsan Fin's son-in-law. Yao Fong became company commander for the CIA's ethnic militia, and in Nam Keung he became *tasseng*. Yao Fong came to the United States around 1978; he was ninety years old when he died a few months ago [in Beaverton, Oregon, in late 2007].[27]

I asked about the big houses. Did they have a shared kitchen? I had heard that from someone. No, they did not have a shared kitchen, he told me; there wouldn't have been big enough pots. He drew me a plan of his grandfather's house, said it had three hearths for making pig food and one stove for the family's cooking, and later it came to have three cooking fireplaces to accommodate the large household. He said that his grandfather's house was the biggest in the village.

> In Ta Fang, Jiem Jien was chief. He had five or six sons, but only two lived with him in his big house. Some lived in houses in the fields, but the big house was like their permanent address. Jiem Jien died in Mae Bong [Chiangrai Province, Thailand] in the early 1980s, he had escaped from Nam Keung in 1972.
> Below the house, there were horse stalls and pig pens. By the house, the roofs were joined. The cowshed was farther away from the house. Father had twenty-thirty cows, some others had more. There was a long-row cowshed below the house. At the downhill side of the cowshed, there was a wall to contain the manure. It was collected and then used in the fields. Cow dung was the main [fertilizer]. Every year before planting poppy, after the corn harvest when the fields had been dug up and cleared and then dried in the sun for a few days, manure was mixed in. Water was necessary for preparing the manure. At a large house, there had to be a schedule for water use, so that the many families would all get their share.
> Manure was mixed in with the soil, and then one or two people were in the field mixing water in with it. Two days later, people would plant the poppy seeds. The availability of water [determined] where people could farm. The whole mountain was farmed. At the bottom of the field were fruit trees and such, bananas, mangoes, peach, also bamboo and pineapple. Only corn and poppy were grown in these big fields. All the rock had been collected and was assembled outside. In some cases a whole mountainside was farmed, and some farmers had fields that stretched even [beyond] one mountainside.
> Households could not grow forever because there was a limit on field size. Grandfather had the best spot at the head of the field, closest to the house. He did not farm himself; I never saw him in the field, but his wife was there very

---

[27] Personal interview, Portland, OR, January 24, 2008.

often. He was inside receiving guests, settling disputes, hosting Chinese people from the city, and so on. When there was work to do in his fields, we [the members of his household] would all come and do the work.

In those days, very few men had more than one wife. One of grandfather's adopted sons had two wives, but others not. When we fled to Nam Keung and Nam Dui, we could no longer farm in this way, with the fields downhill from the house. People couldn't choose, this was in the lowlands and people had to live much closer together than before.

In the village in the old days, there was often a half or a whole mile between houses. Grandfather and his two brothers lived side by side, about ten to fifteen yards between them each way, and all the fields were below. The next houses were maybe a mile away, on another hill.

Akha people would hire themselves out for labor, and they would get daily wages in opium. The Akha villages were a four or five hours walk away from where we lived. Nobody planted rice in the fields down below the house, rice fields could be miles away, and they were shifted with regularity as the soil depleted. Later, slash-and-burn ate up the forest at Nam Keung and Nam Dui really fast; it was forest when we got there, and, later, it was all depleted.

People had horses and oxen for transportation. The rice fields were miles away, and the horses were not enough to transport the rice, so we used the oxen, too. At the house, there was a building that served as a barn for the harvested crops, rice and corn. So, uphill from the house was the chicken coop, below were the horse shed and the pig pen, further below was the cowshed, and to one side of the house was the barn. It was very crowded with buildings around the house.

In the old days, Chinese would come and purchase the opium. They would exchange merchandise for it, or pay in silver coins. There were also some Mien traders [from Thailand, in the late 1940s, who traded consumer goods for opium, which they took to sell in Thailand where the price was high].[28]

WAR ENTRENCHED

In Laos in 1958, CIA agents asked who were the leaders of the Iu Mien people, and were told of Chao Mai and Chao La. The CIA's need for ethnic leaders increased and entrenched the two brothers' prominence. The CIA also established a Khmu leader, Khamsene, for instance, along with establishing Vang Pao as the Hmong leader. In some ways, the quest for ethnic leaders to head militias fighting an international war echoes the strategies that had prevailed in the previous landscape of situation-specific interethnic networks that enhanced certain peoples leadership positions and had various repercussions for how ethnicity became socially meaningful within diverse societies.

Some Iu Mien men went for soldier training, and some served as spies across the border in China. Attacks by Pathet Lao forces on Iu Mien settlements made a real difference, in that people either had to cooperate with them or take the other side and flee. Recollections of this time suggest the violence that was involved in forging the two sides of this national and international war, and the wartime normalcy of killing those on the other side. The following is from Tsan Tsong Chao:

---

[28] Ibid.

In about 1963, communist soldiers came to the village. I was with my grandfather visiting at the other end of the village, about ten minutes walk from our house. The soldiers shot and killed a cow [to eat]. My older brother had got a gun from Chao Mai in Nam Dui just a few weeks before that. After they killed the cow, the leader of the communist army was in the [household's] vegetable garden. Bullets would not enter him, he had *faat* [magical protection; M., *faatv*]. But the Iu Mien caught the leader and then his soldiers fled. They [local Iu Mien] knew bullets could not kill him [the Pathet Lao unit leader], so they did him in with rocks and then a shovel. Later, we [the villagers] went to Nam Keung.[29]

In response to the Pathet Lao capture of the provincial capitals of Nam Tha and Muang Sing, adjacent to China, the two Iu Mien leaders brought their followers from these provinces to the area around Houai Xay, by the Mekong River and at the border with Thailand, about a week's walk from their previous home villages. For some groups, this one-week walk took over a year because the opposition's soldiers tried to prevent migration, so travelers had to bide their time. Some of the Mien people still maintain relations with the Tai Lue people who housed them and helped them out on this sojourn in 1963.

The resettlement in Nam Keung and Nam Dui took shape between 1962 and 1964. There was some tension between the two brothers. Chao Mai, the older, was the military leader, and he set up camp in Nam Dui. Chao La, always more of a businessman, led his followers to Nam Keung. Some people have mentioned this fraternal rivalry, but none has discussed it extensively. Chao Mai passed away from a stroke in 1967, leaving Chao La as the de-facto leader. The basic reason for the Iu Mien affiliation with the CIA-supported militia under the Royal Lao Government was that Chao Mai was a government official, this was his side. Perhaps that also influenced the turn of events when the Pathet Lao soldiers attacked the Mien village and killed a cow, as reported above; there was no relationship between them, so people acted with hostility, just as the soldiers had acted toward them.

To the best knowledge of the people I consulted during 2005–09, two Chinese men ran refineries in the Huai Xay area, and they paid Chao La protection money as his militia guarded their enterprises. Chao La himself had a saw mill and perhaps a rice mill. Journalist Roger Warner mentions a power struggle between the two brothers, and that they "were more interested in war profits than in military gains."[30] Given how things went in the war, I am rather clueless about what military gains the two Mien leaders should have aimed for to impress such American assessors.

One of the famous and somewhat infamous US agents in the war was Tony Poe (Anthony Poshepny). In a description of the various ethnic militias that Poe worked with, journalist Warner states, "The Yao soldiers sat in their bases in their uniforms, collected their paychecks, and did as little as possible."[31] This comes across as a slur; of course, any soldier should be out killing and getting killed on a daily basis, to make a good impression with the Americans.

---

[29] Personal interview, Redding, CA, December 16, 2007.

[30] Roger Warner, *Shooting at the Moon: The Story of America's Clandestine War in Laos* (South Royalton, VT: Steerforth, 1996), p. 259. Warner is an uneven source on these times, places, and peoples, and sometimes it is clear that his American-military biases lead him astray (as a balanced source for my benefit, that is).

[31] Ibid., p. 255.

Warner states that Chao La ran opium refineries. But I have no confirmation of this from my interviews with Iu Mien people, some of whom have no interest in protecting Chao La's reputation. According to one Mien acquaintance, "I know that Chao La did not own an opium refinery. He owned a saw mill and a rice mill, and he had a mill in Vientiane that was in the works but was not completed then the communists took over, and that was that." Chao Mai and Chao La profited from the opium trade, and sold some CIA-donated arms and other equipment on the black market, primarily to armies on the Burma side.[32] The following is from an interview with Longsan Tzeo, and involves Chao La and opium cultivation during the war:

> Chao La could read and write Chinese; he also learned Lao, but his writing was poor. When I was in high school, College Huai Sai, I went on break to Nam Nyou, the military headquarters. Chao La was writing a proposal to the Lao government. The government wanted to eradicate opium growing, and Chao La wanted to propose a grant to supply tractors. This was for opium replacement; people could grow beans and corn in the lowland areas. For that, for Mien to be successful, they needed tractors. Chao La wrote the proposal, and I typed it on one of those old manual typewriters for the Lao script. Chao La submitted the proposal to Prince Souvanna Phouma, brother of Prince Souphanouvong, but it was not successful—nothing happened.[33]

Another acquaintance was a student in Huai Xay in the 1960s. His recollections indicate some of the practice of looking the other way regarding opium and heroin refineries, and also some of the deception that went with getting the goods to the refineries:

> Nam Keung was in the lowlands, people grew corn and rice in the hills around, some grew opium in the mountains farther away. The opium that was refined near Nam Keung came from Burma. I was at school [in Huai Xay], and we'd be offered a *baht* or up to five *baht* to take opium in our pockets to the refinery. I never did it, some guys did. Chao La did not own an opium refinery, it was owned by Chinese, but they may have bribed Chao La to allow it near Nam Keung. One time a helicopter with Americans came to Nam Keung, and they got Chao La to go with them, flew off to somewhere upriver in the Golden Triangle, where there was a large poppy field. Someone had complained to the Americans. When Chao La came back to Nam Keung he looked very different, was very upset and troubled.[34]

There was considerable logging in the area, and most of the mills were owned at least in part by Thailand-based businessmen who sold the wood in Thailand. With these mills and the clandestine opium cultivation and the refineries, there was considerable corruption. According to one Mien man:

> There was a Lao regional commander in Huai Xay; every month he would go around in his jeep to different sawmills, and at every place he would be handed

---

[32] Ibid., pp. 255, 259–62.

[33] Personal interview, Portland, OR, December 13, 2007.

[34] Personal interview, Portland, OR, December 13, 2007.

an envelope [with goodwill money]. The whole thing worked on corruption. This area [Huai Xay] was a favored post for Lao officials; the governor of Huai Xay was the king's cousin.[35]

China's Great Leap Forward campaign during 1958-60 led many Iu Mien families in Muang La, Yunnan, to flee across the border to Laos, and as a result of these conditions relations across that border became more difficult. Many Lao Iu Mien now in the United States have relatives on the China side and speak of previously easy interactions among those who traveled back and forth across the border prior to 1958. Firsthand accounts of the Chinese campaigns for collectivization and against what the communist cadres considered lazy, rich, and parasitical farmers may have contributed to the Lao Iu Mien's willingness to side with Chao Mai and Chao La against the Pathet Lao. "My family had eighteen cows, and they [Great Leap Forward cadres] were assaulting us for being lazy rich people," commented one man who grew up in Muang La.[36]

The war in Laos created antagonistic identifications that hardened at war's end and during the Iu Mien people's exile. Prior to being drawn into warfare in 1958, people in Iu Mien villages in northern Laos had various relationships among themselves, with non-Mien neighbors and traders, and with state institutions, both Lao and French colonial. Several people commented that the hiring of Akha laborers for farm work was common and that many Mien people developed proficiency in the Akha language. It was only through war and exile that Iu Mien people were spared from such particulars and came to a collective identity that drew on the intersections of militia leaders, exile, and refugee resettlement in other countries.

War centers agency on high-level leaders. The process is similar to what occurred with the Iu Mien migration group that traveled from southern China to northern Thailand in the late nineteenth century. The migration leader subsequently reasserted his prominence in settled conditions through ritual as much as through links of tribute and trade with a lowland kingdom, and he and his son are said to have maintained law and order within their highland area. They would arrest thieves and mediate disputes, but outside the context of migration and warfare their command over social life was limited by other people's domestic orientations in farming, ritual, trade, and kinship. This is where war makes a fundamental difference in justifying a leader's permanent command over social life; during war, a leader establishes prowess through his ability to offer protection and provisions, and the largely unquestioned ability to recruit soldiers and other staff for his projects, against the interests of farming households.

The Hmong leader General Vang Pao ran a multilingual radio station at his military headquarters in Long Cheng. The Union of Lao Races radio station, established in 1965, was initiated by an American CIA agent, Vinton Lawrence.[37] An Iu Mien woman who now lives in the United States was one of the radio announcers when she was fifteen years old. Her service for one year at the radio station allowed her brother to stay at home and farm for his parents. The then-teenager would read news and sing traditional songs, and at Vang Pao's New Year festival in 1969 she danced *lamwong* (the standard form of Lao social dance) with the King of Laos. Chao

---

[35] Personal interview, Portland, OR, December 12, 2007.

[36] Personal interview, Portland, OR, September 10, 2010.

[37] Warner, *Shooting at the Moon*, p. 178.

La similarly invited various dignitaries to his festivals in Nam Keung. The militia leaders engaged in national and multiethnic politics even while simultaneously pursuing certain ethnic agendas.

Both dynamics, those of ethnicization and of multiethnic nation building, point to US involvement. But the historical setting also motivated the realignment of society in national terms, and the efforts of Vang Pao and Chao La need to be seen in the context of pervasive lowland urban Lao prejudice against Hmong, Iu Mien, and other highlanders at the time. As the militia leaders entrenched their ethnic prominence and took an active part in the ethnicization of social life, they made various efforts to shape national society toward multiethnic accommodation. During the 1950s and 1960s, the Pathet Lao were also devising schemes of multiethnic nation-building. Their framework of nationals-by-altitude—*Lao Sung,* highland Lao; *Lao Thoeng,* midslope Lao; and *Lao Lum,* lowland Lao—became official by 1975 and has been a significant part of national iconography.[38]

CHAO LA'S ETHNIC COMMAND

Any choice of terms that I use to describe Chao La may place me on one side of internal Lao or other politics. I have heard a range of views about him from among Iu Mien people in the United States. The diversity of views is rather similar to what I had earlier learned about certain past leaders of the Iu Mien in Thailand. To some, these were exemplary leaders whose unique qualities were the key to a good life in the highlands; others were somewhat indifferent and did not recall that the leaders had much power in daily life; yet others suggested that they were cruel and held onto their power through ruthless means.

The range of local views expresses varied social proximity to these leaders and uneven access to the benefits they could distribute. These diverse views are all accurate in their different ways. There is no single way to describe Iu Mien leaders without seeming to take sides in local politics. My aim is not the critique or glorification of militia leaders, but an understanding of the historical process that aligned their respective identities with particular ethnic groups. The engagement calls for some ironic distance, ideally of the sort labeled "true irony" that denies animosity and superiority and rests instead on the recognition of kinship and a sense of indebtedness across some otherwise fundamental divides.[39]

When I started meeting US-based Iu Mien people in 2005 and learning about their lives, I was repeatedly told that they had all been under the wartime leader Chao La and that they had left Laos in 1975. As I got to know more people and they told me more about the past, these facts emerged as radical simplifications that had more to do with people's post-war resettlement. The American people interviewing

---

[38] Grant Evans, *The Politics of Ritual and Remembrance: Laos since 1975* (Chiangmai: Silkworm, 1998); Ing-Britt Trankell, "The Minor Part of the Nation: Politics of Ethnicity in Laos," in *Facets of Power and its Limitations: Political Culture in Southeast Asia,* ed. Ing-Britt Trankell and Laura Summers (Uppsala: Uppsala Studies in Cultural Anthropology, 1998), pp. 45–64; and Jan Ovesen, "All Lao? Minorities in the Lao People's Democratic Republic," in *Civilizing the Margins: Southeast Asian Government Policies for the Development of Minorities,* ed. Christopher Duncan (Ithaca, NY: Cornell University Press, 2004), pp. 214–40.

[39] James Boon, "Kenneth Burke's 'True Irony': One Model for Ethnography, Still," *Irony in Action: Anthropology, Practice, and the Moral Imagination,* ed. James Fernandez and Mary Taylor Huber (Chicago, IL: University of Chicago Press, 2001), p. 119.

refugees in Thailand had particular notions by which they could sort genuine refugees from others. To them, any Iu Mien person qualified insofar as he or she had been under Chao La, whose militia had been financed by the CIA, and left Laos once the communist Pathet Lao took over in 1975. Many people had left in 1973 and at other times that did not match the officially declared year of "genuine refugee" departure (1975), but anyone declaring in an interview a departure year other than 1975 would be turned down for further consideration, as "nothing was happening in Laos at that time."[40] Lynellin Long describes the similar sorting of "genuine" from other refugees in the Ban Vinai refugee camp.[41]

The Iu Mien military headquarters were at Nam Nyou and the civilian headquarters at Nam Keung, where people farmed lowland areas and some hill fields. This big resettlement was multiethnic, but in many ways it was the domain of Chao La, who became the sole Iu Mien leader after his older brother died. Each Iu Mien household had to supply one man to serve as a soldier. Chao La annually sent one hundred soldiers to help Hmong militia leader Vang Pao fight in the northeast, at Long Cheng and the Plain of Jars. I learned of this from various Iu Mien people, who think it took place already in the 1960s, while Warner suggests that it started in 1970.[42]

Some Iu Mien people said that it was rumored at the time that Chao La "sold off" the soldiers because Vang Pao paid him for the services of one hundred soldiers per year. "Many later were able to return," one Chao La supporter added, to disprove the notion. With the money from Vang Pao for his soldiers' services, Chao La was able to purchase his first rice mill. He is not remembered as very generous to his people. When I asked former soldiers if there were any particular difference between Chao Mai and Chao La, most were disinclined to say anything. One man offered that neither leader smoked but that Chao Mai always bought cigarettes and shared them with his soldiers when they returned from a tour; Chao La never did so.

One of Chao La's kinsmen once asked him for help. This young man wished to get married and establish a household; he was fatherless and had lost connection to his mother after she remarried. He hoped that Chao La, with his sawmill, could spare some wood for building a house, and approached him on the matter. Chao La's response was to walk the man past the mill and down toward the river; he said the younger man could have his pick of the wood that was left at the riverbank—scrap that was completely useless for building a house.

In general, households with only one male of working age were exempted from military recruitment. But even those came under pressure:

> The only son of one household was recruited to fight for Chao La in 1971. He went for a year and then came back, and the family did not want to see him go again. They asked that the son stay home because they still had to harvest rice, and Chao La's men came and beat up the mother so the son had to serve another term.[43]

---

[40] Personal interview, Portland, OR, November 6, 2007.

[41] Lynellyn D. Long, *Ban Vinai: The Refugee Camp* (New York, NY: Columbia University Press, 1993), pp. 155–56.

[42] Warner, *Shooting at the Moon*, p. 299.

[43] Personal interview, Portland, OR, March 3, 2008.

I learned of this during a conversation about songs, and asked if people had made up songs about this predicament: "No one dared make songs about this, if they [military officials] did hear it, then they could order the soldiers to strike them [song writers] immediately, or they could be put in jail. People could not say anything bad about our own friendly soldiers." Military command played up authoritarianism and the use of violence, which were naturalized through the equation of the ethnic group and its leader that made alternative priorities of identity, such as families or households, appear subversive or unthinkable. During the war, Vang Pao's leadership was questioned by many Hmong dissenters, and those who had accommodated the enemy Pathet Lao forces were variously arrested, tortured, or executed.[44] I have no interest in critiquing Vang Pao; he was an active participant in war, but had no control over his context—in times of peace, he might have been a genial leader.

There were two kinds of military units under Chao La: Special Guerrilla Units (SGU[45]) and village militias. The former received training in Thailand, while the latter were trained in Nam Nyou. The soldiers' salaries came from the CIA. But the dynamic of ethnicization was not exclusively related to warfare and the CIA. There were also Iu Mien who were trained as medics and operated clinics, and some who were trained as school teachers and taught in Lao, who served only Iu Mien people. Some Khmu in the area were similarly trained and only served Khmu people. The medics and teachers were trained and paid by the US Agency for International Development, USAID, that operated almost like a second government.[46] They were not directly under Chao La's command, but their services primarily benefited his people: "He would stall or end the career of anyone he did not like," suggested one of my sources.[47]

It is rare, if ever really true, that an ethnic group has been unambiguously on one side of such conflicts in Southeast Asia. Statements of that sort are politically charged projections of unity and purpose and should be met with ethnographic skepticism. I do not wish to undermine as somehow wrong or false the claim of my Iu Mien acquaintances that they were all under Chao La and left Laos in 1975. This statement is primarily about the position of refugees in conditions of exile—it is an official fact, and not entirely wrong, but this truth is more positional and retrospective than it is historical.

A number of Iu Mien fled Laos to Thailand in 1973 in response to the capture of the Nam Nyou base by Pathet Lao soldiers with considerable Vietnamese backing. This occurred at New Year, when most of the Iu Mien soldiers were away, celebrating with their families. In response to the Pathet Lao capture of Nam Nyou, the base was destroyed in an American bombing raid.[48] Lao people were not to come into new positions, and the ferocity of American bombing raids—most pronounced

---

[44] Warner, *Shooting at the Moon*, pp. 278–79.

[45] The various Mien, Lao, Khmu, Hmong, and others who have spoken with me about this time always use the English-language acronym "SGU," whereas for village militias they use the Lao term *thahan ban*.

[46] William Sage, personal communication, 2008; Castle, *At War in the Shadow of Vietnam*, pp. 59–60; Fred Branfman, "Presidential War in Laos, 1964–1970," in *Laos: War and Revolution*, pp. 256-64.

[47] Personal interview, Portland, OR, December 3, 2009.

[48] Warner, *Shooting at the Moon*, pp. 341–42.

around Xieng Khuang, but manifest all over the country—imposed a particular character on social relations that was then matched by the massive violence and punitive reeducation campaigns of the Pathet Lao following war's end in 1975.

Many of the Iu Mien people affiliated with the militia unit left for Thailand after the attack on Nam Nyou in 1973. Of those, many returned to Laos after a month, led by Chao La, when it was clear that Nam Keung would not also be attacked. In 1973, a coalition government was formed in Laos following international peace talks. When it lost power in 1975, many Iu Mien soldiers feared being sent to labor or reeducation camps, and people started fleeing across the Mekong River. When the first groups left, many were brought over by boats arranged by a man on the Thai side who had established relations with Iu Mien in Nam Keung as an arms trader to insurgents in Burma.

The internal resettlement in and around Nam Keung created an ethnic space that was unlike the common multiethnicity of the social landscape in these areas, in Laos, and in adjacent regions of China, Vietnam, Thailand, and Burma. Nam Keung accommodated various non-Mien peoples such as Lahu, Akha, Hmong, Chinese, Tai Neua, and Tai Lue, but the wartime configuration also made it an Iu Mien space. Nam Keung provided the conditions for an ethnic consciousness in relation to a military leader that was later reinforced as people fled the country and were placed in refugee camps on the Thai side beginning in 1975.

Iu Mien in Laos who were beyond the resettlement area near Houai Xay lived in villages that were interspersed with those of various ethnic others. Theirs was not an ethnicized space, and I have never heard Lao Iu Mien who were unaffiliated with Chao La claim their experiences as somehow representing those of the whole ethnic group. When I have consulted with the Iu Mien from Nam Keung about what I learned from those who never identified with Chao La's command, their most common reply is a dismissal: "They are ignorant; all Iu Mien were under Chao La." As I understand the history, this last statement could only have become true as a result of the conditions in refugee camps, and the particular ways that the camps played to militia leadership.

The Iu Mien people who lived in the Nam Keung area from 1963 to 1975 often give the impression that their experiences typify those of their entire ethnic group. The statement that "all Iu Mien were under Chao La" erases some important aspects of a more complicated history. Some Iu Mien people had joined the Pathet Lao forces, but their voices are not heard in the United States. The war ended in 1975, with a massive wave of refugees, but only Denmark would later accept people who had been under the (communist) Nationalists and later left the country. (A friend of mine knew of three Mien families in Denmark.) But not all the other Iu Mien were under Chao La. This statement pertains to Mien from Muang Sing and Nam Tha provinces in the north, close to the border with China, who left in the early 1960s and formed the large internal resettlement effort in Nam Keung and near Huai Xay. This group is known as Northern Mien (Lao, *Mien Neua*).

My Northern Mien acquaintances always state that location within Laos made the main difference in determining which leaders they followed during the war. Northerners were from Nam Tha and Muong Sing, and the Southerners (Lao, *Mien Tai*) were from Sayaburi and Luang Prabang provinces. But the few Southern Mien whom I have talked to said that "Northern Mien were under Chao La, we Southern Mien were under [Hmong leader, General] Vang Pao." Then I started to ask specifically about this issue, whether people were Northerners or Southerners.

Among the things I learned then was that yet others called themselves Central Mien (Lao, *Mien Kang*) and insisted that "we were not under any of these leaders." Said one friend in Portland with a puzzled look, "Southern Mien? I don't know why people would call themselves that. They were not with Vang Pao. Maybe they spoke Hmong, but all Mien soldiers were under Chao La."

These divisions were forged in the context of the war within Laos, and the terminology, the words for "Northern," "Southern," and "Central," is always in the Lao language. It is possible that the north–center–south divisions only took effect in refugee camps, when people had to define themselves in relation to militias and their leaders, but these labels indicate divisions that took shape much earlier and were reinforced as the war continued to shape social life.

For many people who were outside the partial safety network of the Nam Keung resettlement area, wartime was filled with movement and lasting insecurities. The following is from an interview with Jiem Hin Tang, in a mushroom-pickers' camp in the mountains of Oregon.

> I was born in Pu-Ping, near Luang Prabang, Ban Than district, in the mountains, in 1957. My dad passed away when I was three months old. I have three brothers and three sisters. When I was about ten years old, there was fighting in my town. Chao La, Vern Chiem, the Captains, they take the soldiers and go to my town. The communists on the other side also came, and there was war in my town. Some people then moved to Ban That, close to Hongsa [in Sayaburi]. Then my mother and brother said, "Let's go to Nam Pai," which is not far from Phulangka [in Thailand]. I was about nine years old. We stayed in Nam Pai for nine months. Then back to Pu-Ping for three months. Then I went to Hongsa to stay with my cousin, my whole family went. We stayed there for three years. Then we stayed with my uncle in Pak Lai, in Sayaburi, they told us it was very good farmland. We were there for seven years. Then my brother and sister each got married, so it was just my mom and me and two of my brothers. Then I moved back to Hongsa, I had cousins everywhere there, and lived in the village of Nam Num for two years. My sister was in Huai Nam Kong, in Nan province [on the Thai side]. They sent for my mom and me. This was 1974, and my relatives on the Thai side said come over to this side to get away from the war. One brother went there and came back, then I and my brothers walked to Thailand from Hongsa. It takes about two days. At that time I needed a Lao travel permit to cross. I was there farming for about a year. Then in 1975 my country fell apart, and a lot of people came to Thailand.[49]

The wartime Iu Mien terms for those on the communist side were *jan-lom* and *jan-sala*. The term *jan* (M. *janx*) marks them as non-Mien, suggesting how at least the people in Nam Keung identified Iu Mien ethnicity with their side in the conflict. *Jan-lom* translates as "bush aliens," while *sala* is from the Lao language and means "to forsake, renounce, abdicate," implying the communists' plan to overthrow the Lao monarchy. Some of my contacts stated that *jan-lom* were the Pathet Lao soldiers and spies, whereas *jan-sala* were the North Vietnamese communists who backed the Pathet Lao and were also involved in the fighting. But there is no consistency in the use of those terms, now over thirty years later, beyond the implication that these

---

[49] Personal interview, Portland, OR, October 4, 2007.

were not Iu Mien people. Many of my sources say that the terms were nonsense words that were invented for the sake of secrecy in case there were spies around, which indicates a lingering anxiety about people transgressing social boundaries without others' knowledge.

The following conversation with Wan Tzo Chao in the mushroom-pickers' camp suggests the general tendency of relating ritual practice to family matters:

> HJ: But did Mien people make offerings to *hung mien* [M. *hungh mienv*], king's spirit or anything like that? Was there a higher spirit than ancestors and village owner spirit?[50]
>
> WT: The largest were *m-ki* (M. *m'geh*) spirits. Five-banner spirits, banner soldier spirits, fighting or war spirits [*m'geh mienv, m'geh baeng, mborqv-jaax mienv*]. In the village before people went off to fight, they would call on the *m-ki* spirits. This is very strong in Laos and in Thailand, too, it is the number one spirit for Mien. When you want to go that way you just take rice and throw it in that direction, and everybody is gone. Then the communists know that someone is going to kill them, they can feel it.
>
> AT: So you throw the rice in the direction you want to go?[51]
>
> WT: They can feel it; if tonight we don't move, then someone will come and kill you.
>
> HJ: Did Chao Mai or Chao La sponsor offerings to soldier spirits for the Mien people?
>
> WT: Not really Chao Mai or Chao La, but many older people knew the ceremony. Each group would do it for themselves; Chao Mai and Chao La were not skilled in doing it. The *m-ki* spirits were the greatest [*hlo-jiex*], most powerful.[52]

This ritual of tossing rice to clear the way also came up in a conversation with another man; the practice has now come into play in contemporary US wars where some young Mien people serve as soldiers:

> There are *m'geh hongh*, red, they need offerings of blood. They are very strong. You have to offer a chicken first, but later the spirits ask for a pig or a cow. They're very mean, very strong. There was a big war in Laos before, and everybody worried about those serving as soldiers, and they called on *m-ki peng* [M. *m'geh baeng*] to cover them. People call on them, and when the soldier returns they have to offer a pig or a cow [for protection]. Here in Sacramento, California, they do it; their children are off as soldiers [in Iraq and Afghanistan]. They throw the rice in the direction that the soldiers are going.[53]

---

[50] The Mien I had worked with in Thailand had come into a relationship with a king's spirit in the 1870s, still maintained in the 1990s, so I expected this to be somewhat general.

[51] As mentioned in the acknowledgements, I was in Anna Tsing's field site for some of these conversations, and we went together to talk to Mien mushroom pickers. I learned much from working with her, and she is one inspiration for my effort to push the ethnography toward carrying the case, rather than seeking comfort in analytical distance.

[52] Personal interview, Portland, OR, October 4, 2007.

[53] Personal interview, Portland, OR, March 3, 2008.

The national and international context of the war in Laos created new options for social alignments that made possible the ethnicization that occurred within the ongoing conflict among royalists, communists, and neutralists. The US-related wars in Vietnam, Laos, and Cambodia brought out diverse social configurations, as did the civil war in Thailand that occurred at the same time, and a still-unresolved ethnicized civil war that raged, with varying intensity, for longer in Burma. These wars were interconnected, but each produced particular configurations of identity and violence in relation to national diversity.

During the war, issues of protection and invulnerability became everyday concerns. Wan Lin Chao told me about *buv*, objects that convey invulnerability and luck. His recollections describe some of the atmosphere in times of war, the general quest to find objects that offer benefits and security, and how people come into such knowledge. If people lack that knowledge, then a beneficial object might endanger them rather than protect them. We talked at the house of his neighbor, Seng Fo Chao, who helped me with translation.

A deer crosses a landscape, and is watched and then shot by an armed teenaged guard on a mountain. The teenage soldier does not know what is going on, but realizes that his life is endangered because any killing releases some forces. If they are not immediately harnessed for some constructive human purpose, then they are not just at large but out to do harm. In drawing together these materials, I was reminded of my teenage years in Cold War Europe that were punctuated—over the radio in rural Iceland—by the targeted violence of Irish separatists, Basque separatists, and the German Baader-Meinhof that took industrial capitalism as enemy number one. Each group made its points with bombs, guns, and kidnappings. With no end in sight, no one felt particularly safe. That may be my link to Laos in some parallel universe. Wan Lin Chao described a sense of omnipresent danger in Laos and attempts to seek protection:

> *Buv* is an object that protects like an amulet. There is *sapv tso buv* that is carried by a large centipede. The centipede is a big thing, over six inches long, and can bite you, and it's really dangerous. If people get the object from the *sapv*, the *sapv tso buv*, then they will become wealthy very quick. The centipede, if it has *buv*, then you can't fire a gun on it [the bullet will miss or not release].
>
> Another kind is banana tree *buv—norm ziu buv*. If a banana tree has a double blossom, [the magic] is probably there; it brings lots of luck. It [some creature that resides in a double-blossom banana tree] flies on the full moon, on the first and fifteenth days of the lunar month. When it flies at night it will have lights, you need to attack it with a knife, a machete. If you get it in one strike then you will have luck. You then carry it concealed on your body or in your house. Only men carry it; if a woman comes too close, then it will dissipate.
>
> A third *buv* item is two stones that look like coupled genitals, this is the best protection for soldiers [the two women present chimed in, "oh yes," they had heard of it as very powerful], it is also very good for wealth.
>
> The fourth is in *jung ji* [M. *jung-giv*], mouse deer. There is *buv* in the tiny horn. The horn doesn't usually show, and I did not know of this at the time. If you have this *buv* then your enemies' guns won't go off. I shot one mouse deer; the bullet went through the body from the rear to the front, but it took another hour or two to die. When it was dead I took it back to where the other soldier guards were. On the way there a snake crossed my path; no one had told me that

the mouse deer was big luck. At the time I was in Nam Nyou, a young soldier guard on the nearby mountains. I had become a soldier before Chao Mai died, I started in 1966 at age sixteen (I was born late in 1949). About a month after killing the mouse deer, I became very sick; I would dream of the deer, and then pass out. This happened several times. Since I did not take the horn with the *buv*, then it became a curse that threatened my life, rather than bringing me protection and luck.[54]

WAR TURNS INTO A DANGEROUS PEACE

In 1973, a coalition government was formed in Laos in an attempt to end the war. This was an uneasy peace, and from the perspective of some Mien people things started to unravel because soldiers were not paid or were otherwise disaffected, and the rival factions did not want to compromise. For this segment, I draw on some extended moments with several people, including Longsan Tzeo—he had an office job with IRCO (Immigrant and Refugee Community Organization), an organization that serves international refugees in Portland, Oregon. When Longsan could reserve some time, I came by his office and he would tell me things. In one of our conversations, he gave me a sense of the uneasy times between the founding of the coalition government in 1973 and its collapse or defeat in 1975, when even socializing and celebrations were often characterized by factionalism, politicking, and vendettas within families. The account also spells out how the lumber mills could offer resources when the need arose, if people had relations there:

> The Lao government had representatives from each province; I think they serve just like senators or state representatives here [the United States]. This was after the ceasefire. One of them, a senator from our region, had some disagreement with his nephew whom he had raised and sent to school, because of the propaganda from the communists. You know how the young people get influenced easily, and the poor, in every country, that's how the communists recruited. They came to Huai Xay and recruited the college students. At that time, I had just left college to join the military, and by this time I was assistant commander. One evening a village that we patrolled in our territory was hosting a fundraising event for the school, so many of us went there.
>
> Many Thai came over [the border] just to enjoy the party. The senator and his niece and nephew came from Huai Xay during the evening, and somehow the two men got into a fight. The nephew was eventually taken away by our forces, because the police there did not dare to do anything to interfere, and they called for help. So our unit went over and then removed him. We actually kept him at our base for one night, and the next morning we just let him go. The senator did not know who rescued him. At the time of the conflict, the tires on his jeep were slashed, so he couldn't go home. And his chauffeur, I think that is when they began to ask help from me.
>
> There was a saw mill, a lumber mill in the area. You know with lumber mills, the owner had a jeep and a chauffeur and this and that. So we walked over to the saw mill, to the manager, and [the mill manager's driver] took the senator home in the jeep. But the senator did not know who had helped him the night

---

[54] Personal interview, Portland, OR, March 3, 2008.

before, so the next morning he came back to the scene, wanting to find out who had helped him. So the villagers dragged him to me, "this is the person who helped you last night." He took me to a small restaurant because he wanted to say thank you, and then he began to tell me the story of Issara, you know, Lao Issara [one of the rival parties to Lao factionalism from the 1950s to 1975]. *Issara* means "independent" in Lao, they formed the Issara party to get rid of the French from Laos. So he was with the Issara and that is what he told me about, getting rid of the French and the taxation.[55]

When Longsan and I talked, he was not telling me things as a politician, but as a one-time soldier who had felt uneasy and then felt betrayed, and had managed to get away.

Khmu [one of the highland peoples who had been organized into militias] were the first to oppose the coalition government, and fought it. In our region, there were two Khmu battalions and only one Mien. Khmu rebelled against the government troops twice; the first time they were just pushed farther away. The government trusted the Mien, and we were stationed between the Khmu units and the town of Huai Xay.

When the second [Khmu] rebellion happened, they came and asked us to join them, every day for three days. Chao La was already away from his post, and they said Chao La and Khamsene have been arrested, we have to join forces to free them, otherwise they will be sent to prison in Vientiane. We did not join them. The third time they came in the evening, at eleven o'clock. Our headquarters was in the local village clinic that was out of use. It had been built by the United States [USAID], they put clinics everywhere. We'd relocate every six months, stay outside of villages, and in this case there was an abandoned clinic we could use.

We had soldier patrols twenty-four hours a day. They [soldiers on patrol] told us that Khmu in full force were coming, and we said, "let the commanders through." We recognized them, since under the CIA the Khmu, the Mien, the Hmong, and the Tai Lue had cooperated. "Can we use your radio, we are short on supplies." What do we get for our radio? There had to be some exchange. They gave us a pistol, Chinese made. "We are going to attack Huai Xay at 3:00 AM." We couldn't sleep. We heard the noise; they had all the Khmu [-driven] taxis transporting soldiers [for the attack]. At 2:30 we heard the explosions. We were afraid and prayed that people would not be hurt. They then took us to Huai Xay. I got there at 6:00 AM, got to military headquarters. "We rounded up thirty Mien soldiers," they said, and they released them to me.

That was the beginning of the rebellion, on December 30, 1974; then we worked together [as the Pathet Lao took over the country]. We had no choice but to work together, from December 1974 to June or July of 1975. So the coalition government used that. "See, Huai Xay already joined, this is how we work together." They used that as propaganda. Then they began releasing soldiers, people can just go home, they said. They interviewed everyone. Seng Fu was on leave. Almost all the Mien left for home. Yao Pu and Seng Fu were commanders; Seng Fu's deputy was Lao. They protested the release of troops, so no one went

---

[55] Personal interview, Portland, OR, September 13, 2007.

home. Then we met and planned, selected a small group of Mien and Khmu, those who could read Lao, and sent them to reeducation camp—a "political seminar."

All of us commanders had to go. This was supposed to be for two months. It was an hour and a half travel by taxi. The instructor said he was a colonel from the communists; there were eight hours of lectures every day. We were lectured on how they worked together in the forest, and how they succeeded; then we were each to write a paper on what we liked about the government. We were let go after one month because there was fear of an attack on Huai Xay. After the seminar was finished, [we were instructed] first you are to campaign in your unit, then in the villages, and so on, you are to spread the word. "This is for the benefit of Laos and not the foreigners" was the message. I thought, this is against ourselves, they may use it to attack the previous commanders; they want us to do the brainwashing for them.

I had a strange feeling after the seminar [that] maybe I should leave the country. Then there was the second announcement that soldiers were being released. I left for home to Longsan village [in Nam Keung] and then to Thailand. All the soldiers were gathered by force and sent to labor camps. Seng Fu and Yao Pu sent me a note from Nam Keung: "We are leaving, we know we are targeted for labor camp." Salaries had been blocked for three months, and they [the government] tried to get everyone to labor camp. When they released you [soldiers], you had to report to base camp to collect your salary from the coalition government. That was a trick. I made an appointment in Nam Keung with my seventeen soldiers, as I had a gut feeling that this wasn't safe.

On the way, I met a Lao official whom one Lao friend knew and called godfather. My friend wanted me to meet him. We had a two-to-three hour conversation, and he told me about the government's plan for the country, including a future plan for soldiers. As we talked, I got more and more worried. When I got to base camp, I did not admit that I wanted to quit. "You can stay or go," they said. I said I chose to stay, but once the interview was over, I said I will go. Everybody thought I was teasing when I packed my things. The names were announced over the military radio.

We were stationed at Huai Xay airport, about one hour's walk to headquarters. Maybe this is a trick, I said, maybe we will be sent to labor camp. I decided to sacrifice my two–three month salary [that was owed me]. Only one older man went to collect his salary. He was forced to labor camp, and his family left the country before he was out again. His family is now in California. At his last post, he was deputy company commander, people were demoted [the Pathet Lao demoted people who had fought on the other side for the brief time in 1974–75 when all were supposedly united]. Before, he was in the logistics office.

This Mien man was married to a Thai Dam woman; he couldn't leave the country because all his savings were held by his in-laws. He stayed at the base with troops and was sent to labor camp. That was stage two; the first had been the political seminar. He was released in 1986. I first met him in 1992, in Fresno (California), at a refugee conference, and we met again last year [2007] at a Mien wedding. They [political prisoners] were initially sent to one area, in Phongsaly, but then there was conflict between China and Laos [in 1979 and 1980, with shelling across the border], and they were all moved to the south. His wife waited for him in Nam Keung, and the in-laws were still there.[56]

Some people got across the border easily, ferried over by people who were friends on the Thai side. According to Seng Fo Chao, "When people were fleeing, Lung [*lung*, Thai, 'uncle'] Phan, a Northern Thai man, was the leader over there; he got hundreds of boats to get people across. After the first two large groups got across, the Lao authorities sent soldiers to shoot people who tried to flee across the Mekong River." Others, like Wan Tzo Pu Chao, had a more challenging crossing.

> When we moved, there were Communists everywhere. My family moved, but we had to separate to cross the Mekong River; some used a boat, others a raft or bamboo. I went on a bamboo raft with a pole. When I crossed the Mekong River, I had really bad luck. The communists shot my father's hand, it broke, I had to take off my shirt to tie his hand, and after that I took off my pants to stop the blood, then my shirt, my t-shirt, everything. I was only wearing underwear when we crossed the river. We got to Thailand and went to Chiangrai Town to the hospital, and stayed there about thirty-three days and then went to Chiangsaen where they had a refugee camp.[57]

I have heard some horrible stories of people who were killed and others who lost their whole family at the river border, where at one point Lao soldiers were under orders to shoot anyone trying to flee the country. These stories are too awful to reproduce, and instead I will relate the difficult and treacherous journey of some friends who were repeatedly robbed and betrayed as they tried to get to Thailand by first going into Burma. The region they fled to is in the Shan State, and at the time there were several rival militias around and considerable banditry. Tsan Tsong Chao told me this story:

> In 1975 we couldn't get through. We went from Laos to Burma and they took us to …
>
> "It's light, we cannot come out," so they took us to a farm. We stayed there until about three o'clock [in the afternoon]. They had about thirty or forty soldiers come out, and they wanted us to pay them because we stopped by their land. We talked to them, first they asked for a lot, but then we didn't have to pay them that much. We paid them, like, ten thousand *baht*, and then waited until it got dark. They had three or four boats to take us from Burma to Thailand. And, they are planning to pull us out on the island [in the middle of the river] again. We have four single persons, we want to go first. If they stop, then we want to fight with them.
>
> But they were smarter than we were, they had us go to that tree, a log in the Mekong River, and we were blocked over there. So my family went all before us, they pulled all of them out so we can not do anything. So we go out … The people were then taken ashore on the Burma side, robbed, and left stranded.
>
> [The bandits] were strange people. They [had us] walk with them about thirty minutes over by the Nam Kok River, and they wanted us to pay them, like,

---

a hundred thousand *baht,* but we talked with them for a while and they let us pay them forty thousand *baht.* They say that after we pay them, they will take us to Thailand. But they did not; they just took the money and ran away.

We couldn't go anywhere. A boat came by on the river; we called them to come pick us up. One boat stopped by, took two of us to Thailand, to talk to the captain of the police. We tried to pay him under the table. We paid four thousand *baht,* [but] he did nothing; he just said he can't do anything. So, we stayed there till about 3:00 PM, and we had nowhere to go. A couple went to their farm, and we borrowed their canoe, then we went back to Laos, to the communists. We told them "somebody lied to us, [they] said they would take us to Thailand and we would have a happy life, but we didn't, they took us to the island and took all our money and left us there, so we had to go back to Laos." We stayed there, in Pang Khwan, one night, and went home to Chalom [a village up in the mountains, a few hours walk from the main Nam Keung settlements, where they had lived during the war]. We stayed there for about seven months. Then one of our relatives from Burma came and told us to go with him. We went to Burma and stayed there for two and a half years. Then finally we went to Thailand, and I stayed in a refugee camp for ten months [before coming to the United States].[58]

In another conversation with Tsan Tsong and Wan Tzo, in the mushroom-pickers' camp, I learned about singing troupes that were sent around Laos in an effort at nation-building. The account expresses the lingering sense or fear that as people became nationals under the new regime, they would never return home. Wan Tso had remarked that if you were twelve years old and not enrolled in school, you had to become a soldier. The conversation between Tsan Tsong, Wan Tzo, Anna Tsing, and I went something like this:

TT: When the communists took over the country, young people, girls and boys, would go in groups together to different cities to sing and dance. They called them *nying num, sai num* [Lao, "young women, young men."] [WT interjected: "These were kids who had no parents, no family."] They were performing for the government. And then one of the communist guys, he told me, you have to go, leave this country. Why? Right now, you are among those wanted most to go to different cities [Tsan Tsong was a popular performer]. ... First, from our village, they want us to go to Huai Pheung, Mung Mom, and then Nam Keung. Then it is Jong Pheng and pretty soon they take us to Huai Xay.
AT: Did you ever join that?
TT: I did, for a year. So he [the communist] told me, if they keep taking you farther and farther, then later they will hand you a gun, they give you a rifle, and you don't get to go back.
AT: Was the group all Mien?
TT: Yes. But the songs were Lao songs. He told me that, so I said we have to leave, so we tried our best to escape.

---

[58] Ibid.

AT: Someone told us that when people were leaving it was like one village would come to another village and so on, the group [trying to escape] would keep growing in size.

TT: Yes, the ones living farther away from the border, they had to tell the government that they were moving, and they got closer and closer to the border [before they could try to cross it].

AT: Were there soldiers in your family?

TT: My three older brothers. One came here last week; he was a nurse for Chao La's army.

HJ: Did you ever go for New Year festivals in Nam Keung?

TT: Yes, there was singing in Lao, and dancing. Before the communist takeover there was an annual New Year festival. Mayors and generals would come to the party—Lao generals. We would only sing love songs. And we would do Lao dances, like *lamwong*.

AT: What kinds of clothes did people wear in Nam Keung?

TT: When they went to a party, people would wear Mien clothes.[59]

The thousands of Lao Iu Mien people who crossed the Mekong River to Thailand in 1975 were not as easily absorbed as were the hundreds who left in 1973. Refugee camps were gradually set up in Chiangrai (Chiangkhong, Chiangkham), Nan Provinces (Mae Jalim, Nam Yao), and elsewhere. The first camp was established in Chiangsaen, but it was replaced by camps in Chiangkhong and Chiangkham. About 300,000 refugees had fled from Laos to Thailand by 1980.[60] Military leaders had considerable say in where their followers were placed. When one temporary camp was dissolved, Iu Mien from Nam Keung were sent with their leader Vern Chien to Suan Ban Tong (near Chiangkhong in Chiangrai), while Iu Mien who had had no previous relations with Chao La were sent with Long Tong, another leader from Chao La's militia, to Nam Yao (in Nan). Others were later placed in the Ban Vinai camp (in Loei), which was heavily Hmong and a Vang Pao stronghold.

The structures of refugee relief tended to reinforce an ethnic imaginary that played to the interests of militia leaders. Asking about one man's experiences in a refugee camp one day, I got a comparative lesson about people and dogs, and about Thailand and the United States. The truth of the comparisons made us laugh, which we all needed, as I tried to learn from people about sometimes difficult and painful times:

HJ: Was it difficult? Some people said the guards, the *O-So*,[61] were very mean to people.

Mien friend: It depends. With Thai people, if you know how to respect them, then they treat you well. If you don't know how to respect them, they treat you like a dog. In the United States, a dog is good, but over there [in

---

[59] Personal interview, Oregon mountains, October 16, 2007.

[60] Van-es-Beeck, "Refugees from Laos," p. 324.

[61] *O-so* is from the Thai abbreviation of *Asa-samak*, "volunteer." Correctly I should transliterate it as *Aw-saw*, but something about the context makes me instead allude to how they were "oh-so" above accountability.

Thailand], a dog is nothing. In this country, a dog is like your kid, but over there, a dog is treated like shit.[62]

Another acquaintance, Kao-Ta Tang, described what it was like to be a refugee:

Ban Vinai was a regular camp, but very big. People could get a permit to come and go. In Nam Yao, people kept coming and going. The camp with the most problems was Mae Jalim, where there were many mean Thai people around. Hmong and Lao people who went off for work were robbed while on the outside. The control of the camp was really harsh.[63]

Kao-Ta Tang said that when he turned eighteen years old in 1979, he felt like he had wasted his life in refugee camp. People were going all over, to the Philippines, Japan, France, Australia, and the United States. His parents wanted him to go to the United States because they already had relatives there. He came to the United States and the rest of his family was going to follow. But a tragedy involving his sister made the parents change their minds, and they instead returned to Laos. Some people never wanted to leave Laos; it was the only home they ever knew. But Kao-Ta also told of the suffering and confusion of camp life:

In Nam Yao, the United Nations sent lots of food, but it was the lowest class food. The refugees complained, and then all of a sudden there were cows, pigs, and chickens [to eat]. Then Hmong offered cows to the gods, the Mien offered pigs to the gods. The [Thai] officials saw it [the rituals] and did not like it, and there was no more [good meat]. That was in 1983. Nam Yao burned down in 1981 or so, it burned for three hours. Dry thatch and such had caught fire. I lost track of my parents for three days, lost my clothes, only had my shorts, and was very hopeless in camp. When the Nam Yao camp was destroyed, people just abandoned it and went either into Thailand or back to Laos, though some stayed in camp. The controller of the camp still received money, didn't tell [any officials about the fire] until 1986, when the UN came to check [and he had to explain the missing camp]. The camp was reopened in Chiangkham and the director had to pay. At the time, some people considered going back to Laos, or going to the United States.[64]

The occasional confusion of refugee camps followed the confusion of war times when people sometimes fled across the border to Thailand. Longtsing Tzeo explained,

In 1973 [when Mien people fled the attacks on Nam Nyou], some people went straight to Mae Bong [a Mien village], there were no camps. In 1974, Thai authorities sent trucks to take them back to Laos. The Mien people all fled to the jungle. My grandfather agreed to go back, and stayed in Nam Keung for one year. He planted rice and corn, but did not have a chance to harvest, because the communists took over and people fled. Thai authorities let the Mien stay near

---

[62] Personal interview, Portland, OR, October 11, 2007.

[63] Personal interview, Portland, OR, October 13, 2007.

[64] Ibid.

Chiangsaen, at Nong Bum Kai. People had to build their own huts, waiting for the completion of the Chiangkham camp. Then grandfather and some others went to Mae Bong, a farming village in Chiangrai Province.[65]

Longtsing Tzeo also told of the man who was in charge of providing food for the refugees in the Chiangkham refugee camp.

A guy we knew as Ai Ne or Phi Ne ["older brother" Ne][66] was in charge of buying food for the Chiangkham camp: vegetables, fish, pork, beef. He asked building-leaders how to distribute to each family. Sometimes he asked people to come work for him at his house in Chiangkham. I went a few times to work for him. First we saw that he had a regular house and an old truck. Two years later he had a new house and had bought a sedan, *lot geng,* with tinted widows. "Look at that, he is so rich," was a regular comment. He would buy inferior meat and save the money for himself.[67]

Jiem Lao Chao spent five years in camp in Thailand:

We started at Ku-tao, a temporary camp in Chiangsaen, for about a year. Most people were then transferred to the Chiangkham camp. In the Ku-tao camp, it was just little huts that people had to build themselves.[68]

I told Jiem Lao Chao that I had heard that the houses were of bad quality, that it would rain through them, and that there was a lot of illness. He replied, "Oh yes, people died, a lot." I asked him about the Chiangkham camp, whether people had some freedom of movement to come and go.

JLC: It varied, sometimes you could go, at other times there were restrictions. There was some favoritism, and in some seasons people had more freedom. At one point, there was a really bad situation due to curfew. I witnessed that and was just lucky not to get in trouble; otherwise, I could have been really beat up by the *O-So.* To make a long story short, that night, because of the curfew, there were some people two buildings over from mine, they were visiting and talking and the *O-So* came and got mad, and the Mien got mad and beat up the *O-So.* Then the *O-So* came back with more people and took those people away. A few more [Mien] came, and the *O-So* took them, too. I heard the wrong word and thought there was a robbery, so I went over there with a really long stick. When I got there, the people had already been taken away, and the rest were scared and had already left for their buildings. When I got there I met one *O-So,* and he asked me, "what are you doing?" I said that I heard there was some problem so I came to find out what's going on. He said, "Oh, no problem here, you can go home. Don't worry about it; we take care of any and all problems." That was the worst time, somewhere up to twenty people got taken away to Chiangrai and put

---

[65] Personal interview, Portland, OR, December 10, 2007.

[66] The terms *ai* and *phi* are used by northern and central Thai, respectively.

[67] Personal interview, Portland, OR, December 10, 2007.

[68] Personal interview, Portland, OR, March 8, 2008.

in jail for about six months. Then they came back to camp. Some of them had been beaten up so bad that they had broken teeth.

HJ: So, generally, people had a good reason to be afraid of the *O-So*?

JLC: Well, we did. We were refugees in Thailand, we had no rights at all. I don't know how it is in other countries. The international organizations sent a lot of money, but we were given very poor food, and a lot of money was taken by some people so it never reached the refugees.

    One time Kouichoy [Saechao]'s father went to visit the Chiangkham camp from the Chiangkhong camp. He is a very nice guy, but he did not know about the curfew. He tried to talk to people, and that person, that *jan-khalom* [northern Thai], beat him up. He threw up blood. It was that bad, and it created tension in the camp.

HJ: Were the guards in Chiangkhong any more humane, was it equally difficult there?

JLC: From what I heard, the Chiangkhong camp was more humane. I heard that Chao La's reputation [may have influenced that]. I heard that people had more freedom to go out, to help cover whatever support they did not receive [to get] firewood, food, and such. I don't know the truth, but my guess is that Chiangkhong is closer to Laos, and the guards had more understanding. I heard that the lives of refugees in Chiangkhong were better than in Chiangkham. People had more freedom to go in and out and to have little gardens for vegetables outside the camp. In Chiangkham, there were times when we were allowed to leave camp, but often we were very restricted.[69]

In another conversation I learned that the administration and rules of a camp might be flexible if people were lucky. There was a front gate and a back gate, and one was guarded less strictly than the other. And there were two minibus taxi drivers who treated their refugee customers very differently:

HJ: Did people ever have a chance to go off to just visit a Mien village?

Mien friend: Some people would steal out; they just left without telling anyone. Sometimes this was to visit Mien people, but also to do work for them, some people did that. [I mention what someone said about going to Sobthu and then to Kamphengphet for ten days to work.] I think they must have gone without permission, and did not use the front gate. Rather, people could take the back gate and walk to the highway and get a taxi there [minibus].

HJ: And then people would be nervous about being stopped and asked to show ID cards?

MF: Oh, yes. The *Jan-khalom* (M. *Jan-kaa lorm*) who handled food for the camp, in some ways he was bad, in other ways he was good. His taxi and another one were the only ones that would allow people to do daily shopping in Chiangkham. He would ask people if they wanted a return slip. If they didn't want it, he just would not say anything. The other taxi driver, he

---

[69] Ibid.

would count people and put all the names down, so you had to return that day.[70]

Men had an easier time than women leaving camp for a short time. One woman told me that she never felt safe leaving camp, that in her recollection there was a lingering fear of rape: "Even if you went with a male companion, the *jan-khalom* bandits could just shoot him or tie him up and rape you." I asked her if there had been the same fear in Laos during wartime, and she said there was not. Thailand, in the late 1970s, was a society of anxious militarization, with considerable authoritarianism and violence. I know of only one case of rape from the Chiangkham camp in the late 1970s; one young woman had gone outside of camp to tend to a vegetable garden or something of the sort, and was raped by the camp guards while outside the camp's perimeter. She returned and told of what happened, but the guards had beaten her so badly that she died the next day.

There was nothing the refugees could do about the guards' cruelty, and it was common knowledge that the guards' disregard had few limits. I have not asked after such episodes, and describing it leaves me only with sadness and despair. But knowing this gives me some sense of why some women at the time characterized their gendered vulnerability as being about Northern Thai masculinity, and why some people more generally thought of the guards' cruelty as manifesting their ethnicity.

Ethnic leader Chao La and many of his closest militia associates were not treated like refugees. They had a general travel pass and enjoyed considerable freedom of travel within Thailand. Chao La did not live inside the Chiangkhong camp, but in a rather nice two-story house outside of it. There he was able to receive visitors, including many Thai military men who maintained relations with him. One Westerner who corresponded briefly with me about this time remembers fondly the elaborate meals he had at Chao La's house, complete with cold beer and delightful conversations. "Chao La was always busy writing letters to help the refugee Mien people," this man once wrote me in an email.

In one of the conversations I had with women about the Chiangkhong camp, I learned that Chao La was continually afraid for his life and had Mien refugees guard his house day and night. "Even if a woman was living alone with her kids, she would have to leave them behind and serve as guard overnight if he demanded it." And some of the time he demanded money of people, added another woman.

Ton Khuon Lor went with his family across to Thailand, but did not go directly to a refugee camp. He lives in Portland, Oregon, is a barber during the week, and is also an active member in his Mien Fellowship Baptist Church, where he plays guitar and sometimes electric bass to accompany the singing. One day I visited his shop; he had the Bible open and was working on turning some Old Testament episodes into songs. He had plans to take a year off and go to Thailand to serve his religion among the Mien people there. Here I share only a few segments having to do with life in Thailand and Laos, gleaned from a full day of talking with Ton Khuon Lor.

On New Year's Day in 1973, Nam Nyou was bombed, and the people fled to Nam Keung. It was about 5 to 6:00 PM, people came and said "the Vietnamese are attacking, you have to leave." People did not even have time to eat dinner.

---

[70] Personal interview, Portland, OR, November 20, 2008.

We were about to celebrate New Year, but had to leave everything and go to Thailand. I was born in Moung Noi in Muong Sing, and was seven years old when the family left in 1973. They had lived close to Nam Keung for four or five years, in *Mu Song* ("village number two"), it had perhaps five houses, my mother's brother was there. When they fled in 1973, they went to Mae Bong [a village in Chiangrai Province, also known as Khun Bong and Mae Khun Bong], and then in 1976 to Khlong Lan in Kamphaeng Phet Province. We lived in Pheung Nom, about fifteen minutes from Khlong Lan. We were there from 1976 to 1979 and then went to "the jungle" in Thang Sut, for farming. There were three groups there, we were Group One. Unless you did something wrong, no Thai would bother you in Kamphaeng Phet. A lot of Hmong were growing opium in the jungle [before 1982]. Some Hmong people then told on those who were growing opium. There was a fight with Thai soldiers. Highway construction stopped because of the fighting, that's why the settlement was called *Thang Sut* ["the end of the road"].

In Kamphaeng Phet, the ones who were born in Thailand would go to school, but the ones born in Laos would just work. I went to school, but then I had to go to the fields for an hour and a half. My mother and sisters would cook, and after dinner I did homework. On weekends there was only fieldwork. All of our neighbors were poor; we could not help each other. When we arrived in Canada I saw Canadians who were always helping each other, here people give money to the homeless.[71]

The settlement in Kamphaeng Phet drew on tensions within Thailand in the 1970s, particularly the emergence of guerrilla warfare between the military and units of the Communist Party of Thailand (CPT) that took to jungle hideouts after fierce suppression in Bangkok and elsewhere. Many Thai college students joined the CPT after brutal violence in Bangkok in 1976, and went "to the jungle." In reaction, the Thai military authorities encouraged upland ethnic minority farmers to settle in Kamphaeng Phet, a forested area that they were welcome to clear and open up for growing corn and rice.

This was a strategy meant to deny wooded hideouts to CPT guerrilla units, and some refugee camp gates were opened up in 1976 and later for people who wanted to relocate to Kamphaeng Phet. The Thai authorities made a similar offer to ethnic Thai in Malaysia to come across the border and open up farmland in the border province of Narthiwat, so as to deny forest areas to the CPT.[72] After CPT members accepted an offer of amnesty in about 1982, the Thai military went after the highland farmers in Kamphaeng Phet as illegal cultivators, or as "strays" who were supposed to be in refugee camps—these farmers had outlived their usefulness for combating Thai insurgents and then came to be seen as a threat to the forest.

---

[71] Personal interview, Portland, OR, August 24, 2008.

[72] Irving C. Johnson, "Paradise at Your Doorstep: International Border Fluidity and Cultural Construction amongst Kelantan's Thai Community," in *Dynamic Diversity in Southern Thailand*, ed. Wattana Sugunnasil (Chiangmai: Silkworm, 2005), p. 303.

ARE THE HMONG DIFFERENT FROM THE MIEN AND EVERYONE ELSE?

From interviews with Hmong people in the United States, political scientist Keith Quincy assembled many graphic and horrible stories from the Second Indochina War in Laos. His effort lends voice to people who lost a war that was not theirs to begin with. It tells about only one side of the many complex engagements that Hmong had in Laos at that time. Quincy uses this knowledge to depict the Hmong as always having been caught up in ethnicized war, and this leads to certain leaps of analogy. He refers, for instance, to Hmong rebellions in pre-modern China as "jihads," and to Chinese violence against the Hmong as "pogroms" and as like the unequal fights between "American Indians [and the] US Cavalry," complete with "slaughtering" and "carnage."[73]

A part of Quincy's iconic depiction of the Hmong concerns "messianic" leaders. One, Pa Chay, was killed in 1921. There were other leaders, but Quincy depicts them as of the same mold. A "frenzied" Hmong rebellion in 1975 demonstrated "that the dead hand of Pa Chay had a very long reach."[74] The origins of Quincy's approach come through in these signifying terms, of Muslim holy wars, Russian violence mostly against Jews, the racist violence of the American Frontier.

This imagery demonstrates how Quincy defines the Hmong as a people, as he assembles the horrendous historic episodes that buttress his understanding. That is, these notions from histories in the Middle East, Russia, and the United States foreground how he comes to define the Hmong in history as a suffering, war-ravaged people, to the point of making any other Hmong unthinkable. The Hmong were always there, clearly distinct from their Others—China and communist Laos in particular. They become knowable through their indistinctness as the general victims of history, similar to what Liisa Malkki has described for "African refugees" as "promising objects of academic specialization, worthy objects of humanitarian attention."[75]

Such accounts do not simply or only describe the Hmong in particular ways. Rather, the descriptions enable a field within which readers can come to a sense of themselves and of history as a particular kind of dramatic field. Any such field may offer certain associations and preclude or discourage others. In one variant of such Hmong stories, the Hmong are somehow a brother to the militarized United States, a good match. Journalist Jane Hamilton-Merritt's book on Hmong in the war in Laos opens with a characterization that insists on precisely that, without having to declare the comparison: "The Hmong have a 4,000-year-old culture which treasures concepts of honor, commitment, loyalty, and freedom."[76] The chapters of her *Tragic Mountains* have titles such as "Massacre on the Mekong," "Men of Courage," "Exodus," "Chao Fa: Mystical Warriors," and "Holocaust in the Hills." The book is largely taken up with detailed accounts of one battle after another; it pictures the heroic and freedom-loving Hmong against the brutal Lao communists. And she is far from alone in this particular American signification of the Hmong:

---

[73] Keith Quincy, *Harvesting Pa Chay's Wheat: The Hmong and America's Secret War in Laos* (Cheney, WA: Eastern Washington University Press, 2000), pp. 23–24.

[74] Ibid., p. 44.

[75] Liisa Malkki, *Purity and Exile* (Chicago, IL: University of Chicago Press, 1995), p. 296.

[76] Jane Hamilton-Merritt, *Tragic Mountains: The Hmong, the Americans, and the Secret Wars for Laos, 1942–1992* (Bloomington, IN: Indiana University Press, 1993), p. 1.

Americans solicited these highland guerrilla fighters; still, US policymakers cannot be held completely responsible for the Hmong losses. The elite in Vientiane and Luang Prabang, who openly viewed the mountain people as little more than savages, were quite willing to sit back and allow their Hmong surrogates to fight the communist trespassers. After all, the lowland Lao army rarely possessed the determination to stand and fight effectively against the North Vietnamese. Moreover, communist proscriptions were anathema to the Hmong way of life. US involvement increased the level of violence, but even without American assistance most of Vang Pao's Hmong clans would have resisted the North Vietnamese.[77]

If Jane Hamilton-Merritt found her freedom-loving and loyal brothers in the Hmong, and Timothy Castle his anti-communist and anti-North Vietnamese ones, Keith Quincy went even further and found there his deep-white or Caucasian brothers:

> It is not unreasonable to imagine [that the Hmong] are related to a people who long ago migrated from the west into Eurasia and later into Siberia. This would account for the Caucasian features so prominent among the Hmong today.[78]

Somewhere deep down, in their political values and their DNA, the Hmong are the United States' brothers, or kin of the democratic and white West. All three authors are so squarely set in their convictions identifying the Lao and Vietnamese communists as evil that they never deal with the diversity of Laos or the contingency of Hmong involvement with the war.

Because the Iu Mien were largely outside the active fighting and bombing raids in the resettlement of Nam Keung, their suffering was, in abstract terms, less than that of Hmong. But in real human terms, it was as bad as that of anyone else. Laos as a country and a society was in many ways destroyed by the violence. The princes and Kong Le, the Vietnamese and American backers and suppliers of the war, and the ethnic militia leadership wanted to keep the war going, and meanwhile the people and the country suffered, during and after the war.

The war shaped the Hmong in different ways than it did the Mien, the Khmu, and many other highland groups. The resettlement around Long Cheng, in Xieng Khouang near the Vietnamese border, was not shown on any map from the period; its existence was a secret. Hmong realities took particular shape through various engagements with the context of war. Vang Pao's forces, which were centered in the Long Cheng area, had, at one point, forty thousand soldiers. I have no population figures for Long Cheng itself, but it was repeatedly under attack from air and land, and there was no way to sustain farming.

For the Hmong, according to Roger Warner, "the wartime economy and the support of the Americans brought luxuries that they were unwilling to abandon.

---

[77] Castle, *At War in the Shadow of Vietnam*, pp. 136–37.

[78] Quincy is assuming that this racial configuration occurred as a result of migration. See: Keith Quincy, *Hmong: History of a People* (Cheney, WA: Eastern Washington University Press, 1995), p. 29. This migration happened perhaps three to five thousand years ago, before Siberia's population shifted from Caucasian to become solidly Mongolian by the beginning of the Christian era.

Nobody needed to farm anymore. Airplanes dropped rice from the sky."[79] I was not there, but from reading and otherwise learning about Laos, I have no indication that anyone in Long Cheng could farm. Warner's tone suggests luxury and easy comfort that are, all things considered, unconvincing, if not insulting, in the way they portray the people and the area at the time.

Comparing the Hmong at Long Cheng to the Mien around Nam Keung, we find two major differences. One concerns Vang Pao's relationship to the United States' wars in the region. The Hmong had a place to guard that they must not leave, no matter how heavy the bombing or the rain of bullets. The Mien could and did escape once, and their settlements were never under extended or heavy attacks. The other difference was that no Hmong people had a normal life anymore; everyone's life revolved around war and death and supplies dropped from the air. By comparison, most Mien and other people around Nam Keung remained farmers throughout the war. A variant of this practice recurred in the Ban Vinai refugee camp, where the Hmong were recipients of aid that depended partly or largely on their militia connections. If that did not suffice to fashion a particular understanding of Hmong identity by highlighting their association with the militia's leadership, there was the shock of post-war violence that may have cemented the image of Hmong suffering and resistance against the evil communists of Laos and Vietnam. According to Grant Evans,

> ... perhaps upwards of thirty thousand Vietnamese troops were used in the large-scale operation launched against the Hmong [post-war militia and civilians inside Laos] in 1977. The fighting was ferocious and included shelling and aerial bombing with napalm. Because the Hmong resistance fighters lived with their families, operations against them included indiscriminate civilian casualties, leading to charges of genocide when these people staggered into camps in Thailand and told their stories.[80]

Vang Pao long insisted to his people that they stay in camp rather than opt for refugee resettlement in third countries, as his forces were going to take back Laos. The clear and rather one-dimensional images of Hmong that come across in Quincy's and Hamilton-Merritt's books may be an outgrowth of how the Hmong as a people were shaped by war. If so, then the dynamic is similar to what Liisa Malkki describes for the Hutu refugees in Tanzanian camps who anxiously guarded their purity and the ethnic boundary enclosing their group. She makes a useful contrast with those who did not become refugees and instead slipped into a multiethnic city life unmarked by any emphasis on Hutu identity.[81]

Throughout and after the war, many Hmong were kept suspended and in harm's way, and then in relief's way, rather than being enabled to move towards a normal life where they themselves might have something to do. Suspending the Hmong people from their own humanity—from life itself—served the various military interests that were entangled in the conflict. Once Hmong resettled in large numbers in the United States, the militia's leaders and agents were also there,

---

[79] Warner, *Shooting at the Moon*, p. 309.

[80] Grant Evans, "Laos: Minorities," in *Ethnicity in Asia*, ed. Colin MacKerras (New York, NY: RoutledgeCurzon, 2003), p. 221.

[81] Malkki, *Purity and Exile*, pp. 197–231.

insisting on ethnic unity and the collection of money on a regular basis so that they might sustain a militia to regain Laos as theirs.

I cannot do much about how the Hmong are sometimes stereotyped. But I can show that for the Mien, people's experiences were quite diverse, differentiated, and particular—as an ethnic group, they are not so easily boxed in or turned into pin-ups for the moral or political fantasies of Westerners, or those of Asian militia leaders.

The glorification of the Hmong as America's wartime brothers is matched by its obverse, Alfred McCoy's critical account of the sinister role of the heroin trade during the war. He easily labels the Mien leader Chao La as "a local CIA mercenary commander and heroin manufacturer,"[82] pins various Lao, Thai, and South Vietnamese politicians as corrupt, and gives an extensive account of Hmong leader Vang Pao, none of it in my view either balanced or fair. I will not itemize any counterclaims, as I think the moralization of Asian nations, ethnic groups, or their leaders, is a very dangerous game for Western scholars to play.

Learning with the Mien people has been a way for me to come into different histories and identities, which also helps put Western scholarship in some perspective. One night in the Oregon mountains with Mien mushroom-pickers, when I had brought some beer and we talked, a man said that he would tell me his story the following night and that I could record it. The next evening we were there, and after some warm-up chat the man, Seng Uei Tang, began:

> In the old days I lived in Laos. Before I left I lived in Phu-Gong [village] in Phalai District [of Sayaburi or Xaygnaboury Province]. That's where I was born. On the twenty-second day of the sixth month in 1988, I came here [to the United States—the date of arrival is an important component of refugee immigrant identities]. We left the house and went to Thailand. During the Vietnam War, our household was attacked and people were killed. At that time, we were in the middle of planting. We left everything, the house and the rice fields, animals, harvested rice, and rice in the fields that we were planting; we only took enough to eat for ourselves. I was not well, and my grandfather wasn't well. For fourteen days we were on the road [walking] until we got to the Thai border. When we got to the border, I really wasn't well, my family left me behind on the road. I was left alone. I only had my brother's gun, the *Kalang* [a rifle, M-1 Garand]. I made a shelter for myself, and [many days later] when my family came back to get me I did not recognize them right away. I was scared and almost shot them. The bullets were in the gun, and I almost killed them.[83]

At this point, Seng Uei was somewhat shaken. The recollection of a teenager left behind and disoriented near the Thailand–Laos border, hiding in the bushes from Lao government soldiers and then hearing rustles in the leaves and expecting the worst, had left him with an easily triggered sense of horror. Not only had Lao soldiers been attacking his home village at war's end, killing his relatives and neighbors, he himself came very close to killing his own family because he had been alone, sick, and without food for days, and initially had no idea who the people were

---

[82] Alfred McCoy, *The Politics of Heroin in Southeast Asia* (New York, NY: Harper & Row, 1972), pp. 146–47, photo caption.

[83] Personal interview, Oregon mountains, October 17, 2007.

who were approaching his hiding place. Had it not been daylight that time, he and I might never have come together over the story thirty years later.

Seng Uei's story is, of course, his own. But it is also a way to situate how Lao people of various political and ethnic identities, and with considerable outside support, lost any restraint against killing their own people and fellow-nationals during the war. Seng Uei was a lucky exception. After the war, much Lao social creativity in exile was brought to making or sustaining militias to fight the communist government. That focus of social and interethnic imaginations after 1975 is depressing, and I have tried to fend off anyone's fascinations with militia intrigues by chasing after other things, because I do not want the violence to replay itself through my work. If people do not know some powerful forces that can be harnessed for a positive purpose, then these forces may, like the mouse deer's *buv* against Wan Lin Chao, freely create havoc and endanger us, others, and worlds.

CHAPTER THREE

THAILAND WITH THE MIEN

French anthropologist Jacques Lemoine's book *Yao Ceremonial Paintings* was based on research conducted among Mien people in the refugee camp of Chiangkhong, in northern Thailand, in the late 1970s. But there is no trace of refugee status, the militia, or the war in his book—instead, the focus is on spirit paintings and on ritual texts written in Chinese characters. Lemoine's book conveys the Yao as timeless ritual practitioners whose traditions reside in Chinese Daoist paintings and texts about which Lemoine has a unique understanding. Lemoine's appreciative readers did not care that an awful war was placing various people in harm's way and enabling others to gain power and wealth, but they wanted to know and hold onto the image of a peaceful and mysterious Orient.

This Orient of *Yao Ceremonial Paintings* was rare and endangered, but still accessible through scholarly expertise and antique shops, and it produced unique enhancements to Western bourgeois living rooms. In their home countries, these paintings were allegedly "burned at the order of some Christian missionary groups or destroyed by communist zealots."[1] This suggests the enlightened and secularist world of upper-class connoisseurs as the intended readers for Lemoine's work. Any owner of a Yao ceremonial painting is made into a redeemer; she has rescued a valuable thing from destruction by fanatics of Christian or communist bent. This cements virtue to bourgeois privilege, and completely erases the possibility of recognizing the role of scholarship in violent encounters. To buy the paintings was not simply about object-rescue and the acquisition of home decor with intercultural allure. The paintings offered a novel opportunity to invest in objects that produced fantastic returns: "Since 1975, [the price for the paintings] in the open market has risen no less than fifteen fold."[2]

Lemoine's case suggests the curious intersections of scholarship, representation, politics, wars, and the Western middle class that make it impossible to recognize the situations in which the Iu Mien people have found themselves, to recognize them for who they are or were, or to comprehend the extent to which educated Westerners are also in this picture while perfectly out of sight. There is no way of adequately representing who and what the Iu Mien people are without situating them in specific times and places, and paying attention to both internal diversity and their position within larger social fields of ethnic labels, state control, warfare, ritual practices, gender, and social geographies. There are many ways of entangling Iu Mien peoples in social or moral geographies beyond their control; this happens in the scholarship that does not recognize that there are actual people in the portrayal, scholarship that offers only types.

---

[1] Jacques Lemoine, *Yao Ceremonial Paintings* (Bangkok: White Lotus, 1982), p. 7.

[2] Ibid.

Any representation can become an object of contemplation and learning, and the understanding it provides can inform identity work. The idea of Zomia contributes to particular kinds of identity work within divided Western societies. So does the Orient of *Yao Ceremonial Paintings*. It would be safe for me and might lend me academic credibility in some quarters to go critically after or through Lemoine's work. But there is better reason to suspend such games that have no currency outside of academia, and instead use ethnography to offer people other intersections with the world. Knowing something about life in the camps, I would rather tell a different story. But first I make some comparative remarks about the display of Mien and other Yao through images and objects.

With his book, Jacques Lemoine captured the market for signifying Mien spirit paintings in much the same way that others had captured the market for an interest in ethnic dress. This left still others only with written texts as a way to say something new with a Yao display. Yao texts became the province of certain German scholars. There is a book commemorating an exhibit of Yao manuscripts and related objects held at the Bavarian State Library in Munich, Germany; the exhibit on display for less than two months in late 1999. The book remains, and stands as a major effort to present Yao through a display of texts. There is no comparable work on Yao manuscripts, and thus the book is likely to serve as an inventory of Yao texts. I found the effort interesting but frustrating, in that the scholars only know Yao people and religious practice from books, and they present the Yao as a people whom outsiders may come to know and understand from their collection of texts. Perhaps it is fitting for work done at a library, and while the effort is important, it is certainly no final word on the topic.

Some of the most compelling pieces in the German catalog show that Yao people have not just carried books about. They have used them in rituals. One example is the text of a chant most likely used for ordination rituals, written on the unprinted side of a recycled American military care package, a relic from the war in Laos. The catalog also contains a photo of the other side of the cardboard that identifies the country of origin and states that the stuff is "not to be sold or exchanged."

Another reminder from the war in Laos is on a single sheet, drawn in comic-book style, found within one of the manuscripts. The cartoon is written in Lao and shows an encounter between an old Lao couple and two soldiers. The grandfather asks for mercy from the soldiers, who reassure the elderly couple that they are genuine Lao soldiers and here to protect them from harassment by the Vietnamese army. After this revelation, the grandmother declares her great relief that the two are "our Lao soldiers."

A third reminder of the world within which Mien and other Yao have found themselves is a 1951 addition to Kia Shen Pong, or Emperor Ping's Charter (not shown in the exhibit catalog). It declares how Yao are going to cooperate with the Han Chinese now that they have been liberated and can benefit from the leadership of Chairman Mao.[3]

---

[3] Thomas O. Höllmann and Michael Freidrich, ed., *Botschaften an die Götter: Religiöse Handschriften der Yao* [Instructions to the Gods: Yao Religious Manuscripts]; *Südchina, Vietnam, Laos, Thailand, Myanmar* (Wiesbaden: Harrassowitz, 1999), pp. 34–35, 60–61, 31–32. Chinese communist authorities incorporated many Yao leaders into local administrative structures. While the first decades of communist rule saw many attempts to curb "feudal superstitions," the post-Mao era was characterized by a different gaze on Yao customs, representing them as the bedrock of social morality. See Ralph Litzinger, "Reimagining the State in Post-Mao

Nations, like scholars, often fashion themselves and the world through displays and signification of ethnic Others. In a glass case in a Hanoi, Vietnam, museum, there is a hollowed-out buffalo horn of the kind that Yao mediums blow when communicating with the spirits during some rituals. The horn is identified as a Yao object. The museum is not concerned with Yao or with spirit mediums and their paraphernalia. Rather, the object is there because of its connection to the theme of the museum. As the label declares, this was "a horn used by insurgents of Dao [Yao] ethnic people to fight the French in 1914." The display is in the Museum of the Vietnamese Revolution.

The horn itself is not revolutionary; it looks very much like the ones I have seen Mien spirit mediums use during rituals, and it does not look like a weapon. The label does not say if the Yao used the horn to call on spirits to aid their fighting, which would have suggested something about the social and ritual lives of Vietnam's Yao people. The museum fits its objects within a grand narrative of the awakening of revolutionary consciousness and the long struggle against foreign aggression—dominant tropes in twentieth-century Vietnamese nationalism and historiography.

Now I revisit the Mien in refugee camp, before examining Thailand more generally and historically.

IMPOSSIBLE SIMILARITIES

One morning, when Thai guards in the Chiangkham refugee camp set about their daily routines, they found a sentence written on the blackboard. This was in a classroom where refugees from neighboring Laos were taught the Thai language, and perhaps it was not unusual for the refugees to practice after hours. But the statement on the blackboard was no inadvertent remainder of some earlier exercise in the written language of the country of refuge. It was deliberately aimed at the guards and what they stood for. The sentence was written in Thai neatly and correctly. It said, according to the recollection of several friends; "we left Laos to flee the communists, but here it is just the same [oppression]," or "we escaped the communists, and now we find them again here [in the camp]."[4]

The guards took photos as if the blackboard were a crime scene, and set about finding the culprit. After they found the individual responsible for the message, they beat him up so badly that some of his teeth broke. Then they sent him to prison in the provincial capital of Chiangrai. After he had served six months he was ready to be returned to camp. But the Chiangkham guards did not want this troublemaker back in their camp, so they stipulated that he be sent to another camp. He was instead sent to Chiangkhong, also in Chiangrai Province. Both camps were adjacent to Thailand's border with Laos.

Humor and irony may avail different intersections through displacement.[5] I cannot easily use humor about war, governments, inequality, or suffering, but I can

China," in *Cultures of Insecurity: States, Communities, and the Production of Danger,* ed. Jutta Welds, Mark Laffey, Hugh Gusterson, and Raymond Duval (Minneapolis, MN: University of Minnesota Press, 1999), pp. 293–318.

[4] Personal interviews on various occasions from December 2007 to August 2009, Portland, Oregon.

[5] James Fernandez and Mary Taylor Huber, "Introduction: The Anthropology of Irony," in *Irony in Action: Anthropology, Practice, and the Moral Imagination*, ed. James Fernandez and Mary Taylor Huber (Chicago, IL: University of Chicago Press, 2001), pp. 1–37.

try to wield irony to create an element of safe distance. I think of this with the analogy of handling burning-hot coals: Without some protection or a tool, whoever is handling the coal will burn her or his hands. The safe distance provide by irony may serve to keep in check the moral and political pretensions of academic posturing—like any form of invulnerability, irony as such is morally neutral and situation-specific.[6] Humor is sometimes appropriate in response to awful times, for it suggests that life goes on; the horror was not the whole story or its conclusion. Irreverence is sometimes justified in relation to particular episodes and situations, because without it only destruction, oppression, and desolation are imaginable. I do not wish that on my colleagues or students, on the Iu Mien peoples I have been with, or on anyone else.

A sentence on a blackboard used for teaching Laotian ethnic minority refugees in camp to read and write Thai may easily disappear from analytical or ethnographic focus if the aim of the analyst is either to describe the Iu Mien as a reified ethnographic object, or to discuss Cold War alliances, animosities, and the related questions of who was on what side during the Vietnam War and whether an academic writes, consciously or not, to take sides. The war was over by this time, the refugees had migrated from Laos, and this happened in Thailand. The sentence was erased, the writer was beaten up and imprisoned, and camp discipline ran in part on violence and fear. There was no way to speak out against the oppressive conditions in refugee camp. Thailand was helping its suffering neighbors, and received financial assistance and favorable recognition from international bodies such as the United Nations.[7]

Had the statement on the blackboard been written clumsily or incorrectly, it might not have had any electric current with which to shock the guards into reaction. It could have been erased, brushed off as a sign of the inability of the ethnic minority refugees from Laos to master the Thai language and the script. As such, a clumsy looking sentence could have stood as one more sign of the ostensible uniqueness and superiority of the Thai: the country, the nation, the culture and language, the guards in camp, and the then-pervasive and militarized anti-communist climate. However, not only was the sentence correct and very neat looking, suggesting that the ethnic minorities from across the border were quite capable of mastering the markers of Thai-ness, it also declared that Thailand's treatment of the refugees was not different from the communist oppression in Laos that the people had fled.

The Lao refugee's Thai sentence struck a national nerve among the guards. The statement left a serious question about Thailand's superiority over Laos and the helpless refugees from across the border, and about the country's claim to being the opposite of its communist neighbors. In multiple ways, the offense resonates with the issue of representation through difference and displacement. The distinctions introduced by such representation are apparent in the contrasts between the Thai and the Lao, between the refugees and their caretakers, and in the deference the semi-prisoners are expected to show their guards. The statement written on the blackboard was transgressive in what it said, who and what it represented, and regarding its author: Some stateless, powerless, non-Thai refugees on Thai soil

---

[6] Nicola Tannenbaum, "Tattoos: Invulnerability and Power in Shan Cosmology," *American Ethnologist* 14,4 (1987): 693–711.

[7] Khajadphai Burusaphathana, *Phu Ophayop-Liphai Indojin* [Indochinese Refugees] (Bangkok: Phraephitaya, 1993).

suggested that the anti-communist Thai were indistinguishable from oppressive Lao communists.

The extreme vulnerability of the refugees in camp may suggest the condition that Giorgio Agamben calls "bare life," biological life, which "constitutes the original—if concealed—nucleus of sovereign power."[8] Agamben's concern is, in part, to understand Nazi Germany's concentration camps as a manifestation of sovereign power. He brings out a distinction, what he calls a biopolitical fracture, regarding the meaning of "the people": on one hand, there are citizens or the people who have some basic rights, and on the other "the poor, the disinherited, the excluded." He characterizes the difference lexically as that between the People and the people, and suggests that the extermination of the Jews in Nazi Germany was an extreme case of the struggle built into the notion of "the people." According to Agamben, the Jews in Germany refused—or were refused, his case is ambiguous to me—integration into the political body: "the Jews are the representatives par excellence and almost the living symbol of the people and of the bare life that modernity necessarily creates within itself, but whose presence it can no longer tolerate in any way."[9]

This theoretical discussion is widely cited, and I might be considered lacking if I did not mention it. One may characterize the episode in the Chiangkham camp as a case that involves sovereign power and bare life, but this characterization risks completely stripping the situation of what made it meaningful and set it in motion in the first place—it was about the equation of Thailand and the ostensible oppression of communist rule in Laos. It was written by a refugee, and it was aimed at the guards. They need to be situated in time and place; they are no mindless agents of "sovereign power" that has been shaped by the same logic since Ancient Rome and through Nazi Germany.

The episode in Chiangkham happened in about 1976 or 1977. At the time, Thailand had been increasingly militarized with heavy US support, and the violent suppression of political diversity had taken particular shape and grown since at least the late 1950s.[10] In the early 1970s, assassinations of peasant and labor leaders, and of student activists, became increasingly common. After a violent confrontation in 1973, a democratic government was installed and the violence decreased some, but it returned in full force in a bloody suppression of student and labor agitation in Bangkok in 1976. There was widespread political panic across the countryside; anyone suspected of sympathizing with the communists would be shot.[11] Within Thailand, Iu Mien, Hmong, and many other highland farmers had increasingly come under attack for suspected subversion. Arrests were common. One news story from the English-language *Bangkok Post* from 1974 gives some sense of the period:

Four Yao [Iu Mien] tribesmen arrested earlier in [Chiang Mai] province were released [after] finishing an agricultural training course given by local

---

[8] Giorgio Agamben, *Homo Sacer: Sovereign Power and Bare Life*, trans. Daniel Heller-Roazen (Stanford, CA: Stanford University Press, 1995), p. 6.

[9] Ibid., pp. 176–79.

[10] For anyone wishing to get beyond my surface discussion of this matter, see: Chalong Soontravanich, "Small Arms, Romance, and Crime and Violence in Post-WWII Thai Society," *Southeast Asian Studies* 43,1 (2005): 26–46.

[11] Jeffrey Race, "The War in Northern Thailand," *Modern Asian Studies* 8,1 (1974): 85–112; and Chairat Charoensin O-Larn, *Understanding Postwar Reformism in Thailand* (Bangkok: Duang Kamol, 1988).

government authorities. [The four men] were charged with sympathizing with communist terrorists. [The] training course was aimed at encouraging the tribesmen to help themselves and their families. [The] Yao tribe is a small group in Chiang Rai [province]'s communist infested areas. Quite a few tribesmen are being detained in Chiang Mai and will be released soon after they finish their vocational training courses.[12]

Within Thailand, highland peoples such as the Iu Mien were viewed with complete incomprehension and mistrust, and were being arrested for a range of made-up reasons because national Thai identity had been fashioned, in part, based on the sense of ethnically non-Thai highlanders as aliens and a threat. These developments occurred in the Cold War context of the late 1950s and lasted into the 1980s.

There was nothing timeless about this rendering of the nation and the dangerous Others who were alien to it, but by the early 1970s this sense appeared not only inevitable but a cause for constant fear and vigilance. In some areas, highland peoples such as the Iu Mien had been in multiple relations with lowland Thai worlds since the nineteenth century and some other highland peoples for much longer, but the interplay of categorical notions of Thai and Mountain People that intensified in the late-1950s made that reality unthinkable. The incomprehensibility of highland peoples was not the result of a timeless disconnect, but had been actively produced as the Thai nation was reimagined and reordered, first with national integration around 1900 and then in the Cold War context.[13]

THAILAND'S PEOPLES

When Mien, Hmong, Lahu, Lisu, and Akha peoples established themselves in the northern Thai highlands in the late nineteenth and early twentieth centuries, some were able to make contracts with the rulers of lowland kingdoms or provinces, including the Mien leader with whose descendants I later worked. He and some of his followers had formal contracts to a Royal Opium Monopoly. This was a national economic structure, but the deal with these particular highland farmers does not appear to have ever been known beyond the northern provinces. Only farmers with big households were considered worthy of this trade connection—no one else qualified. In other words, certain people in five settlements were (for perhaps seven decades) legal poppy growers, but for everyone else, in over one thousand settlements, poppy growing was illegal and violators were vulnerable to official abuse. Mien fellow villagers in small households, and Mien, Hmong, Lahu, Akha, Lisu, or other poppy-growing highlanders elsewhere in northern Thailand, were continually at risk of arrest and subject to police demands for payment.

The arrests of highlanders growing poppy illegally or taking it to sell on the black market can be traced back to the early twentieth century. Only exceptional cases such as the opium trade monopoly, which made several hundred thousand people into illegal cultivators, have created situations of animosity and distrust that led people to try to stay out of reach. Prior to the twentieth century, most, if not all,

---

[12] "Tribesmen Freed," *Bangkok Post,* March 8, 1974.

[13] Hjorleifur Jonsson, *Mien Relations: Mountain People and State Control in Thailand* (Ithaca, NY: Cornell University Press, 2005), pp. 55–85.

states maintained relations with highland populations, for trade, security, and more. Networks of relations were predominantly regional, unhampered by different relationships with particular rulers, and never impeded by a relationship to the state in the abstract.

The isolated status of the highland people was a result of how the Thai nation state had actively undone previous relations in the highlands. By 1900, government officials came exclusively from Bangkok, and they did not make an effort to learn various local languages or establish relations other than to impose Bangkok superiority.[14] Most highlanders across northern Thailand stood outside any relations with lowland structures and instead dealt with Chinese traders who exchanged various goods for highlanders' opium. This dynamic—a combination of regular trade and a black market—went on for many decades and accentuated what seemed to be the natural isolation of exotic peoples in the forested mountains, exotics whom ethnographers then "discovered." The black market responded to how national society denied accommodation to highlanders. It delayed negotiation across highland difference, which may have contributed to the intolerant and violent character of Thailand's national integration in the 1960s to 1980s.

Between 1968 and the middle 1980s, Thai highlanders were the object of considerable discrimination and military violence, on the assumption that they were alien immigrants, communist sympathizers, rebels, unsanctioned opium growers, a threat to the national environment, and much more. The notion of hill tribes as a national threat served to mobilize various hostile, aggressive, and violent forces and to focus them on highland farmers as much as against student activists, labor organizers, and peasant advocates. The typecasting of a threat not only brought violence against the Hmong and others, it also diluted the considerable diversity that had previously characterized Thai society.

In my view, these are political pathologies that represent neither nation nor state but can instead shape them in particular ways with specific (but perhaps unintended) destructive consequences. The violence does not reflect the state or the Thai. Instead, a particular ethnological typecasting lent a new shape to national society that was anchored to militarized fear and hostility and which denied highlanders the potential for peaceful coexistence. The Bangkok elite had taken over in a new way. Around 1900, it destroyed many northern kingdoms and their networks of relations. The violence in the 1960s to 1980s was not a continuation of the typical Asian state's practice of attempting to corral the free highlanders. Quite the contrary, this two-part process eliminated for the most part the channels of connection between hills and valleys.

The isolation of highlanders was actively produced by hostile policies that are quite specific to twentieth-century Thailand; the phenomenon had no precursor, and things played out differently in Laos, Burma, Vietnam, Cambodia, and Malaysia. By accepting the tale of Zomia, which theorizes that isolation is the preferred condition of the highland people, we are participating in some Western self-fashioning that thrives on some very particular tragedies far afield.

---

[14] Michael Moerman, "A Minority and Its Government: The Thai Lue of Northern Thailand," *Southeast Asian Tribes, Minorities, and Nations*, ed. Peter Kunstadter, vol. 1 (Princeton, NJ: Princeton University Press, 1967), pp. 401–24; and Michael Moerman, *Talking Culture: Ethnography and Conversation Analysis* (Philadelphia, PA: University of Pennsylvania Press, 1988), pp. 70–86, 162–72.

Contestation regarding national identity has been a major impetus for Thai ethnography and ethnology. Only by taking Thai-language ethnology seriously does this pattern ever become visible. One needs to know something about the characters of ethnography, and there is some advantage to looking alongside and past the Bangkok elites. Bunchuai Srisawat's foundational work, *30 Peoples of Chiangrai*, was written in order to acquaint a national audience with his home province; the author represented Chiangrai Province in the national parliament. His text includes descriptions of the natural riches of the province that suggest economic opportunity, and he includes information on travel arrangements for people arriving from and going to Bangkok. In the book, Bunchuai laments that Bangkok people dismiss the lowland peoples of his northern province as "Lao." He insists that they are *thai thae*, "true Thai."[15]

Roughly twenty years earlier, Seri Phetyaprasert, a member of parliament for Nan Province, wrote about the "conditions of different ethnic groups" for a Bangkok audience, trying to convince them that the lowlanders of Nan were not Lao, but instead "true Thai," while the highland people were exotic and different.[16] Both writers insisted that there had been no mixing of blood with non-Thai peoples. Thus, one can see Thai ethnography and the creation of knowledge about mountain peoples as a way to establish certainty about who are Thai and who aren't, based on ideas of ostensibly pure blood that emanated from the Bangkok elite, and which asserted its superiority and centrality.[17]

Nationalist discrediting, if not harassment, of northern provincial politicians by the Bangkok elite appears to have accentuated the marginalization of highland ethnic Others as an object of Thai knowledge and politics. This process was already initiated by the dynamics of national integration that replaced local royalty with provincial governors sent from Bangkok and dependent on Bangkok for their position, salaries, and promotion. The politicians Bunchuai Srisawat and Seri Phetyaprasert were not in a position to critique or argue against Bangkok prejudice regarding the peoples of some northern provinces. Instead they asserted the true-Thai credentials of their northern lowland populations, and made this seem even truer by accentuating the strangeness of mountain peoples.

There have never been pure Thai, while there are many real Thai, and some real Thai have been more willing and interested than others to facilitate inter-ethnic accommodation of the diverse social networks that have often characterized Southeast Asia and adjacent southern China. This is old history, but it matters if we are to come to some sense of contemporary national realities in ways that do not present marginalization, disconnect, and abuse as inherently in the cards for certain people, as if dealt by some (Asian?) hand of fate. The national disconnect, historically and socially specific, helped Western and other ethnographers maintain that they had pure ethnic samples.

---

[15] Bunchuai Srisawat (Boonchuay Srisawasdi), *30 Chat Nai Chiangrai* [30 Peoples of Chiangrai] (Bangkok: Uthai, 1950), p. 12.

[16] Seri Phetyaprasert, "Saphap Chonchat" [The Condition of Ethnic Groups] in *Nakhorn Nan, Chabab Phathomruk* [An Introduction to Nan], ed. Nai Bua Chok-di (Bangkok: Bamrungkulkit and Thaphrajan Presses, 1933), p. 273.

[17] Jonsson, *Mien Relations*, pp. 45–55; Hjorleifur Jonsson, "Encyclopedic Yao in Thailand," *Asian Ethnicity* 4,2 (2003): 295–301; and Ronald D. Renard, "The Image of Chiang Mai: The Making of a Beautiful City," *Journal of the Siam Society* 87 (1999): 87–98.

During the Cold War, Thai nation-building was fashioned in relation to a feared communist threat from neighboring countries such as China, Vietnam, and Laos, with considerable US involvement. The phrase "mountain people" (*chao khao*) emerged as shorthand for some of these anxieties, as it described alleged border-crossers who showed no particular allegiance to king or country. There was a domestic communist movement, but it was defined as foreign, somewhat like the mountain people. Any agitation for farmer or labor rights was interpreted as an alien communist threat and was fiercely suppressed. Militarized violence escalated in the late 1960s, and came to involve attacks on highland settlements by 1968, after which large tracts of mountains were declared free-fire zones and many people fled toward the lowlands.[18]

During and after the violence that lasted into the 1980s, Hmong in particular were singled out for their alleged communist sympathies. The label *meo daeng* (Red [communist] Meo/Hmong) stuck, in some ways as a gloss for all mountain peoples. In the lowlands across the country, there were many analogous attacks on suspected communist sympathizers.[19] The incidents were varied, but all assumed an image of Thailand as a "bounded entity under threat," where anxiety and violence were constitutive of the object that they sought to defend through the image of threatening Others.[20]

CHANGING LANDSCAPES

The Thai dynamic that opposed national sameness against difference was never exclusively about inter-ethnic relations. Rather, the process has sometimes focused on ethnicity, and sometimes had ethnic consequences while its focus was elsewhere. One example is what happened to forests and the members of the Communist Party of Thailand. The CPT was offered amnesty by the late 1970s in an effort at national reconciliation, and its members may all have given up their forest-based struggle by the early 1980s.[21] CPT members' surrender was enacted as a spectacle of national identity (for the media) that rested on the iconic contrast between the forest and society. In rituals of re-incorporation into Thai-land, CPT members would publicly "[hand] over their rifles and red flags to the government officials. In return, they would receive the tricolor flag and a picture of their majesties, and, finally, they would join in singing the national anthem together."[22]

---

[18] Robert Hearn, *Thai Government Programs in Refugee Relocation and Resettlement in Northern Thailand* (Auburn, NY: Thailand Books, 1974); Race, "The War in Northern Thailand"; Jane R. Hanks and Lucien M. Hanks, *Tribes of the North Thailand Frontier* (New Haven, CT: Yale Southeast Asia Studies, 2001); Jonsson, *Mien Relations*, pp. 55–60.

[19] Charoensin-O-Larn, *Understanding Post-War Reformism*.

[20] Walter Irvine, "The Thai–Yuan 'Madman' and the Modernizing, Developing Thai Nation as Bounded Entities Under Threat: A Study in the Replication of a Single Image" (PhD dissertation, University of London, 1982). See also Malkki, *Purity and Exile*; and Bruce Kapferer, *Legends of People, Myths of State* (Washington, DC: Smithsonian Institution Press, 1988).

[21] David Morell and Chai-anan Samudavanija, *Political Conflict in Thailand* (Cambridge: Oelgeslager, Gunn & Hain, 1981).

[22] Thongchai Winichakul, *Siam Mapped: The History of the Geo-body of a Nation* (Honolulu, HI: University of Hawaii Press, 1994), pp. 169–70. See also a photograph of one such event in Chris Baker and Pasuk Pongphaichit, *A History of Thailand* (Cambridge: Cambridge University Press, 2005), p. 197.

As a ritual of affective transformation, the event turned the participants from hostile aliens to docile members. With the threat of insurgency and insubordination erased, the forest was later remade, with uninhabited nature, as *thammachat*: the "birthplace of the Buddha's teachings." It had earlier been labeled, from Bangkok, as *pa theuan* (forest wilderness), with connotations of illegality and wildness. This now transformed domain invokes Buddhism and national identity in a way that defines non-Buddhist, ethnically non-Thai farmers as an alien and destructive threat.[23] The alienation of mountain peoples was further entrenched as national identity and space were reworked in an act of closure on a period of civil war.

In 1981, the Royal Forestry Department (RFD) established a Wildlife Sanctuary in the subdistrict of Phachangnoi, in Pong district of Phayao province, to close off a former area of CPT insurgent bases in the forest. This sanctuary is adjacent to the area where I once conducted field research. By 1992, the RFD declared five of six registered villages illegal and announced that they must be evacuated. Nothing happened at the time. After a major protest in 1999, when some official buildings were burned down and a hundred heavily armed government soldiers threatened the local people, there was still no change.[24] In 2003, the RFD declared the whole subdistrict a Primary Watershed (Class A1); all settlement and farming in the area was illegal and would have to be erased. When I visited the region in 2005 and 2012, it appeared the villages are still in place and farming continues, though wage-labor (in Thai cities as well as in Japan, Hong Kong, Taiwan, and elsewhere) has been of growing importance since the mid-1980s.

Within Thai society, there is an ongoing debate about whether farmers are compatible with forests. One aspect of this factionalizing debate is a counter-discourse against the notion of Mountain People as troublemakers. It is remarkably slanted in favor of Karen peoples and against the Hmong, leaving other minority ethnicities somehow less marked.[25] This can be understood as a refraction of the Thai national self, with the "good alien" Karen as the most compatible with Thai notions of society and the environment, and the "bad alien" Hmong assumed to be the least compatible.[26]

Such representations often enter academic discourse: "The Hmong are notorious for their former practice of burning forest to prepare fields for opium cultivation. When fields were exhausted, they would repeat the process in a new area. This highly destructive practice drew relatively little attention until 1970."[27] In contrast,

[23] Yoko Hayami, "Internal and External Discourse of Communality, Tradition, and Environment: Minority Claims on Forest in the Northern Hills in Thailand," *Southeast Asian Studies* 35,5 (1997): 572–73.

[24] Jonsson, *Mien Relations*, pp. 131–47.

[25] Tim Forsyth and Andrew Walker, *Forest Guardians, Forest Destroyers: The Politics of Environmental Knowledge in Northern Thailand* (Seattle, WA: University of Washington Press, 2008).

[26] Hayami, "Internal and External Discourse"; Yoko Hayami, "Negotiating Ethnic Representation between Self and Other: The Case of Karen and Eco-tourism in Thailand," *Southeast Asian Studies* 44,3 (2006): 385–409; Andrew Walker, "The 'Karen Consensus': Ethnic Politics and Resource-use Legitimacy in Northern Thailand," *Asian Ethnicity* 2,2 (2001): 145–62,; and Pinkaew Laungaramsri, *Redefining Nature: Karen Ecological Knowledge and the Challenge to the Modern Conservation Paradigm* (Chiangmai: Earthworm Books, 2001), p. 54.

[27] Neil Engelhart, "Resource Conflict and Ethnic Peace in Northern Thailand," *Asia Pacific Viewpoint* 49,1 (2008): 100.

"highlanders such as Karen have been living in harmony with the conservation of the forest in the mountainous north,"[28] for centuries or perhaps forever. These examples show not only the common practice of taking ethnic labels for granted as referents that indicate coherent clusters of ideas and practices, but also demonstrates the uncritical academic recycling of national-moral valuations.

"[Value] transforms every product of labor into a social hieroglyphic," writes Karl Marx.[29] Viewed in the context of political confrontations, festivals in the Thai countryside—which I discuss next—point to the ongoing negotiation of social relations in terms of the value assigned to various categories of people and place. The politics is much more complex, mundane, and problematic than is suggested by the assumed antagonism between the state and a community, or the nation and a minority; politics is the realm of resource conflicts, power, and resistance. It is about signifying the national setting and its components (e.g., forests, mountains, ethnicity, and gender) in such a way that the contingency of particular configurations of identity, power, and history disappears. Representations of identity are about social relations within and beyond ethnic labels or administrative units, while they appear to simply express a "thing" in itself.

SPORTING CULTURE, 2001 AND 2005

In the Thai public sphere there were many suspicions about highland Others in the early 1980s, after pervasive militarized violence against the CPT and assumed sympathizers had come to an end. At that time, Mien people in certain villages started to assemble for contests in soccer. As far as I can tell, these events did not involve any ethnic markers, but rather played to notions of national sameness and apolitical fun. In my research area, ethnic minority Mien and Hmong school students started to come together for subdistrict-wide sports contests in 1988. In early 1993, the annual competition of running and volleyball was framed by national loyalty (flags, the anthem, and a politician's speech) and ethnic markers (evening displays of dance and song by people in ethnic dress). The event also played to male desire, with dance partners for hire during two nights of evening entertainment.[30]

In 2001, Mien people came together for their first national ethnic event. It began with flag-raising and the national anthem, and included four days of sports contests and two nights of cultural displays. This event was organized by the national Mien Association, and supported largely by the host village. It did not aim for a Thai audience and did not feature sexualized dance, unlike festivals in 1993 and 2005 that did both. The village did not succeed in attracting a national-level politician to visit and give a speech, but one official donated money and trophies.[31] At that time, all the sports played were those already common in Thai schools. The subsequent

---

[28] Chusak Wittayapak, "History and Geography of Identifications Related to Resource Conflicts and Ethnic Violence in Northern Thailand," *Asia Pacific Viewpoint* 49,1 (2008): 123.

[29] Karl Marx, *Capital*, vol. 1., trans. Ben Fowkes (New York, NY: Penguin, 1976 [orig. 1867]), p. 167.

[30] Hjorleifur Jonsson, "Serious Fun: Minority Cultural Dynamics and National Integration in Thailand," *American Ethnologist* 28,1 (2001): 151–78.

[31] Hjorleifur Jonsson, "Mien through Sports and Culture: Mobilizing Minority Identity in Thailand," *Ethnos* 68,3 (2003): 317–40. See also my video documentary, *Mien Sports and Heritage: Thailand 2001*, at http://asiapacific.anu.edu.au/newmandala/2008/03/27/mien-sports-and-heritage, accessed February 24, 2014.

introduction of traditional or cultural sports is a relatively new feature, in part related to the growing acceptance and endorsement of ethnic markers as apolitical heritage.[32]

The Mien Sports and Culture Festival[33] that was held during February 1–4, 2005, was the fourth annual event of the Mien Association. It had an opening ceremony, contests in "international," "local," and "cultural" sports, and evening entertainment. The event made various statements about belonging in national society, blurring the boundaries among the event itself, the host village and its school field, the dispersed members of an ethnic group, and national space.

The parade that marked the opening of the festival can be viewed as a symbolic condensation of the intended message of the festival. Prominently at the front were national flags, carried by people in ethnic-minority dress. Following the flag-carriers were ethnic markers, including an enlarged photo portrait of Phaya Khiri Srisombat, the man alleged to be the founder of Mien settlement in Thailand over a century ago. Processing behind that photo were people carrying a scroll, about fifteen feet long, that is promoted in a provincial tourism brochure as "the world's longest passport." This is an old document attributed to a Chinese emperor of uncertain historical provenance, that declares the Yao people (Mien are a kind of Yao) free from duties to the Empire.[34]

This "passport" has come to represent the collective heritage of the ethnic group, through parades organized by the national Mien Association. Behind the photo of the ethnic group's indexical leader and its now-heirloom object were live expressions of heritage—an elaborately dressed bridal couple with several attendants, and a group of men dressed as high-level spirit mediums. Trailing them were people carrying a "Mien Games" flag. It is modeled on the International Olympic flag, with twelve rings (in place of the Olympic five), in reference to the twelve lineages of the Mien people. Last were groups of contestants and others in ethnic or sports dress, with signs for each of the competing villages.

The parade suggests a play on difference and sameness. With people in ethnic dress (in styles no longer used for everyday wear) carrying national flags, ethnic minority markers are cast as manifesting national loyalty, having previously been associated with its opposite. The portrait of the founding ancestor is granted a place analogous to that of the king's portrait in Thai public events, and this is suggestive of its intended message. Embodiments of ethnic religion, heritage, culture, and society—the scroll, the dressed-up spirit mediums and the bridal couple, and the registered villages—actively fuse difference as devotion in a statement of the legibility, appeal, and belonging of an ethnic minority people in modern Thailand.

---

[32] Hjorleifur Jonsson, "Mien Alter-natives in Thai Modernity," *Anthropological Quarterly* 77,4 (2004): 673–704; Jonsson, "Encyclopedic Yao"; Michael K. Connors, "Ministering Culture: Hegemony and the Politics of Culture and Identity in Thailand," *Critical Asian Studies* 37,4 (2005): 523–51.

[33] Thai: *ngan mahakam kila-watthanatham chon- phao iu-mien-samphan*.

[34] Jonsson, *Mien Relations*, pp. 26–34; Eli Alberts, "Commemorating the Ancestors' Merit: Myth, Schema, and History in the Charter of Emperor Ping," *Taiwan Journal of Anthropology* 9, 1 (2011): 19-65; Huang Yu, "Preliminary Study of King Ping's Charter," *The Yao of South China: Recent International Studies*, ed. Jacques Lemoine and Chiao Chien (Paris: Pangu, 1991), pp. 89-123. For the look of the scroll and book, see collector Jess Pourret's many examples in his delightful study, *The Yao: The Mien and Mun Yao in China, Vietnam, Laos, and Thailand* (London: Thames and Hudson, 2002).

They draw on state imagery in an active denial of the state's monopoly on representation, modernity, and important heritage. Through these events, Mien assert equality and equivalence within Thai society. What these particular Mien were doing might be viewed as an echo of events in nineteenth-century China (Chapter One), where a hundred Yao dressed up and brought nice things to the lowland ruler, making and maintaining an intersection that could be of importance and give pleasure to parties on both sides of a relationship.

The opening ceremony further connected the ethnic group and various aspects of the nation state. The national anthem was played, and then there was a welcoming ceremony in the manner of Mien weddings, honoring visiting dignitaries, including the director of the Provincial Administrative Council, who later gave a speech. Another aspect of the opening ceremony was a collective bowing to portraits of the king and queen of Thailand, which were set above the event's billboard and below a display of national flags. This act of deference draws on performances that had been customary for a Mien bridal couple on the eve of their wedding, who traditionally bow to the spirits of the patrilineal ancestors of (usually) the groom. The social creativity of this event expresses multiple cross-references between Mien and Thai, the minority and the nation, and ancestor spirits and royalty through pleasure and play.

The organizers had assembled about twenty committees of referees and judges for the various sports. For the event as a whole there were forty-five committees with a total of 396 positions. The ethnic and traditional event was also both modern and bureaucratic—these qualities need not be at odds. Equally important, the games defined people as representatives of villages that competed for recognition and prizes. The village as a socially relevant unit is very much part of the intersection with the modern nation state; villages are the state's smallest administrative unit. Households and kin groups, previously the exclusive focus of Mien and Hmong ritual and social life, do not get activated in public engagements with the nation, and village festivals contribute to making them unthinkable in contemporary social life.

At the cultural (or ethnic) sports festival, people competed in the name of villages. But these events also turned into sports activities that had been everyday practices of livelihood (crossbow shooting), ritual (calligraphy, the making of spirit money), and dress (embroidery). As contests or sports, these are novel, but previously there had been a competitive element to singing and dancing, primarily at weddings, where people represented the kin groups of either the bride or the groom. Previously competitive practices have increasingly been turned into collective and noncompetitive expressions of heritage pertaining to the ethnic group, and the group typically involved in dancing has shifted, from adult men to teenage and younger girls. The festival expresses the making of history and identity through the assembly of ethnic markers and the assertion of their relationship to national loyalty and membership in registered villages, under the umbrella of a national ethnic minority association. All of this fashions an ethnic group as a knowable entity, that then can become a party to negotiating with state structures and international entities such as ethnic Iu Mien settled in the United States, who sent a team of athletes from Sacramento, California.

The combination of cultural, local, and international sports is as important as the Mien's insistence on their distinctions for envisioning themselves as a transcendent ethnic group whose heritage is guarded by the Mien Association and whose identity is as profoundly Thai as it is squarely ethnic. The Sports and Culture Festival successfully brought in a powerful provincial government official, and received national attention through coverage on (Royal Thai Army-owned) TV Channel 7, with its display of ethnic heritage, apolitical fun and games, and loyalty to the nation. During the following months, the video segment was shown at least three times on national television, in an evening slot devoted to cultural matters and human-interest stories. To Mien acquaintances in my research area, this was a good thing. It showed that they were in view as a presentable component of modern Thailand, generating publicity that might also bring them visitors at future festivals and more positive national attention.

Evening entertainment teams representing individual villages were predominantly made up of young school girls ranging in age from about five to fifteen. They wore ethnic dress, Mien and Hmong, and performed sexualized dances akin to the televised presentation of performances accompanying contemporary pop music. Such performances take place within a national domain that is strongly gendered, at an event focused on ethnic heritage and loyalty to the nation.

Leslie Jeffrey notes changes in rural entertainment in lowland Thailand during the 1960s with the "expansion of roads and radio through the countryside." New musical styles, notably *luk thung,* that drew on urban and international sounds but were promoted as rural and Thai, involved "backup dancers (usually females) in flashy costumes."[35] Encouraging men to watch sexualized young women has become routine at village fairs in Thailand, in ways that connect to the national domain of political rallies, musical performances, televised entertainment, and, also, moral panic.[36] This is part of the national reality that Mien and Hmong people are claiming a space within, through the presentation of girls at festivals who invoke, through the multiple play of representation, the Thai Other as a male and desiring subject.

Contemporary Thailand is fashioned through a standardization of displays and contests that rests on national terms of engagement and interactions. Festivals place communities in the national public sphere in the hope of generating some beneficial interactions. This brings its own risks. When the 2009 Mien Sports and Culture Festival was held in the village of Huai Chomphu, "some gangsters came and destroyed the whole event, it was really bad."[37]

MARKETING AND LOCAL BEAUTIES

The Festival of Lychee (fruit) and Local Treasures, in Phachangnoi Subdistrict,[38] was held on May 7, 2005, and was part of an effort to establish Phayao Province's reputation as a source of quality products for national and international markets. It was on a smaller scale than the Sports and Culture Festival, but can be viewed as an analogous attempt to place people within a national domain, in this case by

---

[35] Leslie Jeffrey, *Sex and Borders: Gender, National Identity, and Prostitution Policy in Thailand* (Honolulu, HI: University of Hawaii Press, 2002), p. 42 On *luk thung,* see Amporn Jirattikorn, "*Lukthung*: Authenticity and Modernity in Thai Country Music," *Asian Music* 37, 1 (2006): 24-50.

[36] Jeffrey, *Sex and Borders*, p. 163; see also Graham Fordham, *A New Look at Thai Aids: Perspectives from the Margin* (New York, NY: Berghahn, 2005); and Katherine Bowie, *Rituals of National Loyalty: An Anthropology of the State and the Village Scout Movement in Thailand* (New York, NY: Columbia University Press, 1997), pp. 174-75.

[37] Kittisakr Ruttanakrajangsri, personal comm. February 11, 2009.

[38] Thai, *Ngan thesakarn linji lae khongdi tambol phachangnoi.*

publicizing cash crops. There was a contest for the best-tasting lychees, and also a lychee-eating contest, a beauty pageant, singing, and dance shows. The festival also awarded prizes (as had been done for the athletes and other contestants at the sports and culture festival): first, second, and third place for the best lychees and for the top three beauties. A Lychee Queen was selected, and she went on to compete in a pageant in the provincial capital.

If the lychee festival is explicitly about quality crops for national and international markets, it is implicitly about the gendering and sexualization of entertainment, with one after another troupe of girls dancing in the style of back-up or chorus-line dancers. The girls performing dances for the (male) audience's pleasure were like the contestants in cultural, local, and international sports who represented their registered villages. That is, as the dancers reproduced the gendered and sexualized inequalities and pleasures of the national domain in the context of an extensive commercialization of women's bodies, they were representing the smallest administrative units of the modern nation state.

An official from the Provincial Agriculture Department spoke at the opening of the event: "People need to know that forest is water and water is forest. You have to help protect the forest so that there is water for the lychees, so that lychees in Phayao province are of good quality." He continued, and shifted to tourism: "There is a rally today from Phayao City; they will come here and visit to see the lifeways of people in Phachangnoi Subdistrict, the Yao and the Hmong people."

As a representative of the provincial authorities, the man evoked the image of mountain peoples as a threat to the forest and the provincial economy, and the ethnic lifestyles as something to be observed by tourists, dissociated from daily practice. Tourism and cash crops imply revenue for the province, and the festival was in some ways a distillation of the subdistrict's commercial potential, where culture had emerged as another product. The event rendered a particular political–economic regime of dispossession as an opportunity.[39]

The beauty pageant was not without surprises. An announcer with a cordless microphone called the contestants out, primarily girls in their late teens. When they introduced themselves, they did so in their local languages, Mien and Hmong. The announcer was somewhat baffled, and teased them in Thai about their incomprehensibility with this insult: *"ching-ching-chong-chong, fang bo hu heuang"* [blah-blah-blah-blah, I do not understand]. The contestants reintroduced themselves in Thai, identifying the villages they were from and the names of their parents. Later the announcer asked them, in the manner of interviewers on national television and maybe with reference to national marketing, "What is the importance of the Lychee Festival for the subdistrict?"

The contestants took things in stride: "This brings together the people from different villages, and we get to know each other better. People will know how far the quality of lychees in different villages has improved." Another girl said, "It is an important event because the Welfare Department will learn about lychees from our subdistrict. Traders will come and buy our lychees, and the public will know that

---

[39] Scholars of Indonesia and its minority regions suggest very much the same thing, and my terminology borrows some from them. See J. Peter Brosius, "The Forest and the Nation: Negotiating Citizenship in Sarawak, Malaysia," in *Cultural Citizenship in Island Southeast Asia: Nation and Belonging in the Hinterlands,* ed. Renato Rosaldo (Berkeley, CA: University of California Press, 2003), p. 121; Anna L. Tsing, *Friction: An Ethnography of Global Connection* (Princeton, NJ: Princeton University Press, 2005), pp. 55–77.

our lychees are a quality product. Thank you." Said a third: "The festival is a good thing. People have love and friendship. Outsiders will know more about lychees from our subdistrict. And I think that there has been a lot of lychee production, so the price has gone down. I would like those in charge [of market prices] to work on improving the price. Thank you."

The contestants were on stage to create a display that was fun to watch and follow, a presentable and desirable spectacle that would not be out of place on national television. But they had to be teased into translation, away from their local and ethnic-minority linguistic register to that of the nation's. The girls were obliging when asked about the relevance of the festival for the administrative unit. There was no alarm when one of them voiced the concerns of farmers, who are cognizant of and concerned with the unstable returns for cash crops. The girl spoke intelligently on behalf of farmers' issues, proving that she was not just another pretty face in ethnic dress.

Neither event was a collective representation in any uncomplicated way. There are various internal differences regarding how Thailand's Mien people engage with matters of their culture and identity. Some, notably school teachers and officials at the levels of village and subdistrict, were particularly keen on displays of presentable culture for a general and national audience. Others, such as NGO workers, were concerned with ways of manifesting ecological wisdom and responsible rural practices that might boost claims to legal settlement and land.[40] Older men and women with little social clout were in general more concerned with household continuity, while teenagers were for the most part immersed in realms of Thai popular culture. All of the people can be viewed as equally local, Mien, and national, but they had very unequal means of manifesting their sense of identity in the public sphere, and of engaging with the nation as regular members or as representatives of an ethnic group.

Individuals, too, embody contrary agendas. For instance, the headmaster of the local school, Khe Kwin Srisombat,[41] is central to some aspects of national integration. Khe Kwin attended the festival and was also the president of the Mien Association, which is invested in the codification and presentation of ethnic culture. At the same time, he has actively promoted the importance of Phaya Khiri Srisombat as a founder of Thailand's Mien. The headmaster is a fourth-generation direct descendant of Phaya Khiri Srisombat, and his promotion of an ancestor was meant to claim his legacy and assert the importance of his ethnic group within Thailand, of his kin group and village in relation to other lineages and villages, and of himself in relation to his cousins, who compete with him and each other for local prominence.

Many of the dances on display at minority festivals are either copied or fashioned by Thai school teachers, who draw on the (trans-) national public sphere. Attempting to distinguish such elements from who the Mien or the Hmong really are, or from how they represent themselves, would introduce an artificial purity to this situation. Ethnic minorities are inextricable from their immediate, national context. It is in many cases impossible to assign a single source to the representations

---

[40] *Ongkhwamru kan Chai Samunphrai lae Rabob Kandulae Raksa Sukhaphap Phuenban Iumien* [Iu Mien Local Knowledge of Herbs and Healthcare], compiled and ed. Kittisakr Ruttanakrajangsri (Chiangmai: IMPECT, 2002).

[41] His Mien name is variously Tang Khae Kwin or Khe Kwin Srisombat. In Thai, he is Khe Win Srisombat, and in English he goes by "Kevin."

that concern mountain peoples in Thailand; some draw on Chinese television features showing Miao, Yao, and other minority peoples of China's south.

The binary opposition of lowland peoples to mountain peoples is significantly involved in the fashioning of Thai realities—not simply those of ethnic and national identity, but also those of state control, military command, border concerns, forests and watersheds, enjoyable culture, and enticing entertainment. In this national context, mountain peoples' identities have always been defined relative to the nation, their assumed opposite, as elements within shifting fields of relations.

A MOVING MOUNTAIN

A sign on the Lychee-festival stage read, "Angel Mountain" (Thai, *doi thewada*) and gave a phone number. This is a recent tourist destination in the province, and in 2005 a road was laid to a scenic spot (*chom wiu*) at the top. Angel Mountain refers to Phulangka, a well-known local mountain. The divinity or angel reference is said to draw on local Mien people's reverence for a mountain spirit. Prior to the mid-2000s, I had never heard of anything that could be called "mountain spirits" or of a Mien reverence for mountain spirits.

Some older-generation locals later told me that this was a new association. The headmaster of the local school, Khe Kwin, who is well connected in the province, had made up the name "Angel Mountain" and successfully pitched it to provincial tourism authorities. A nearby mountain, not Phulangka, had been known as a spirit mountain (Mien, *fin-ja-bo*), but not because it commanded any reverence. Instead, the name drew on an episode from approximately the late 1940s, when a Mien farmer made several attempts to clear and plant a field on that other mountain. The man would repeatedly get lost in fog, get dizzy, faint, or fall asleep, and ultimately he gave up. The word spread that some spirit on that mountain was decidedly uninviting, so no one tried to farm there. Thus, *fin-ja-bo* defined the place as unappealing and as useless for farming.

Through a domestic tourism effort decades later, the "*fin-ja-bo*" reference was simply moved to another mountain, which was then reframed as an object of reverence to create something of local significance that was nationally interesting. A brochure from the province's tourism office states that some local people also refer to the mountain, because of two rocks, as "Mt. Maiden's Breasts" (Thai, *doi nom sao*). Again, this name did not originate from local traditions, but is an expression of a drive to make "the Thai" into a subject of desire that travels around the country with particular carnal or spiritual interests.

The national geography of pleasure has its counter in the public promotion of domestic tourist destinations that is largely confined to waterfalls and Buddhist temples, and suggests the official denial of male vernacular desires and subjectivities. The spiritualized and sexualized mountain has a parallel in the exaggeration of ethnic culture and of girls' sexuality at village festivals. These binaries are variants in the contemporary fashioning of subjectivity in relation to a national domain, from different perspectives.

A hard-surface road now leads from the highway to a scenic spot near the top of Angel Mountain, as noted above. It was laid by a company owned by the brother of a democratically elected provincial representative in the national parliament, who won a contract of Thai Baht 20 million (half a million US$) from the Provincial Administrative Council. This is some indication of who can now make a living off the forested mountains, and how. A press release that appeared (as news) in two Thai-language newspapers mentioned the road project's budget, but not those who were involved in awarding or receiving the contract. The report focused instead on how the road benefits tourism and the preservation and enjoyment of nature. When the road was laid toward the mountaintop, "only one big tree was cut."[42]

People's identities are fundamentally intersubjective and relational, products of history and productive of social relations. Ethnicity in modern Thailand rests on objectification and the dynamics of nation building. The social and natural landscape (villages, fields, roads, mountains, forests, ethnic labels, and the like) is, like any commodity, "abounding in metaphysical subtleties and theological niceties."[43] The road, the renamed mountain, and the combination of domestic tourism and nature preservation conflate the landscape's character and use-value in an active dispossession and redefinition of the local farming population in relation to the market for crops, labor, culture, and entertainment.

The genealogy of this new reality lies equally in state–minority relations, variant national–cultural forms, the ongoing contestations over national identity, capitalist transformations, and modernity, and in the conclusion of a civil war that was the precursor to the Buddhist nationalization of forests as aspects of pristine and enjoyable nature. Any enactment of identity by Thailand's Mien or other minority peoples is an engagement with this complex history. The enactment shapes its ethnic or other intersection, at a historically particular moment that allows certain representations as it makes certain others unthinkable.

There is considerable alarm over Thailand's sex-trade and the sexualization of girls' and women's bodies. I acknowledge it, but wish to be comparative and historical about the current transformation regarding girls' and young women's dances as expressions of Mien ethnic frontiers. In some odd way, it appears that the shift from male to female dancers (starting in 1992, as far as I know) tells more generally of a changing intersection. Men used to handle spirits and the matters of kin groups, and they learned to dance as they learned to deal with spirits. Young men might apprentice with a medium in order to become competent in taking care of household rituals. But some households had ritual rank and thus access to soldier spirits, which could grant benefits beyond the ancestors' reach. Soldier spirits are also more demanding and potentially dangerous than ancestor spirits, and they might damage the household's crops as they fended for themselves if they were not fed often enough.

While in fieldwork in the early 1990s, I observed two rituals of calling in the soldier spirits, *syo peng* (M. *siou baeng*), to appease them and protect the crops. These are the same spirits that have been cited in reference to the war in Laos, where all the recollections concern the spirits' ability to protect their constituents from harm by the enemy during war. The ritual of collecting the soldier spirits involved a competent spirit medium and a group of young men not already attached to the spirit world. The men would work themselves into a trance and then fling themselves on a pile of glowing-hot coals. "You feel warm and think this is a pool of refreshing cool water," said one after the event in answer to my question about what made him throw his body with such abandon into a dangerous spot.

---

[42] *Chiangmai News, Lanna Business* section, June 6, 2005, p. 15; *Northern Citizen*, June 6–12, 2005, p. 10.

[43] Marx, *Capital*, p. 163.

Before they are awakened from their trance, the men dance around as a group, each with a live chicken in one hand; the chicken is later killed and offered to the spirits. In the other hand, they hold white and red flags for the "soldiers of five banners." Blood from the animals is smeared on door posts and then dripped into cups of liquor that are offered to the spirits, since they are fierce and have a particular appetite. After the event, the young men checked themselves out to see whether anyone got burnt. All were fine, and that was a sure sign that the household's ancestors had a good handle on things and that the effort to control the soldier spirits was successful. Each young man acquired one soldier spirit guardian as a result of taking part in the ritual. That is, these otherwise fierce spirits enter into a relationship with the young and spiritually unattached men, becoming their individual guardians, once the men have made a serious effort to help recruit, please, and feed these spirits.

After one of these events in northern Thailand in 1993, one of the participants visited the house where I stayed late at night. He was nonchalant and chatted about sexuality to another young Mien man. They talked about things that could happen with girls in the big city of Bangkok. The young man was dressed very nicely for a regular day in the village. He was going to a club in the town of Chiangkham, where there was alcohol, new music, and young women who might perhaps be willing to talk or dance.[44]

Learning to act across the spiritual frontier has some similarity to acting across the contemporary ethnic frontier. It exposes the unattached participants to some risks, but it is for a local purpose of managing relations beyond for everyone's benefit. Currently villagers are proud to be able to muster a troupe of accomplished resident dancers, which they consider a significant asset, whereas previously they were more inclined to value resident men who could handle things with the spirit world. Girls and young women can become familiar and competent in wielding their physicality and attractiveness in ways that were previously not an option. The whole process is about being a village in a modern nation state in a manner that can bring in interested outsiders for interactions and potential negotiation of exchange and benefits. For these exchanges to work as politics, they must not look like politics, but rather like the fashioning of potential crossings where people can come to recognize each other's humanity and the benefits of ongoing relations.

If dealing with assertive and playful Thai masculinity is an important component of being a village that tourists find attractive, then I offer the ethnographic analogy of having access to soldier spirits. If people manage their relations (with tourists, with spirits) with skill and care, then there is no damage done. Instead, there is the chance of reaping some benefits greater than those available locally. There is also the pleasure of watching a good performance that did not leave a scratch. People need time, practice, and some familiarity to engage with spirits, and the same holds for their engagements with national society. These are in some ways always potentially volatile intersections.

The Mien and other hill tribe societies that ethnographers found in the 1960s were in many ways defined through relations with ancestor spirits, and part of the

---

[44] In the early 1990s, there was prosperity in some hinterland regions. Ethnic minority men enjoyed going to bars in towns like Chiangkham and some even had a Northern Thai mistress or girlfriend. Ethnic minority women experienced the time very differently, and if they had any engagements with the Thai market in sexuality it was only as the workers in low-class venues.

reason for this was the generally precluded intersection with Thai society. Government officials viewed highland peoples as aliens and made no effort to establish relations. Ethnographers fooled themselves, I suggest, by not taking the practice of ritual as an expression of the world people found themselves in. The issue is similar to what N. J. Enfield describes for linguistics, that is, we assume origins in the past and sameness within a category, rather than ask challenging regional and historical questions about the ongoing production of identity and difference through interaction.

The moving mountain, Phulangka, that became Angel Mountain and Mount Maiden's Breasts, expresses a Mien theory about the Thai: it is a way to fashion intersections that will bring Thai peoples to this minority region. Angel Mountain is explicitly anchored to Buddhist expectations about spiritual landscape connections, and it invites the Thai who generally only visit temples and waterfalls if they leave their urban abodes on a weekend. Mount Maiden's Breasts, in contrast, appeals to the Thai who would only travel in search of some physical and sexual titillation. Accommodating both the spiritual and the carnal Thai, the Mien have attempted to situate themselves as a destination. They don't control any of the tourism traffic, but can try to influence the flow in some ways.

One of the apparent ironies of the setting that I found in 2005 emerges from a contrast to my research in 1992–94. At that earlier time, there was much fear of the spread of HIV, and many campaigns to keep girls and young women from the evils of the sex trade. I was brought into one effort of writing a proposal to help keep girls in school longer (to encourage them not to leave school after grade six and to stay at least past grade nine). But the sexualization that was pervasive at festivals in 2005 was, in general, the work of school teachers, who had the means and skills to organize activities and training to make the students able to pull off a seductive entertainment that would be interesting to Thai audiences.

Whether the girls were doing a modified plate dance as an expression of Mien ethnicity, or were performing the disco shimmying that showed how they might pass for Thai entertainers, they were sharing with their audience what they had learned or practiced at school. And the "product" engaged with two different notions of who and what are the Thai who might visit the countryside and join the audience. They are, on the one hand, the people who seek "community culture," expressions of tradition and morality in the village. On the other hand, they are males in search of enjoyment and sexual pleasures.[45]

There is no average Thai, and there is no necessary match between chauvinist nationalism and the ideas of ordinary people. The common anthropological sense that minorities are inherently threatened by national integration, modernity, capitalism, the state, or whatever needs serious revision if we are to arrive at some

---

[45] Yukti Mukdawijitr, *Aan "Watthanatham Chumchon"* [Reading "Community Culture"] (Bangkok: Fa Diowkan, 2005); and Fordham, *A New Look at Thai AIDS.* There are innumerable "Thai." Kasian Tejapira finds five kinds of them among the educated middle- and upper-class individuals engaged in national political discourse. From their biases, he glosses them as state-civilizing, national-consensus, authoritarian, liberal, and communitarian. That diversity is from only a small segment of the national population. See Kasian Tejapira, "*Thammarat/* Good Governance in Glocalizing Thailand," in *Words in Motion: Toward a Global Lexicon*, ed. Carol Gluck and Anna L. Tsing (Durham, NC: Duke University Press, 2009), pp. 306–26. For an alternative approach that undermines or questions prospecting for "the national," see Ward Keeler, "What's Burmese about Burmese Rap? Why Some Expressive Forms Go Global," *American Ethnologist* 36,1 (2009): 2–19.

intersections other than the looming destruction of the peoples we use as pin-ups for particular political or academic fantasies.

Contemporary Thailand's Mien people are nationals, and much of their public action aims to enhance their ability to pass in Thai society. The shows and festivals in 2005 were important performances that played to local, provincial, and national vistas. The Thaksin Shinawatra government had been populist in emphasis while also in many ways authoritarian.[46] Prime Minister Thaksin came up with various schemes to counter the effects of an international financial crisis, and he directed booster funds directly to villages and subdistricts. The administrative changes he made, which some gloss as neo-liberal, led to the formation of Subdistrict Administrative Councils (SdAC) and Provincial Administrative Councils.

Mien and other people in my research area had access to SdAC funds in support of their 2005 festivals. When I returned in 2012, I was eager to see in what directions the dance performances had developed, and I wanted to talk to the young dancers and their trainers to see whether I could learn something. But there was nothing going on. The networks of interested people were no longer there; they had dissolved. The new director of the SdAC seemed uninterested, while he was keen on the national reputation of Phulangka Mountain as one of the top-five spots in Thailand for hang-gliding competitions.[47] And in the preceding years, some new dynamics had come into place: the district and the province were now demanding monies from the subdistricts (their inferiors in the administrative hierarchy) to stage public events sponsored and organized at these higher levels. With that, there was much less energy and enthusiasm at the village level for engaging with public events, since the shows only called attention to some other place and were not of any particular local benefit.

Prime Minister Thaksin had been ousted in a coup in 2006 and barred from re-entering the country, so he could no longer shepherd finances to local levels. While he lasted, his rule was a major break from the pervasive Bangkok focus on national politics, and many rival politicians and urban elites disdained his rural supporters. The SdAC had provided the first opportunities for well-paid office work in my ethnic-minority research area, and educated locals had started to return home from city careers in Bangkok and elsewhere to work in the subdistricts.

By 2012, more than ten years after these changes were set in motion, the dynamic was again shifting. The village people who had well-paid administrative posts were increasingly buying homes in the town of Chiangkham, thirty kilometers away, and commuting weekdays to work in the countryside. As with the renamed mountain that I interpret as the symbol of a local, Mien theory about what moves some Thai people, one may look at the SdAC office as refracting notions of Mien and Thai selves and others and how they may differ and connect. The context of the office has changed; rather than promoting local festivals, welfare, and non-elite tourism, it tends to concentrate on the national domain of sports as well as to manage ever-more demanding relations with the district and the province.

---

[46] Pasuk Phongpaichit and Chris Baker, *Thaksin: The Business of Politics in Thailand* (Chiangmai: Silkworm, 2004).

[47] I have only found reference to one such event at Phulangka, the "Thailand Paragliding Princess's Cup Open 2010." See http://asia.hangpara.jp/2010/wp-content/uploads/file/20091119092631Bulletin.pdf, accessed November 19, 2013.

I did not see the hang-glider contest, but it seems to me that Phulangka Mountain is coming into competition with other Thai mountains for the attentions of athletes, advertisers, and travel writers—a different crowd from those moved by Buddhist spirituality or carnal delights. Phulangka is no longer just a local mountain; it is squarely national, and its signification avails some networks and benefits as it precludes others. The Mien and their landscape have become increasingly national, and, like the Thai, they are diverse, differentiated, and unequal in various but always particular ways that can be situated if one gets to know people and places.

AN OLD TIGER

In some contrast to the ideas of French anthropologist Jacques Lemoine, I do not think that Mien people or culture should be defined in relation to notions of an endangered past. And while the scheme of ritual ordinations that the spirit paintings pertain to has been of some importance, one should not assume that religion is any less of a time and place than are patterns in farming, festivals, or anything else. People are continually being shaped by circumstances and by engagements with their surrounding worlds. I offer a brief discussion of ideas about witchcraft that took hold during the war in Laos, but which later lost hold in refugee camps on the Thai side, to emphasize the need to historicize the ethnology of Southeast Asia.

The Mien ideas that crystallized during an episode of witchcraft fear are an expression of time and place. At that time, in that place, militias controlled the region, exaggerating ethnic boundaries, leading to social instability and complexity, and considerable interethnic traffic in religious ideas and practices that centered on invulnerability and protection. The scare over witchcraft was specific to a historical moment; had it been simply about the inner logic of an ethnic culture, then the ideas would have resurfaced in refugee camps later. They did not, however, and the main difference is that the militia did not have the command that it did during the war, and Christianity offered some people new options—people's decisions were based partly on gender and family particulars, issues that completely disappear if one expects people to act in ways that simply express their ethnicity.

As the Iu Mien in Laos became drawn into the war, they moved across the country and into a different environment. A number of children had died from illness in the process of a resettlement to Nam Keung, a lowland area near the Mekong River and about a week's journey by foot from their previous mountain home areas. At least some of the deaths were attributed to the old-tiger spirit. Yet the Iu Mien asserted that: "No Iu Mien will become [a host body for the] *lau-hu-gwe* [old-tiger spirit], it is the Akha, Lahu, and Lue," referring to other ethnic groups in northern Laos and neighboring areas of China, Burma, and Thailand.[48] Children in particular might become victims of this spirit, but Iu Mien people were by (ethnic) definition never its host.

The *lau-hu-gwe* was not an issue of any apparent concern in the Iu Mien settlements where I based my previous research in Thailand. Only once did I see a spirit medium drive such a spirit from an afflicted child, wielding a tiger claw—the medium was Le Tsan Kwe, in Phale Village, in the early 1990s.[49] At that time, the Iu

---

[48] Personal interview, Portland, OR, December 10, 2007.

[49] Even ordinary spirit mediums are diverse, particular, and interesting, but Le Tsan Kwe was no ordinary man or medium. For some sense of his importance and how knowing about him

Mien did not begin a search for a resident witch whom they could hold responsible for the illness, and the treatment for the affliction was analogous to how people would drive off a "wild spirit" from a household. Because the events in Nam Keung came to focus on Mien people who had been adopted as children from other ethnic groups, I must note that there is no indication from my research or that of any other scholar that there has ever been such an anxiety. The fear of witchcraft manifest social collapse at a very special moment when a militia (that also has no precursor in Mien history) saw its duty as to guard the ethnic boundary with violence, something that, in fact, could not be done.

One Iu Mien woman in Nam Keung had been acting strangely one day, and some people grabbed her and asked her to identify herself. After she gave her name and was recognized, people released her. "But when they got to her house, she was there before them. For an adult to be in two places at the same time is a sign of being *lau-hu-gwe*."[50] She was then accused of hosting an old tiger spirit that had made a child sick and caused its death. At a village meeting, some Tai Lue people suggested that the woman be released if she would agree to leave the settlement and live far enough away. Her husband was at the meeting, and he was made to convey to her the notice of eviction. If she would not leave, then militia leader Chao La would send his henchman, Fu Tsing, to arrest her. The woman had children and did not accept either alternative, that is, to leave or be arrested. The husband and children were not thought to be afflicted by the spirit, as victims or hosts. This is different from lowland Shan and highland Lisu notions, where contagion results from living together or eating repeated meals with someone who has a witchcraft spirit.[51] The accused woman used poison ("the kind we used for fishing"[52]) to take her own life that night, and the husband later remarried. Another Iu Mien woman was later accused of hosting this spirit; she promptly took off and was never heard from again. She did not have any children.

Both women were said to have been "adopted" as children, probably from Akha or Lahu families. The practice of purchasing children available for adoption was among the strategies employed by better-off people to increase their pool of laborers and household members. When the children grew up, they had the same rights and duties as other children of a household. Some of my contacts recall the hardship of French colonial taxation, when many Iu Mien were forced to sell off children in order

---

provides an entry into many and complex worlds and histories, see Peter Kandre and Lej Tsan Kuej, "Aspects of Wealth Accumulation, Ancestor Worship, and Household Stability among the Iu Mien Yao," in *Felicitation Volumes of Southeast Asian Studies Presented to His Highness Prince Dhaninivat Kromamun Bidyalabh Bridhyakorn on the Occasion of his Eightieth Birthday*, vol. 1, ed. Phitthayalāpphrutthiyākǭn (Bangkok: The Siam Society, 1965), pp. 129–48; Hanks and Hanks, *Tribes of the Northern Thai Hills*; Tim Forsyth, "Obituary: Le Tsan Kwe," *Journal of the Siam Society* 89 (2001): x–xv; Hjorleifur Jonsson and Sudarat Musikawong, "Khwam lak-lai thang chon-chat nai phaphayon thai yuk songkhram yen: Yon klap pai du khon-phu-khao khong Khunawut" [National Diversity in Cold War Thai Film: Revisiting Khunawut's *Mountain People*], *Warasan Nang Thai/Thai Film Journal* 17 (2013): 97–132.

[50] Personal interview, Portland, OR, December 10, 2007.

[51] E. Paul Durrenberger, "Witchcraft, Sorcery, Fortune, and Misfortune among Lisu Highlanders of Northern Thailand," in *Understanding Witchcraft and Sorcery in Southeast Asia*, ed. C. W. Watson and Roy Ellen (Honolulu, HI: University of Hawaii Press, 1993), pp. 47–66; and Nicola Tannenbaum, "Witches, Fortune, and Misfortune among the Shan in Northwest Thailand," in ibid., pp. 67–80.

[52] Personal interview, Portland, OR, December 10, 2007.

to pay the tax. This critical awareness is generally absent from discussions of purchase-adoptions by Iu Mien people from other groups.

Ideas of *lau-hu-gwe* did not emerge for the first time during the war. Nor is the notion specific to the Iu Mien peoples. It resonates, for instance, with Chinese ideas of evil spirits, *gui*.[53] Some of the remedies that Iu Mien people employed they had learned from Tai Lue neighbors, and in some Iu Mien- and English-language conversations people used the Tai Lue term for witches, *phi-pop*, when answering my questions about *lau-hu-gwe*. But as much as there was a regional, interethnic continuity in ideas about witchcraft spirits, the form these ideas took reflected an anxiety about ethnic boundaries that had emerged in the context of war and was reproduced in relation to an ethnic militia leader's command over "his" people.

Only non-Iu Mien people were the supposed hosts of *lau-hu-gwe*. Some Tai Lue people were suspected of harboring the witchcraft spirit, but Iu Mien people took action only against members of their own ethnic group, particularly women who had been adopted as children. Adoptions are not rare, but in previous research I never heard of those who had been adopted being accused of witchcraft or raising other anxieties. In conversations about life in refugee camps, subsequent to the resettlement in Nam Keung, people never mentioned any allegations or fears about witchcraft. Instead, many related conversions to Christianity in response to the unexpected deaths of children.

In Nam Keung, in about 1967, a boy around age seven died after only a few days of illness. He had not been in bad health as a child, and this led some people to suspect witchcraft. As people explored a likely source, they settled on a Tai Lue noodle vendor, speculating that the boy had at some point gotten a bowl of noodles from her after school with a promise to pay her later. Someone supposedly overheard the woman wonder out loud why the boy had not paid her. But there was no action against this woman. The policing against witchcraft was limited to the Iu Mien people, and came out, for instance, in occasionally ruthless acts of imprisonment, beatings, and expulsion by Chao La's henchmen.

The context of war militarized everyday life. While ostensible witchcraft was seen as a potential threat to the ethnic group's members, actual harm was rare. By comparison, deliberate violence was never signified in the same way. One young man, a soldier, based in the militia's camp at Nam Nyou, had interest in a young woman who was a niece of sorts to the leader, Chao La. But she had another suitor, and was meeting with that suitor when the first man decided to take his gun and kill both of them. He killed the young woman but the other man got away. In despair, the soldier then tried to kill himself. He was badly injured, but, because he was with the militia, there was a way to get him on an emergency flight to a Bangkok hospital, where he was treated successfully. He recovered, and I met him once, twenty years later and now about twenty years ago (long before I had any inkling of these stories and lives). The point is, in contrast to the perceived threat of the witchcraft spirit, violence involving local soldiers was not marked as a collective danger.

Iu Mien people acquired many of their defenses against witchcraft from non-Mien sources within the multi-ethnic resettlement of Nam Keung, especially from neighboring lowland and Buddhist Tai Lue peoples. If witchcraft spirits marked an ethnic boundary for the Iu Mien and expressed their anxieties over social boundary

---

[53] Norma Diamond, "The Miao and Poison: Interactions on China's Southwest Frontier," *Ethnology* 27,1 (1988): 1–25.

transgressions, then it is particularly telling of their situation that the defenses they chose relied on crossing these same boundaries. There was no way of maintaining an ethnically sealed-off space. The Tai Lue neighbors suggested such remedies as chili peppers, Buddha amulets, and relocation. For the first, "the person would sneeze and the spirit would leave. The Buddha image would scare off the spirit because of the amulet's greater power. Regarding the third remedy, Tai Lue people stated that if a person hosting this spirit lived a two-hour distance away from other people, then there was no danger when the spirit took off at night in search of a victim; it could not travel that far.

In one conversation, in Portland, Oregon, I asked a man if he had heard *lau-hu-gwe* stories.

> Yes, we heard, but did not know so much. Some people carried it [the spirit], but we can't see it. People did not necessarily know if they carried the spirit. *Lau-hu-gwe* goes mostly after young children, they [the spirits] are after the blood, and the young children get sick. [The spirits] have to have something to feed on, if the person feeds it then all is okay, but if the person [host] does not feed it, then it goes out on its own.[54] Some people can see it as it goes about at night. A shape, looking for something dirty or blood, and going into someone's body. Some women would go into labor, and the blood would come out, and the *lau-hu-gwe* wants to eat it. People were scared of this because nobody could do anything. You know, with *lau-hu-gwe*, you have to take the tiger teeth and scratch the body to scare the spirit off, or shoot off a gun to chase it off. Lots of people did that in Nam Keung. One plant scared it off; it is mint, *nam-zoi-nyao*. You put it on the body, and the smell scares the invading spirit away.[55]

Unlike lowland neighbors, such as Tai Lue and Lao, the Iu Mien were not Buddhists. But during the war that raged across Laos with varying intensity between 1954 and 1975, many Iu Mien soldiers and others took to wearing Buddha amulets for protection, and the ease of wielding a Buddha amulet to fight the witchcraft spirit may have come from their ubiquity at the time.[56] Hmong General Vang Pao had

---

[54] Framed in this way, the old-tiger spirit is represented as a force that can be domesticated in ways that do not endanger others, but it is an invasive and demanding spirit in contrast to soldier spirits that are invited. Soldier spirits can endanger the self (household, fields) if hungry while old-tiger spirits only endanger others (children, women in childbirth, and so forth). The old-tiger spirit invades a person, whereas a wild spirit invades a house. *Yienh fiu mienv* (whistle-lure spirit) takes up residence in a lone tall tree from where it tries to snatch a human soul for company, by whistling in the daytime or through an erotic dream at night. I witnessed one expulsion of such a spirit in 1993, and the spirit medium commented that, had the exorcism not been successful, then the next step would be to identify the tree and chop it down to drive away the spirit. This spirit has different attributes among the Iu Mien from Laos and those in Chiangrai, Thailand. See Herbert C. Purnell, *An Iu-Mienh—English Dictionary with Cultural Notes* (Chiang Mai: Silkworm Books, 2012), pp. 438, 738.

[55] Personal interview, Portland, OR, March 3, 2008.

[56] For comparisons, see Tannenbaum, "Tattoos"; Richard Ruth, "Dressing for Modern War in Old-Fashioned Magic: Traditional Protective Charms of Thailand's Forces in the Vietnam War," in *The Spirit of Things: Materiality and Religious Diversity in Southeast Asia*, ed. Julius Bautista (Ithaca, NY: Cornell Southeast Asia Program Publications, 2012), pp. 129–46; and Chris Baker and Pasuk Phongpaichit, "Protection and Power in Siam: From *Khun Chang Khun Phae*n to the Buddha Amulet," *Southeast Asian Studies* 2,2 (2013): 215–42.

detailed notions about amulets that worked against bullets, which he potentially derived from a Lao and Buddhist colonel in his army.[57] An Iu Mien soldier suggested that rifle bullets might work, since they were partially fabricated from bronze like the Buddha images—this may be a distinctly non-Buddhist understanding of the quality of amulets. Amulets, even from a different cultural scheme, made local sense as *buv*, objects that create a protective barrier around a person, in contrast to the protection of *faatv* (see Chapter 2) that draws on verbal formulas.

Invulnerability became an ongoing concern as people were brought more deeply into war. At various times, I asked people whether Chao Mai or Chao La had been in charge of rituals having to do with the militia, but the answers were always negative; each family took care of rituals for the benefit of its members. But in one conversation, I learned that when one unit successfully returned after some major military action, the elementary school in Nam Keung was closed for a day to accommodate the militia leaders who had to repay the spirits for guarding their men.

When I asked whether people had feared witchcraft in refugee camps, no one recollected that anxiety. Some people had converted to Christianity following the death of a child, I was told, and it seems to me that Christianity offered some spiritual support and an alternative to the ancestors whose efficacy people came to doubt during hard times. And that process implies a reworking of the ethnic boundary, no longer defined exclusively in terms of farming households and the spirits of the ancestors, on the one hand, or the ethnic militia, on the other. When settled in a refugee camp and dependent on food supplied by outsiders, people completely lost some of the scaffolding for certain former practices and assurances.

The general point of my discussion is that ethnography needs to be comparative, regional, historical, and reflexive in particular ways so that it can specify with more clarity and relevance what it describes. The various dimensions of the witchcraft-fear episode teach us about a complex field that was shaped by a very particular war. To suggest, as some might, that the elements are telling of "the Mien" or their cosmology would be an absolute denial of the complexity and historicity of our fields and the particularity of our encounters. The structural quality of the field, as a method, suggests that, as with time and space (in Einstein's work), the ethnic group and the state have no independent existence. There are fields of relations and networks of relations within which people arrive at particular ideas and practices, and these need to be specified and situated before any generalization can be made.

I make no claim toward abandoning the study of peoples in relation to ethnic terms. Rather, I suggest that the tendency to situate the Mien, say, as an ethnic group, as highland peoples, as refugees, or a minority, generally imports mistaken expectations about who people are and what happens in their interactions within and across ethnic frontiers based on high-theory notions regarding identity, history, politics, and more. My effort is not to arrive at some timeless description of the Mien ethnic group. I am turning the analytical table to arrive at some better understanding of how to do anthropology, based on what I know about Mien and some of their others and contexts.

---

[57] Roger Warner, *Shooting at the Moon: The Story of America's Clandestine War in Laos* (South Royalton, VT: Steerforth, 1996), p. 170.

If we aim to preserve anthropology's uniqueness and its difference from other academic fields, then we are engaged in something we should recognize as the jealous guarding of ethnic boundaries. Anthropology, like the Mien, needs to be understood in terms of patterns of interactions across difference, and from the social consequences of such patterns.

CHAPTER FOUR

FINDING HOME IN THE UNITED STATES

The Chiangkham refugee camp was being shut down in 1992, which is about when I first settled into research with Mien people in Phayao Province, Thailand. The little I learned at that time about Mien living in the United States came from listening to recorded music on cassette tapes that people had been sent. In Thailand's Mien villages, people would sing at wedding festivals, and the singing was always in the archaic song language *nzung waac*. At one of the first weddings I attended, the old people would *ooh* and *aah* over someone's skillful wielding of uncommon words. Younger people had, for the most part, no understanding of the singing and no appreciation for the skill involved. School and everyday life brought them into Thai language worlds, and at social events they might get together and sing Thai pop tunes when the older people were no longer in charge. The young people's general comment was that the old-style singing was in "Chinese" and meant nothing to them.

But judging by the cassettes, the Mien in the United States were singing in the everyday Mien language, *mienh waac*, and that was fundamentally new to me.[1] Fifteen years later, I learned some things about how the Mien came to sing in new ways, shifting to the everyday language. Kao-Chiem Chao, the first Iu Mien to come to the United States (along with his mother and wife), was one of the early singers.[2] The first time he and I met, a friend had introduced us and we had a little time to chat at the Beaverton Public Library, in Oregon, in one of Portland's suburbs. Kao-Chiem Chao told me:

> The first to write Mien [pop] music was Ee-Yun, he lives now in Richmond, California. He had worked for [Vang Pao's Union of Lao Races] broadcasting station in Long Cheng. There he asked a composer, "how can I write some music in Mien?" You should use Laotian tune and write Mien words to it. He did one or two songs then. Another guy was Tzeo Jo-Yun. He had gone to France first,

---

[1] On language, see Herbert Purnell, "Developing Practical Orthographies for the Iu Mien (Yao), 1932–1986: A Case Study," *Linguistics of the Tibeto–Burman Area* 10,2 (1987): 128–41; Herbert Purnell, "The Metrical Structure of Yiu Mien Secular Songs," in *The Yao of South China, Recent International Studies*, ed. Jacques Lemoine and Chiao Chien (Paris: Pangu, 1991), pp. 369–96; Herbert Purnell, *An Iu-Mienh–English Dictionary* (Chiangmai: Silkworm, 2012); and Christopher Court, "Fundamentals of Iu Mien (Yao) Grammar" (PhD dissertation, University of California, Berkeley, 1985). On music, see: Lynne Picker, "Where Has All the Music Gone? A Case Study on the Effects of Migration upon the Musical Practices of an Iu-Mien Community" (MA thesis, Northern Illinois University, 2004).

[2] For a long time refugees feared going to the United States. Kao Chiem may have had less of that fear, as he had worked directly with US military people during the war. On his story, see Tracy Jan, "Leading Mien to a 'New World,'" *The Oregonian*, August 20, 2001.

then he came to the United States about five years ago, and he now lives in Seattle.

I was lonely when I came to the United States, and thought, "maybe I can follow up on those [composers] and write Mien songs." I had lots of Lao friends who knew how to write music. I was embarrassed about my songs and did not tell them about it. Another guy in Seattle, Wuen Seng, he wrote songs using Lao or Thai tunes, he recorded Mien songs in a studio and made a cassette. We listened to Hmong songs written to Thai/Lao music and thought it was fascinating. Wuen Seng recorded twelve songs; we listened to them, and thought they did not compare to the Hmong songs. Then I couldn't wait any longer, and did my first album with my wife and other singers. We were pretty popular, and we were surprised by that. People loved it and sent cassettes with the music to Thailand. It was played in the refugee camp, and also on the Chiangmai radio station [for hill tribe audiences], in 1985.

I was still hesitant to show my music to my Lao friends. Then they found out and learned that I was one of the Mien songwriters, after the music became popular. The band was called Lam Hlang Hle [M. Lamh hlang hleix], or Highland Star; we used that name for a long time. Then we stopped for a while because our drummer died. He was Tzeo Ziep Wuen, who died in about 1995 or '96. He lived in Portland, and he was very good-looking. Later we recorded more songs, and now we are recording again, with a new band name, Friendship Star. The name is in the Lao language, *Wong Dontri Phantha Mitr*. The first album had various kinds of songs, including love songs. The most popular was a song that asked how everyone was doing back in Thailand and Laos. It was played a lot in Thailand.[3]

Later, when I had a day talking with Ton Khuon Lor in his barbershop, I learned what the Thai Mien thought of the new-style Mien pop music:

On the Chiangmai Hill Tribe Radio Station, they played Kao-Chiem's music. People wrote in to complain, "why do you always play the same music?" The announcer talked back to them, saying, "you Mien in Thailand, you are destroying Mien music with your *ae-aw* [music in the archaic song language] …"[4]

Ton Khuon later had his own engagements with the worlds of pop music:

In the Ubon refugee camp in Thailand, there were Laotians who played guitar really well. My friends and I would go watch. One of them now lives in Richmond [California]. My friends did not know songs, but I knew some Thai songs. The Lao guys said, wow, you know how to sing. Come here; you sing and we'll play guitar. So at night they would play music and I sang. I watched their fingers, but they never taught us how to play. They were kind of selfish, didn't want other people to use their guitars. Then they became tired and put the guitars down. I picked one up, but had not touched a string yet, when one of them said, "Hey, you touched my guitar. Put it back." So I put it back, but from

[3] Personal interview, Portland, OR, October 24, 2007.
[4] Personal interview, Portland, OR, August 12, 2008.

time to time I would "steal" one to use it until I knew the D cord, and later I learned A-minor.

Me and my friend, we don't know anything, but at one point we sang ten songs. Then I went to Canada, and there I formed a band. The songs [we performed] were Lao and Thai pop songs, but this was a Mien band, in Kitchener, Ontario [not far from Toronto]. We had this band until 1990, when I went to Surrey. [In Ontario] we found the church people, and there was one man who was an excellent musician. He could pick up and play many kinds of instruments. They invited us to a picnic, and the man said, "You know something, right?" I said, "Yeah, we just have a band up there." He invited us to come to the church and sing a special song, so we started there.

One time they sold tickets in the Seattle area and in California. [The promoter], he is an older brother, he said that this singer from Toronto is famous. The guy just hired the place. Lots of people came, the ticket was fifty dollars. All my friends went to see the performance, but they could not find the address. This guy was cheating, he hired a huge gym, but he hid the address. He thought we were not that good, but we were a good band; we were called the Toronto Band. We had really good musicians on keyboard, base, guitar, drums [Ton Khoun's brother]. The band then played a few parties, but after that concert we split up.

I asked Ton Khuon whether people were upset with the band.

No, at the guy [promoter]. He is a Laotian, not a Mien. I had used my credit card to pay for the place. He said he would write us a check for $5,000, but he did not give us money. He sold over two hundred tickets before the party started ($10,000). We did not want to do this anymore. So, after that I started looking for a wife.[5]

For me, asking people about music and singing, and about religion, was a way to learn about things without sticking to the topic of war and camps. But dealing with the war and refugee status is unavoidable, in part because post-war fighting pushed Mien people in the United States to reconsider their identity in some fundamental ways and with, ultimately, profoundly constructive consequences.

THE BETRAYALS OF WAR

In the late 1970s, Thai authorities and military personnel cultivated and maintained relations with anti-government militias from Laos, Cambodia, and Burma. This changed in 1988, when Thai authorities made official deals for economic relations with their neighbors' governments.[6] When these new deals were made, and Thailand gained access to vast areas for logging in neighboring regions, the Thai government promptly declared a logging ban within its own country. The Thai prime minister, Chatichai Choonhavan, won an environmentalist award from some

---

[5] Ibid.

[6] Philip Hirsch, "Thailand and the New Geopolitics of Southeast Asia," in *Counting the Costs: Economic Growth and Environmental Change in Thailand*, ed. Jonathan Rigg (Singapore: Institute of Southeast Asian Studies, 1995), p. 236.

unit of the United Nations. Of course, one must not joke about international awards and recognition for the official plundering of someone's war-torn and cash-strapped neighbors, or about how the Burmese government took this opportunity to further dispossess its ethnic minorities. Chatichai Choonhavan called the effort "turning battlefields into marketplaces." But that was in the late 1980s, whereas the refugee crisis occurred in the 1970s, at a time when refugee militias were accommodated and encouraged to fight against Thailand's communist neighbors.

Refugee camps in Thailand that sheltered people fleeing the wars in Burma, Laos, Cambodia, and Vietnam have produced various configurations of humanitarian relief, people-making (subjectivities), political manipulation, insurgency, and social reproduction since the 1970s.[7] Journalist Roger Warner characterizes the refugee camps along the Thai border as "the strangest place of all: part prisons, part feeding and vacation centers for resistance fighters, part travel bureaus, where Iron Age tribesmen could sign up to emigrate to the West."[8] His tone may reflect the prejudice of the people who gave him the information, who were mostly the Americans involved with the war in Laos and who later settled in Bangkok.

The Mien leader Chao La wanted to keep fighting after 1975, as did Hmong leader Vang Pao. Both men organized militias in 1976 from among their former soldiers, and both received encouragement and support from exiled former leaders of the Royal Lao Army. Chao La was visited many times by some of those leaders in a refugee camp in Chiangkhong, and Thai military leaders arranged for refugee soldier training and orientation in military camps in Chiangrai Province, Thailand. The Iu Mien militia unit was promised supplies, but many people have told me that the men took off with only one rifle for the whole group. In the first year, militia members managed gradually to arm themselves by killing Lao government soldiers and taking their weapons. The promised support never materialized. This guerrilla unit was defeated in 1984, when the leader, Seng Fu (Pien, or Sae Phan), was captured in Burma and handed over to the Lao authorities.

Before it was defeated, the guerrilla group had alienated many potential supporters and allies among Iu Mien people within Laos and in the refugee camps, and also among those in the United States. The soldiers relied on supplies from local Iu Mien villagers, who were in a bind. They would be punished by the Lao authorities if it became known that they were supporting the post-war militia. Sometimes the insurgents would steal food from people, or rob them at gunpoint. "When he took off in 1976, Seng Fu went about like a *jan-tza* [M. *janx-zaqc*], he knew which households had wealth and that's where he would go." The man who told me this glossed the Mien term in English as "freedom fighter," but I had only known it

---

[7] See Lynellyn D. Long, *Ban Vinai: The Refugee Camp* (New York, NY: Columbia University Press, 1993); Lindsay French, "The Political Economy of Injury and Compassion: Amputees on the Thai–Cambodia Border," in *Embodiment and Experience*, ed. Thomas Csordas (New York, NY: Cambridge University Press, 1994), pp. 69–99; Lindsay French, "From Politics to Economics at the Thai–Cambodian Border," *International Journal of Politics, Culture, and Society* 15,3 (2002): 427–702; W. Courtland Robinson, *Terms of Refuge: The Indochinese Exodus and the International Response* (London: Zed, 1998); Hazel J. Lang, *Fear and Sanctuary: Burmese Refugees in Thailand* (Ithaca, NY: Cornell Southeast Asia Program Publications, 2002); and Ashley South, *Mon Nationalism and the Civil War in Burma* (New York, NY: Routledge Curzon, 2003).

[8] Roger Warner, *Shooting at the Moon: The Story of America's Clandestine War in Laos* (South Royalton, VT: Steerforth, 1996), p. 374.

as reference to a robber or a bandit. *Jan* marks an alien, a non-Mien, the ethnic boundary assumes honesty within; *tza* (*zaqc*) is a thief.

What seems to have ended the general Iu Mien exiles' support for the group was that the militia killed all the members of an Iu Mien household in revenge for being denied supplies. This was one of several violent attacks by the militia on Iu Mien people in Laos. Word of the killing spread to the victims' relatives in the refugee camp of Chiangkham, where one in-law of the victims made up a song about it in the archaic song language. The man, whose name is Fu Pu, made a cassette recording of his song and sent it to relatives, who were by then living in the San Francisco Bay area of California. Chao La's relatives were also living in the Bay area, and they learned of the song. They wrote out the words and sent them back to Chao La in the refugee camp.[9] He fined Fu Pu *baht* 6,000 for the offense. The song blamed and criticized (*hemx*) Chao La and Seng Fu, said one man. According to another:

> It was purely cursing. The song did not mention Chao La's name, but in the words, every bullet was shooting at Chao La's name. [HJ: I asked, were there any other songs like this?] No, this was the only one, and because we were in a refugee camp we were safe, but still not safe. If this man had been in Laos, you know what would have happened: bang! This was not just criticism; it was a cursing of Chao La for what had happened.[10]

People in refugee camps lived under surveillance and authoritarian control to a considerable degree. The camps resembled prison-like institutions that were monitored by ethnic militia leaders and their agents, as well as by the Thai guards. Songwriter Fu Pu would probably have been beaten up or killed if he had performed his song where he was, in the refugee camp, because of Chao La's authoritarian command over his subjects, which was enabled by the war and the conditions of exile. Instead, by making the cassette and mailing it to Iu Mien relatives in the United States, Fu Pu transcended the total institution of the camp by reaching a transnational audience of people who were in a position to hear and respond to the criticism.

Ton Khuon Lor experienced the militia and its betrayals firsthand, and in ways he had never wished for. The following interview excerpt is from our time together in his barbershop. Few customers came that day; Ton Khuon Lor provided inexpensive haircuts, and a generous customer might leave him a one-dollar tip. The scenario he describes evokes human trafficking. As teenage boys were deceived and sold off to cross-border militias, various people behind the scenes were making considerable money on the whole thing:

> TKL: We were in camp and doing nothing. Dan, this leader guy, said, "why don't you go to Nong Baen, you know? Mien people have a little village there and do gardens."
> HJ: A northern Thai village?

---

[9] At this time Chao La was living outside but next to the camp, and he had documents that allowed him full freedom to travel within Thailand. He was not (technically) in charge of running the camp, but his position was certainly not that of a regular refugee.

[10] Personal interview, Portland, OR, March 3, 2008.

TKL: A-ha. And then they came out and said, "hey, build a house for us, we will pay you fifty *baht*." One of my friends went there for a couple of days and made some money. I said, hey, that's a good idea. So I asked my mom and dad, because my parents loved me so much that they never let me go hungry or anything, they'd give me money to spend. They were okay with this; I would go for a few months, and then come home. This was from Chiangkhong to Chiangkham, so when I got there it was evening already. The people there brought some meat and made *larp* [a Lao delicacy, usually made with raw meat, onions, mint, and many other good things] and provided expensive whiskey. They said, "just come and join us for dinner, we are so happy that you are coming to work for us." They did not even tell me that I was going to work as a soldier; it was all a big lie. I found out that each soldier [was supposed to get] a monthly salary of *baht* 1,500, but we got nothing.

About 6:00 PM, six Thai soldiers came to see me. I knew there was something wrong. They said about me, "this person who is going to be a soldier." My tears dropped, because my parents had loved me so much that they never even spanked me. Everything they taught me was in a good way, so [I thought], why are you lying to me? I did not say it, but that is what I thought. They asked why I was crying. I said, "this is not right." The Thai guy said, "at 3:00 AM, seven of you guys have to take him," meaning me, "and catch the minibus, go to the other camp, and walk to the border, about a three-hour walk." I asked why they were doing this. They said, "oh, you go there and you get money." It's true, we would have had a salary. The money was from Vang Pao. Vang Pao actually sent money to Thailand, but the leaders in camp, they took all the money. They'd sell them [the recruits] to the Mien leaders. The Mien leaders couldn't do much; they would have to go by what the Thai authorities decided. The Mien leaders in camp, they had no problem, they had Thai ID cards.

HJ: The Mien leaders like Chao La and Wuen Chiem?

TKL: A-ha. These two did not do much, but other people jumped in with the hope of getting some money. They'd go ask Chao La, who gave them permission. They'd go to the Thai government and say, we have money. But they had to prove that they had soldiers, so they had to send pictures. This would go to Vang Pao in the United States, and then he would give money. We give to you, so this is not against the law in Thailand. That's what happened, the Thai got some money, the Mien leaders got some money, and the soldiers—they got nothing. We would just suffer in Laos.[11]

We went over to the Lao side for a week of training and put on uniforms. We went to a city called Pangmuan, in Xaygnaburi. We trained at a sawmill that had been shut down. It was a big building. They took a lot of pictures, and my friend still has one of them. He showed it to me a few years ago, and I could still remember. I guess he was the only one to get a picture, the rest were sent to Vang Pao to get money. So they trained us and got us ready and took our pictures. They did not let us go home,

---

[11] This unpolished, verbatim account is the only insider information that I have. It comes across as describing some combination of a sham and a scam.

but I tried. I thought to myself, this is going to be for one or two months. One day I just sat down and thought, I just have to be sick, you know? So I lay on the bed and did not eat. When people ate, I did not. When people went to sleep, I ate, but I didn't let people see me eat.

I played that way until, one day, a Mien who was called a *kong roi* [leader of a hundred men], he had seen me before in the Chiangkham camp, he asked; "oh, why are you here?" I said they sent me. He was nice to me and talked to me. He said, "why didn't you stay in [the refugee] camp; you are not supposed to be here, this is no good." I told him my story, and I said I'm sick. I'm not really sick, but I am weak.

The first thing he did was to send his soldier to the city, to get a chicken in the city of Pangmuan, and they barbequed it. They also made sticky rice. Then he said, "okay, you go home. This is my permission. In this area, no one can say anything. If I open my mouth, you can go home. If you cannot walk, I'll let my soldier carry you." I said, I can walk, I am sick but I can walk. He said, "I know you, that's why I help you out," and he gave me *baht* 200. I got over to the Thai side, but the camp had moved, so I stayed one night and was told "tomorrow you have to go back [to the Lao side] again." I said no. This was in Chiangkham. They said that tomorrow a soldier would come again for me and if I didn't go back then, I would die. I said, I don't care; if you want to kill me, do it now, I will die.

The next day I heard the news, a car would come from the *mulanithi* [Thai, foundation]. I waited and the car came, and it was going to go back to Chiangkhong. So I said I will go with that car. The guys said, "no, you cannot do that, because you don't have ID, nothing." I said I have my own ID here right in my mouth. If I go to the refugee camp in Chiangkhong, I am going to tell them everything. So I went there, to Chiangkhong, and the *O-So* [guards] did not even ask me anything. Then Chao La's wife, I think the first one, came and asked me, "what happened to your hair? It used to be long." When I left, I had long hair, but in Chiangkham they [*O-So* guards] just grabbed the scissors and chopped it up really short. She, Chao La's wife, came and asked me, "are you from the other side now?" I said, "the other side." She asked, "how did you get here from there?" I said I just walked. When I was back in camp, my parents said, "we have to get out of here." I stayed for another two or three months. I knew another Mien, he worked for the UN; he told me to come work with them.

HJ: When you were in Kamphengphet or in camp, did you hear anything about Seng Fu's army over on the Lao side, which was formed in 1976 or later?

TKL: Oh yeah, yeah. This is how they lied. Chao La, if he sent soldiers to Laos, he would get a huge amount of money from Vang Pao. Each month, Vang Pao sent him money. It's the same story that I just told you, people just sell each other. That's why, who would want to be leader? No one wanted to be leader, but he just took Seng Fu. He said [to Seng Fu], "you go to Laos, take the people, and I will support you, I will send you money." But there was no support. So over there they had only twenty or thirty people, just hiding in the jungle. Now they had nothing to eat and were in the jungle, they had to go out to the Mien village, to rob the Mien people.[12]

The Iu Mien who had resettled in the United States abandoned their support of this militia group. Chao La is still an indexical leader, but he now stands for the Iu Mien past in Laos in a way that suggests their route to the United States and France more than anything else. When I learned of the song critiquing the militia's actions, I was keen to hear it and to get help with a translation. But no matter how many people I visited who were said to have a cassette, I never found it. Now it seems to me that this was just as well; the song very likely would simply, only expose old wounds and grief, things better left untouched. Not everyone was as lucky as Seng Uei (Chapter Two), who put his gun down before causing irreparable harm to himself and others.

Chao La died in 2005, in France, where he had settled in 1992. His ashes are kept in a memorial structure in Laos. "It looks like a Ming tomb," said one friend. Some say that the reliquary cost the equivalent of US$10,000 and that the Iu Mien people who go there to make offerings are charged a high fee by the guard, a son of the old leader. This I cannot tell. All I know is that Chao La is not completely gone, and that now people may relate to him in new ways. His son changed his family name so as not to call attention to his elite past in the communist present.

I know of only one person who challenged Chao La regarding his militia's violence against fellow Iu Mien people after 1975. Already resettled in the United States, this man learned that the militia intended to kill his uncle for not giving them the support they demanded. He wrote to Chao La in the refugee camp that, if anything were to happen to the uncle, he would hold Chao La responsible. "I know what to do to take care of you."[13] This threat came from a man who was descended from one of the several *Phya*-titled chiefs in the region—people who in some cases did not take for granted or perhaps even accept Chao Mai and Chao La's general command over the Lao Iu Mien population, or that of their father (Tzeo Wuen Tsoi Lin, Phya Long Hai) before. Even if it did not take place, the proposed vendetta hints at the generative quality of militarized violence. Killings become a mode of communication and reciprocal interaction.

The loss of support for the militia from among the Iu Mien in Laos and those in exile was in response to Seng Fu's transgressions of the ethnic boundary that was central to the ethnicization of Chao La's and his militia's agendas. By attacking Iu Mien people, the militia undermined any justification that people supported their cause because they represented the Iu Mien ethnic group. Anyone who identified with the victims of these attacks could see the situation as an assault on themselves, personally or ethnically—the kind of threat that had crystallized in ideas about witchcraft spirits.

After American support came to an end and Chao La did not have the resources to equip the militia, Seng Fu and many other militia leaders looked to the communist Chinese for support, equipment, and training. Sometime around 1980, Chinese military leaders offered the assembled Neo Hom resistance groups, then in Yunnan,

---

[12] Personal interview, Portland, OR, August 12, 2008.

[13] Personal interview, Portland, OR, March 8, 2008.

backing to take Laos.[14] This was soon after China had staged aggressive attacks across the borders with Vietnam and Laos in protest of Vietnam's support of Hun Sen's faction, which had taken power from the Khmer Rouge. One Mien contact told me that resistance leader Kong Le had turned down the Chinese offer of military support at this meeting, since it would result in too much bloodshed, but on this front I have no idea what to take seriously.

Seng Fu had been supplied with weapons, and, as the story goes, he sold them off to some militia in Burma and came back to Yunnan for more. Members of the Chinese army had an inkling of what had happened, and gave him a letter that they said would insure his safe transport to Thailand. He was to give the letter to one of the militias in Burma. Because he did not read the letter, he was taken by surprise when members of the other militia arrested him and handed him over to the authorities in Laos. War is betrayal. Chinese authorities also abandoned their support of Communist Party of Thailand guerrillas, who then gave up their struggle once they lost their Chinese backing (Chapter Three). The communist Chinese authorities made a deal with the staunchly anticommunist military government of Thailand in order to negotiate weapons transport to the Khmer Rouge, who by this time had lost power but still continued their violence against their own fellow nationals.[15]

When Seng Fu had been in prison for four or five years, he was eligible for release if some people would vouch for his return into Lao society. "But no Iu Mien person would sign for him, so he could not be released and he later died in jail."[16] The popular notion that no one would take responsibility for Seng Fu's release emphasizes a uniform discrediting of the guerrilla leader among the Iu Mien people in Laos and more widely. That belief is retrospective, and may do more to situate Iu Mien group identity relative to—that is, opposed to—internal diversity than to describe what really took place. It directs attention away from Chao La's role in creating the militia and defining its mission, and from Vang Pao's active role in keeping the process going. It also disconnects Iu Mien identity from the deadly violence that accompanied the agendas of the ethnically defined militia after 1975.

Seng Fu's wife had left the Chiangkhong refugee camp and moved to live near the prison so she could assist and care for her husband. This is one indication that there certainly were people around who would have been willing to sign for his release. The prison was a rather open place, on an island in the Nam Tha River in the town of Louang Nam Tha, where Seng Fu received some visitors. Several people suggested that he was badly treated and even poisoned by Pathet Lao guards (someone told me "his hair fell out, he looked scrawny"). One man added, "you know how the communists treat people," turning wartime ontology into a historical explanation. Seng Fu died in 1990 or 1991, and soon thereafter Chao La left the refugee camp for France.

---

[14] Geoffrey C. Gunn, "Resistance Coalitions in Laos," *Asian Survey* 23,3 (1983): 316–40; US Department of Defense, Joint Chiefs of Staff Message Center, "Briefing on Resistance Groups in Laos, 12 May 1981," a "secret" file that came into my possession.

[15] The motivation for Chinese support of the Khmer Rouge was, in part, that China's big communist rival—the Soviet Union—was supporting Vietnam and Laos. These were big-time family squabbles.

[16] Personal interview, Portland, OR, October 12, 2008.

While the post-war Iu Mien militia lasted, there was an effort to collect money for its support among the Iu Mien in the United States, and the money was passed on to Hmong leader Vang Pao for delivery. Some United States Iu Mien were also collecting for Vang Pao's more general support of an anti-government guerrilla unit in Laos. I was told that Vang Pao's people asked US$100 per household per year, and in exchange people received a card that guaranteed their admission to a future Laos that would be governed by Vang Pao once the militia had taken back the country. None of this can be proven, but I heard these things from several sources and find it credible.

Vang Pao was arrested in California in 2007 for allegedly arranging to buy weapons for the purpose of retaking Laos. This final resistance effort was either a last attempt to satisfy a decades-old promise to followers, or a stunt by an FBI spook who wanted to make a name for himself or to justify a bonus on his pay. But the collection of money among refugee immigrants did not stop. Among the deals that people could supposedly get—this report is impossible to substantiate—was the reward of being named mayor of a town or city in Laos for a payment of US$6,000. Such posts were available on installments. An acquaintance with connections among US Hmong suggested that the Iu Mien might be charged extra; the amounts that Hmong people mentioned were lower.

I learned of some elderly Iu Mien women of meager means who were still paying, in late 2008, US$50 per month, over a ten-year period, for their sons' future prominence in the old homeland as the mayor of some unspecified town under a phantasmatic Vang Pao regime. From what I learned, these young men had no interest in returning to Laos. In his book, Roger Warner mentions considerable corruption regarding the selling of such future government posts. Some very desirable positions had been sold to more than one person, and a good portion of the money had been skimmed off by US-based members of the resistance unit and then by Thai customs agents and the police.[17]

In the United States, most Iu Mien, Hmong, and other refugee immigrants from Laos have abandoned wartime orientations. The point is not to suggest that the money collection was widespread, but that it sustains a worldview that defines identity as it structures social relations in favor of militias and their leaders. Such efforts and taxation sustain wartime identifications long after their original context has expired, so that ultimately a collective ethnic identity and a particular wartime orientation become mutually constitutive of individual and collective subjects in exile in ways that continue to reinforce militarized, masculine leadership. It is this kind of dynamic that informs the "people-making" in refugee camps that I referred to earlier.

General Vang Pao passed away in early 2011, and the wartime orientation may have finally come to an end once the old leader was gone. But he was never alone in prospecting for a new–old Laos through an overthrow of the Lao PDR government. Instead, he was just the most visible and recognizable of the campaigners because he had been the major ally of the US effort. Many militia leaders, including a good number of ethnic Lao, came into prominence after the fighting stopped, and multiethnic alliances took shape as soon as the war was over and leaders were actively organizing, signing agreements, and sometimes looking for international sponsors. It is this that Mien people moved away from as they created new forms of

---

[17] Warner, *Shooting at the Moon*, p. 383.

community and identity in the United States. One man told me, in terms that I initially could not comprehend, "Iu Mien stopped being political in 1984."

CONVERSIONS AND COMMUNITY IN THE UNITED STATES

When Iu Mien people settled in the United States, they generally moved into low-income apartments in low-income neighborhoods and received social-services support.[18] People had no particular skills for this new life, but they were told that, in cases of domestic violence and other troubles, they should call the police. Many people have, now thirty years later, indicated to me that nothing much has changed. "The police come and they arrest someone. They are not trained to help. A week or two later the person is released and returns home and things are even worse than before. Only family and community can help." The point is that, initially, they had no skills, and if they did not come up with new ways of coping, then bad things would keep happening.

It is with those dynamics in mind that I situate Christian conversions and Buddhist, Taoist, Kuan Yin, and Lao Iu Mien Culture Association influence in the United States since 1976. People have come up with ways to enable coping and competency in otherwise alien surroundings. Religious and cultural organizations have been involved in workshops on citizenship, language and culture matters, and emotions. One of the realizations was that US-based Iu Mien children have American needs, that they need to be told by their parents, "I love you." This was not something that Iu Mien had a habit of saying. Based on my exposure to village language in Thailand in the early 1990s, *hnamv*, "love," came up in conversations primarily in the context of worry or serious concern, and not regarding romantic feelings or familial affection.[19]

Mien community leaders and social workers saw a crisis coming with regard to intergenerational tensions and miscommunication, and tried to be proactive. Young people obtained jobs, learned English, and organized activities and communities.

[18] I provide no literature review on this matter. Among the sources for Mien are (based on work in Portland) Jeffrey L. MacDonald, *Transnational Aspects of Iu-Mien Refugee Identity* (New York, NY: Garland, 1997) and (mostly from work in Oakland, CA, but also in Thailand and a brief visit to the Chiangkham refugee camp) Jonathan Habarad, "Spirit and the Social Order: The Responsiveness of Lao Iu Mien History, Religion, and Organization" (PhD dissertation, University of California, Berkeley, 1985); Jonathan Habarad, "Five Villages: Culture and Resilience among Lao Iu Mien," *Kroeber Anthropological Society Papers* 65–66 (1984): 83–100; and Jonathan Habarad, "Refugees and the Structure of Opportunity: Transitional Adjustments to Aid among US Resettled Lao Iu Mien, 1980–1985," *Center for Migration Studies Special Issues* 5,2 (1987): 66–87. Also from the Oakland area, Eric Crystal and Kaota Saepharn, "Iu-Mien: Highland Southeast Asian Community and Culture in California Context," in *Minority Cultures of Laos: Kammu, Lua', Lahu, Hmong, and Mien*, ed. Judy Lewis (Berkeley, CA: Center for Southeast Asian Studies, 1992), pp. 331–401. On some of the changing conditions of Hmong and Mien women in this new world, see Lynn Fujiwara, *Mothers without Citizenship: Asian Immigrant Families and the Consequences of Welfare Reform* (Minneapolis, MN: University of Minnesota Press, 2008). But recently Chaylium Saechao published her memoir, *From Broken Jar Mountain: Laos to San Francisco* (Berkeley, CA: Minuteman Press, 2013), which changes the whole field of knowing and learning with and from Mien people. Anything I write should be checked against her book.

[19] Smith Panh's *Modern English–Mienh and Mienh–English Dictionary* (Victoria, BC: Trafford Publishing, 2002), p. 95, has an entry for *hnamv camv*, which translates both as "love very much" and "sorrowful thought."

Parents and grandparents expected that a new daughter-in-law was at their beck and call, while young people would go out dancing and otherwise embrace various post-refugee-camp freedoms in a land that they—and not their elders—had learned to navigate. Social and cultural issues and differences, such as respect for elders and religious orientation, were now influenced by gender and generation.[20]

There were various immediate challenges. An unsuspecting neighbor might call the fire department when someone burned spirit money at the conclusion of a ritual. In other cases, non-Mien people called the police and reported drug use when Iu Mien people smoked their tobacco from a bamboo water pipe on their front porch ("we had to shift to the back yard"). The influx of Asian refugee immigrants was met with an often racist backlash and attacks on school playgrounds and along city streets. And as Iu Mien people earned enough money to move into their own apartments, sometimes drunkenness would lead to brawls and fights, followed by police intervention and arrests. There was, in short, a growing crisis that called for new forms of self–other help through community organizing.

When organizations were first formed among refugees from Laos, they were multiethnic, and there used to be soccer matches among the various Southeast Asian immigrants. But over time, many multiethnic organizations were replaced by ethnically focused groups. The case I know best is Portland, Oregon, where the rivalry between two Lao candidates for leadership led them to each form his own separate Lao association in 1978, and from then on the Mien, the Hmong, and others each formed their own groups.

Longtsing Tzeo told me about this time in Portland, Oregon. The "Halsey Square" noted here is a large housing complex where many of the refugee immigrants initially lived. The apartments are called something else now, and practically no Mien people live there anymore.

> A lot of Southeast Asians were labeled Vietnamese or Chinese. If there was fighting or gangs at Halsey Square, it made the Portland news. This is like in northern Portland, which is a black neighborhood; there is always some shooting, so the media will pick it up and characterize the neighborhood as bad.
>
> I was asked by a teacher where I lived, after some Lao kids beat up a white kid and it made the news. There was a general perception that Halsey Square was a bad area to live in, not safe. I told my teacher, I live in Halsey Square, it is fine. "Oh, maybe it's not a good idea," was the reply. But what makes the news is a one-time thing that could happen anywhere.
>
> Many kids attended Madison High School [but had] limited English; it was tough for them to survive high school. American kids assumed that [Asians] were all Vietnamese. One Vietnamese stabbed a white guy in a school fight. The next day a carload of white guys approached as I and three or four others were walking, they had baseball bats and were seeking revenge. "We're not Vietnamese, we know what happened; we had nothing to do with it." They

---

[20] Some of these issues are on view in the few Mien-based films there are, all of them very well done: *Death of a Shaman,* directed by Richard Hall, produced by Fahm Fong Saeyang (KVIE Public Television, 2004); *Kelly Loves Tony,* directed by Spencer Nakasano, produced by the National Asian American TeleCommunication Association in association with the Independent Television Service (San Francisco, CA: National Asian American Telecommunications Association, 1998); and *Moving Mountains: The Story of the Yiu Mien,* directed and produced by Elaine Velazquez (New York, NY: Filmmakers Library, 1991).

would yell, "You are all the same, go back to your country," and other remarks of the sort.

In the 1980s, there was sometimes tension at Halsey Square. There was a paved volleyball court, it was okay. Mien and maybe a few Lao would play volleyball all day long, with small bets of one or two dollars on the outcome. One day a white guy stopped by, looked menacing, out of control, and said, "you guys beat up one of my friends," and we had to call the police. Another time, four or five white guys with knives and baseball bats, wanting revenge for something, came up to us as we walked home from school. Yet another time, some random guy came from nowhere to Halsey Square, maybe drunk; he wanted revenge and to stab someone. There was an automatic response at the time that bad stuff came from Halsey Square; the media used to mention it that way. There were Lao guys, maybe four or five, who were brothers, they were like a gang, they beat up some white guys badly.

In 1983, welfare payments were cut and many Mien moved to California. That was the first move out of Halsey Square. Many went to Redding, California. For the most part, the ones who stayed on in Portland had jobs already. After 1985, [Mien people in Portland] started to buy homes. They'd use savings, a bank loan, and borrowed money from relatives. Houses were a lot cheaper then. The [Mien Fellowship Baptist] church cost $300,000, with the land; three- and four-bedroom houses were $40,000 to $50,000. Most people left Halsey Square in order to buy their own house. Rent during that time, for a two-bedroom apartment, was $250 per month, and $300–400 per month for a three-bedroom apartment. Back then the minimum wage was $3.25 or $3.50 an hour.

The accounts that I heard describing people's conversion to Christianity are varied. Some mentioned the difficulty of procuring live chickens in an American city, for the purpose of making offerings to ancestors. In Portland, there was an open-air market open for only one day during the weekend, and sometimes people had to stand in line for a long time in cold rain to buy a live chicken. On top of that, very few people had cars, and one young man continually had to drive to fetch a spirit medium and then return him home afterwards. One man converted to Christianity for love, it was the only way that his future wife's family would accept him. Some people talk of the healing power of the Lord, which I also heard in relation to conversions to Buddhism, Kuan Yin, and other Asian divinities. For the most part, other family members then join the convert.

In some cases, repeated illness or death within a family led people to give up on their ancestor spirits. While Iu Mien lived in farming villages in the Asian hinterlands, such occurrences might lead people simply to change ancestors by moving into a different household or otherwise establishing relations with a different set of spirits. Livelihood and social identities do not play out in the same way in US cities, nor do they offer the same options in moments of crisis.

Community organization has depended on context, and there is considerable difference from one city to another. In Oakland, California, the police force is much more aggressive and overtly racist than is the case in Portland, Oregon, so people in Oakland have networked around issues involving legal advice, self-defense in cases of police brutality, and the like. Another reason for community organizing through religious or cultural frameworks is the sense that bureaucrats don't care. To obtain advice or help that matters, people have to be self-reliant and competent, and then have some community they can approach in cases where family resources are insufficient or overstretched.

In both Oakland and Portland, the Mien are quite dispersed and this increases the value of community centers, including churches. In contrast, the Iu Mien in Redding, California, brought about something resembling a village atmosphere by purchasing houses adjacent to one another within three city blocks. There the need for a community center has not come up. One of my friends in Redding does not like the crowded atmosphere and has a house about a twenty-minute drive from the Mien concentration; as one who has resisted a trend, he confirms the diversity of everyday life. In yet another contrast, the largest settlement of Iu Mien in the United States is in Sacramento, California, where there is no community center.

In Sacramento, in notable contrast to some other settings, Iu Mien Christians and non-Christians have collaborated actively and extensively on educational issues and many other shared concerns. As elsewhere, this comes down to individual motivation and energies, and while it is often a thankless task, it is the only way to sustain a community. There has been a purportedly national Iu Mien organization for a long time, but most people did not show much interest in it at the time that I was learning about these things. For the most part, people say that conditions from one place to another are so particular that a national organization would not be helpful. Some are also skeptical of the influence any national leader could acquire, perhaps because they know how badly things went during the war and in camps under a strong leader who had considerable command over people's lives.

Tsan Tsong Chao gave me some indication of how people in Redding worked things out among themselves:

> We Mien help each other a lot. Some American people, they don't know where their family is. We help each other, we marry. You have to go to the party on New Years or to a wedding [to see how this is], there will be several hundred people. When my next son gets married, I will call you; you have to check it out. I invited my co-worker when my first son got married, and he asked, "who cooked all this food?" I said, we have all these people, a hundred people cooking. When my son got married, we killed two cows, and five pigs, and we had about four hundred people for one day. It was a big party. Friday night you prepare everything and then the next morning, by 4:00 AM, you start cooking, then people come about 11:00 AM and stay until 11:00 PM.[21]

Currently, all forms of Iu Mien religious practice have an international dimension. A translation of the Christian Bible involved Westerners as well as Mien people in Thailand, France, and the United States, who worked on the project for over a period of at least twenty years. The Romanization of the Mien language was triggered by missionary concerns, but the development of the script later became nonsectarian.[22] An American linguist with missionary connections worked with Iu Mien in the United States (non-Christians and Christians alike) on developing the current script, and they made the necessary connections in China, where the government's Nationalities Affairs Commission must authorize the proper way to

---

[21] Personal interview, Oregon mountains, October 11, 2007; and in Redding, CA, December 15, 2007.

[22] Purnell, "Developing Practical Orthographies."

Romanize a written language that uses characters or a different script. The effort to have a uniform written language thus involved Chinese and Yao from China, and Iu Mien from the United States, France, and elsewhere, in a collaboration that sidestepped factional concerns. Some of this work was continued when people went from the United States to an International Yao Studies Conference in Hong Kong in 1986.[23]

In the United States, one of the impacts of Christian conversions was the establishment of churches where people congregate once a week or more. Once established and running, these churches provided a model that others could respond to or try to counter. The King Pan Buddha Light Palace, completed and inaugurated in September, 2008, is the most elaborate response, and it is a ritual center on the same lot as a very active Iu Mien community center serving the Oakland–San Francisco Bay area. The community is so spread out that it is divided into eight districts, each with two or three leaders who organize activities among their constituents. Kouichoy Saechao, one of the organizers, made a parallel between the current districts and the twelve lineages of the Iu Mien. He said that the districts and lineages are united and equal through their relationship to King Pan, a founding ancestor and now a focus of veneration, "According to our myth and history, whenever we settle down permanently, then we have to build a permanent place of worship."

The King Pan temple has a parallel and precursor in an elaborate temple in Hunan Province, China, where the Chinese government is actively involved in promoting and influencing matters of minority identity for tourism and nation building.[24] There is a third King Pan temple in Chiangrai Province of northern Thailand, a small one-room building that holds some images.

In 1995, one or more Mien people each in China, Thailand, and California, at roughly the same time, were visited in a dream or a trance vision with the message that they had to establish a temple to King Pan, otherwise their culture and identity would fizzle away. This ultimately led to building the King Pan Buddha Light Palace. Because people have made connections, through migration histories, kinship, and the Romanization project for the Mien script, word got around, through letters and phone conversations. The dream message and people's response have increased contact among Mien in the three countries, not just through visits but also help. Because the Mien in Thailand did not know how to do the chant for King Pan, the most accomplished and involved spirit medium in the United States chanted for them, and it was transmitted by cell phone live to Thailand, where it was amplified by loudspeakers. "We just bought [telephone] calling cards and did it, that's all" commented one man in the United States.

King Pan (Bienh Hungh) is a founding ancestor of the Mien. He is too big a spirit to be called on by a household for everyday concerns. Only when the survival of the Mien people (as "the twelve lineages" or "King Pan's descendants") is at stake is it justifiable to call on him. The revival of Bienh Hungh as a focus of ritual veneration and community speaks in part to contemporary conditions of globalization and dispersion into ever more new surroundings where people must adjust. It also speaks to a structure of expectations and relations that was established a long time ago and was preserved in stories. The establishment of the temple in Oakland drew

---

[23] MacDonald, *Transnational Aspects of Iu-Mien Refugee Identity*, p. 255.
[24] Ibid., p. 252.

on the combination of dream messages, an existing community center and organization, and, perhaps, on the wish among non-Christians to offer an alternative to Iu Mien Christian churches as the focus of community life, identity, and communication. There was also a need to come up with religious forms that did not require the sacrifice of a chicken or a pig, as did ancestor worship, since most American Iu Mien youth wanted no part in such activities; they didn't get it.

As Christianity connects Iu Mien across distances and links them to Western missionaries and churches, King Pan is enabling new connections among China, Thailand, and the United States, and various forms of media make this veneration of King Pan accessible to Mien people in Canada, France, and elsewhere. People pool their resources to establish and maintain their community centers and religious institutions. The organizing committee has requested funds from city authorities in Oakland for the King Pan Buddha Light Palace—in part because the temple contributes to upgrading a rather run-down area—but, so far, as of 2013, they've had no success. Iu Mien people themselves have contributed practically the whole amount, with the rest provided through bank loans. The same holds for the Christian church that I went to most frequently in Portland; community members taxed themselves to pay for the land and the building. Having abandoned wartime orientations, Mien people shifted their efforts and resources toward making community and a future in the United States and elsewhere.

Kouichoy Saechao told me the following, about what led to the construction of the King Pan temple in Oakland:

> One of the reasons that we need to do this—I had been talking to our priests, grand priests, and senior priests—is that prior to migrating from China, a long time ago, we used to have temple, right? Even now, when they do a ceremony, they will call on empowerment from certain temples, they are still doing that, the shamans. So, since we have been pushed up to the mountains and then we used the temporary temple everywhere, every time we lived in the mountain area doing slash and burn. And when you get here, and this is time according to our *kia shen pong* [M. *jiex sen borngv*] and other texts of history that were passed on, that whenever the Iu Mien come down to the lowlands after a certain war and so on.
>
> You have to look at that history, the trend of our life. And we also have the belief that there is a message from a higher being to our individual mediums. They got the message in a trance that we really have to build a temple. The spiritual power of the ancestors from King Pan has gotten different in the recent past of the Iu Mien, so we need to honor him. Let me tell you why we have to have the King Pan Festival.
>
> I was the head of a delegation that went to China in 1995 for the grand opening of the King Pan Palace in Jang Hua, Hunan Province. Then I came back, and we started searching to buy property for our Iu Mien community to call our home. During that negotiation, I had this property [sale] pending, but we can never [close the deal], there were various problems with the city or neighbors or lenders or the owners. There were all these little challenges. This was in a residential area, so we had to have a conditional-use permit. After we moved back from West Virginia, then I had been searching. At one point we tried to establish a home in Dawson, West Virginia. We failed and then we moved our community to Montgomery, Alabama. Then finally we all moved back. We still

needed a place. This was about thirty-seven people, about ten families. We settled back in Oakland and San Francisco [California]. Our community said we feel strongly that we cannot rely on outsiders to give us money or to get us land. We have to invest ourselves.

We gradually [collected] donations from our members, who understood that we wanted to build a center and a temple. Our main goal is to have balance in life; we have social space and spiritual space. I always had some obstacles with paperwork moving [the project] through. And then we got a special message from our ancestors, from our Buddha. This came to a spirit medium in a trance. They [spirit mediums] called me up and said, "you have to show up here, you have to come listen to this." When I came there, they said, I, we, Iu Mien, especially me, have to be responsible to have this for honoring our ancestor, King Pan. Then things will be able to move smoothly. Right there I accepted that responsibility for [the request] that came in that spiritual trance, for the high being that we have to honor.

This is to tell us that we cannot forget our ancestor. We have to honor our ancestor, honor our Buddha, and the Bodhisatva, in order to have the blessing. We already have the blending of Buddhism and Daoism in our culture, in our religion. But nobody really practiced, due to our life in Laos, where we did slash and burn agriculture. So now we are settled down permanently here. According to our myth and history, whenever we settle down permanently, then we have to have a permanent place of worship. Not a temporary temple, like when people [are in a place for a short time]. I accepted that responsibility and said that, as soon as I have these papers signed, then we will have our festival honoring our King Pan.

That was in 1996, that's when we bought the property. This was in August or September. Then two weeks after that we got the conditional-use permit, all the obstacles were lifted. For the [King Pan] Festival, we had to have a Grand Priest [to do the] offering and honoring, because we had a lot of karma in the twelve clans, the six brothers and sisters had done a lot of good things and a lot of unpleasant things over their lifetimes. So we had to start doing something good. That's the reason we started our first King Pan Festival. We had also been talking about how we could come together as a community; we had to build a place for our people to worship our ancestors and high beings.

Instead of doing the same thing that we used to do [we changed the traditions], because nowadays when you sacrifice a chicken or a pig for a ceremony the younger generation will not get involved. That's the only way that we will bring our people together, that's what the [spirit] message said. So, our obligation is that every clan has to do the King Pan [festival], and we take turns, so that in twelve years each lineage will have been at the center at one point. So that's why this year [2007] was the most significant and important one for the completion of the twelve clans.[25]

The elective conversions of immigrants from ancestor worship to Christianity or other faiths, as individuals or as families, actually confirms their sense of ethnic belonging, though this may seem counterintuitive to Westerners. Being Christian is a way to be Iu Mien, in much the same way as Thomas Pearson suggests for refugee

---

[25] Personal interview, Oakland, CA, December 16, 2007.

immigrants in the United States and Montagnard–Dega in Vietnam.[26] This dynamic, of conversion as a way to become ethnic, may seem new because it combines Christianity and Asian refugees, but it has long been important in Southeast Asia. From what I related about the landscapes of regional history in Mainland Southeast Asia, we see that ethnicities and other identities are continually being shaped and reshaped within various networks of relations. Suggesting that ethnicities happened only in relation to states or to colonial regimes, as some academics do at times, occludes much longer histories as much as it denies the present.

As Iu Mien people became urban wage-workers in the United States, their engagements with ritual and ethnicity necessarily took new forms. But for the Iu Mien, their spiritual and ethnic orientation ranges among ancestors, Daoism, Christianity, Bienh Hungh, and Buddhism (with or without a Kuan Yin focus). People have come to divergent expressions of their identity, but not for the first time. Previously, difference was manifest in a ranked scheme of ritual contracts. The most exclusive were ordinations with expensive offerings. Veneration of the ancestors was more generally attainable and affordable, while those people with practically no means could not engage in exchanges with the spirit world and had no status in social life.

Seen from that angle, the new religious and social forms are more accommodating of economic difference than were the old, and do not divide people as "poor," "getting by," or "rich," as ritual activity in Laos and Thailand did previously. While competition and rivalry a century ago connected people as it differentiated them by household, village, and kin group, the shared sense of minority identity in the urban United States may be separating immigrants by religious affiliation while, at the same time, uniting them in the creative fashioning of ways to be Iu Mien in a new land.

Rivalries among chiefs during the 1880s to 1930s offer a context for examining community dynamics among the refugees who settled in the United States. In the old settings, in Laos and Thailand, young, aspiring upland leaders came to place themselves in relations with lowland kings and to focus on farming, which enabled them to assemble a household that would outdo their rivals. In the United States, the men who shape new forms of community and identity acquired English language skills in refugee camps or through work with the US military agents in Laos and Thailand. When they settled in the United States, they received training and sometimes jobs in social work and came to mediate a new reality for their Iu Mien constituents in the 1980s and after.

Kouichoy Saechao told me how they came to a workable community organization in the San Francisco Bay area of California:

> Prior to 1991, we used to have one chief, using the same model from the Lao village, to oversee the well-being of the members in Oakland, in Richmond, in San Francisco, in San Jose, and in other communities. Time went by, and we found that it was very difficult for communication, to share messages and so on. I am one of the founders of the cultural association [LIMCA, Lao Iu Mien Cultural Association], we decided this [that we needed more than one chief] among many elders and leaders. This is only internally, we respect them as

---

[26] Thomas Pearson, *Missions and Conversions: Creating the Montagnard–Dega Refugee Community* (New York, NY: Palgrave, 2009).

caring and loving individuals, that's why we call them leaders; they are like spiritual leaders, healers, and elders. Then we thought we had to find a way that was comparable to the US system [of local government]. We came up with district, that the best way to [coordinate and care for each other] is if people come from the same village. They are related, they know each other, they care [because] they […] live together and share experiences together.

Each district is made up of two or three villages. You mentioned Taa Fang, Pin Hoi, and Ban Sam Sao [in Laos]; [people from there] know each other, so [here] we group them together as one district. In a district, we have two or three leaders as the contact persons. By doing this, we save a lot of money for the [local] cops, the government, because we solve problems ourselves inside the community, instead of going to the police. Why eight districts? Because we looked at the puzzle and tried to figure out how many communities are here, for San Francisco and Oakland. Now in Sacramento, they adopted this model, too, but there they have more people and have eleven districts. When they say "Oakland District One," then they know who is the leader. The district leader has a term of four years. Three district leaders [in one district] have to coordinate with each other. For information, events, graduation, emergency, whatever, they have to call to support each other.[27]

Settlement in Laos and Thailand over a century ago played to rivalries among farmers with chiefly ambitions, and settlement in the United States has also brought leadership opportunities. Some contemporary leaders have been ambitious and claimed credit for making the settlement possible and for paving the way to reinforce connections back in China and Southeast Asia. But most people dispute such claims and insist that this has very much been a collective effort that rests on multiple collaborations, for which no individual can take sole credit. And for all of the occasional rivalries, the many people who have contributed to shaping Iu Mien forms of community and identity in the United States have managed to produce constructive organizations and networks. Each of them has found ways to bridge generation gaps by informing parents about their children's different orientations and needs, and, at the same time, found ways to give older people—whose capabilities usually were no match for new forms of language, education, social life, and transportation—a role in maintaining and contributing to new ways of being together.

There has been considerable creative innovation in religious practice. One non-Christian example are the *jouh en lua* offerings to ancestor spirits that are supposed to make people wealthy. I have not seen the practice carried out, and the friend who told me about it commented that he never once heard of it back in Laos. But certain innovations are actively blocked. For instance, young women are still not taught how to deal with spirits. To the ones interested, this would be useful and a sign of greater equality. The response to them has been that only men are pure enough to engage with the spirit world. This has in general discouraged young women from engaging with the traditionalist community. When Thailand's Mien formed an ethnic association in the early 1990s, the issue played out in precisely the same way. There, the young women who were interested in learning how to handle rituals and otherwise take a more active part in religious life and ethnic traditions later married

---

[27] Personal interview, Oakland, CA, December 16, 2007.

outside the ethnic group, where they sought measures of equality and participation that their own communities had denied them in the name of ethnic traditions.[28]

While refugee immigrants have come to learn and appreciate various things about their new home country, they sometimes comment on the social isolation of white American lives, commenting that such people sometimes either get lost or value their freedom at the cost of mutual social obligations. One perspective was offered by Jiem Lao Chao:

> The meaning in our language and culture needs to be passed to the younger generation. I find this very important in many, many ways. I work with the general public, mainstream American people here [as a social worker]. Every day they come to see me. I look at them; some people, they are just lost. They don't know where to start, they stay low; their lives continue to get worse. Those who have connections [over generations] and good family functions, they would have a better life.[29]

In Portland in 2007, Kao-Chiem's pop music band once rented a dance hall and did a show. Not many attended, and the group may have lost money on the evening. A Hmong woman had the band's synthesizer player perform the background to her rendition of the Hmong-language version of Lionel Richie's "Love You More than I Can Say." This had never been a song I much cared for, but, for me, it took on a string of positive associations once it had been flipped through a Southeast Asian refugee immigrant language at an event with some friends. Some of the women were teaching the steps to various line dances and square dances that were too complicated for me, so I just watched and chatted. One of the women told me, "We learned [the dances] in Minneapolis; there are nine Hmong discos there, and they have lots of dances."

Learning to move differently, and to different tunes, has been one way immigrants have learned to move into different times and selves with various others. That is the image I want to keep of the Hmong from Laos: people creatively engaging with ostensibly trivial things, such as pop songs and square dances, in the United States, finding their feet in a more peaceful world. For the longest time, the effects of prolonged war had denied them their humanity, and these little things help reassert what and who they might be: skilled, playful, good company, and carefree for a change.[30]

PERSPECTIVES

Thirty years ago, anthropologist A. Thomas Kirsch argued that "any future anthropology will also be an anthropology of the future." In his opinion, this was not about abandoning studies of past or present, but instead about "opening up the

---

[28] Hjorleifur Jonsson, *Mien Relations: Mountain People and State Control in Thailand* (Ithaca, NY: Cornell University Press, 2005), p. 116.

[29] Personal interview, Portland, OR, November 20, 2008.

[30] For an introduction to the Hmong, see Chia Youyee Vang, *Hmong America: Reconstructing Community in Diaspora* (Urbana, IL: University of Illinois Press, 2010).

temporal and the spatial boundaries within which anthropologists work."[31] I have tried to aim for something of the sort in this book. My concern lay in finding ways to traverse some landscapes of scholarship, history, warfare, festivals, refugee camps, and community organizations with Mien people and some of their others.

The past is not only the past. As an academic, I suggest that we engage with the past and present with a purpose, and that the whole point must be aimed toward equality and justice and some constructive futures. In my case, this effort revolves around Mien peoples at home and away as much as it does anthropology and area studies in parallel universes. I do not treat Mien identity, culture, or history as an ethnographic object, but as a way to specify and engage with the intersections of history, identity, national scholarship, politics, and epistemology that our work has tended to ignore.

With the Mien in the United States, I went through something similar to what Jane Guyer described regarding how changes happen in anthropology. I personally absorbed much of the academic work that I have subjected to critical examination here because I was "challenged, criticized, shamed, or inspired by 'another' to whom [I am] absolutely committed to listening."[32] Having been somewhat critical of scholars whose work I have learned from, I resist any dismissal of anyone's work. There is no telling where and when we learn things; we only find out when we apply that knowledge to particular situations.

Learning with the Mien, I know that they and I cannot claim any political innocence, but suggest that acknowledging some uncomfortable pasts is a way to insist on shaping more positive futures, and to do so together with particular people in specific circumstances. When Tom Kirsch published his piece on the anthropology of the future, no one noticed or appreciated it, as far as he could tell. I found this out later when I studied with him. He may not have been the first to have the idea, but I see it as my task to pass it on.

Rather than suggest that anthropology can see through what the Mien have been doing and toward some reality that is only accessible to academics—which is an old elitist refrain that implicates academics in social stratification and its justifications—I think that we can learn from and with the Mien. They had, in many ways, lost everything and several times over: their farms, a home country, security, friends and family, and, finally, any previous convictions about their identity once the militia started robbing and killing its own people. And they came through with very constructive and generally democratic forms of community that stressed interactions, competence, and intergenerational relations. What the ethnic militia did has its parallels elsewhere—in China, Laos, French-ruled colonies, Germany, Thailand, Cambodia, and the United States; there have been many such cases, involving some people who are motivated to kill their fellow nationals or fellow humans because they represent an alien threat. I do not present the Mien as being saints, but it seems to me that, as an ethnic group, they have been better than many people at coming to new terms of identity and community after one such crisis, and in ways that preclude a repeat of that crisis.

---

[31] A. Thomas Kirsch, "Anthropology: Past, Present, Future—Toward an Anthropology of Anthropology," in *Crisis in Anthropology, View from Spring Hill, 1980*, ed. E. Adamson Hoebel, Richard L. Currier, and Susan Kaiser (New York, NY: Garland, 1982), p. 108.

[32] Jane I. Guyer, "Anthropology in Area Studies," *Annual Review of Anthropology* 33 (2004): 518.

I close this chapter with a Mien exorcism of sorts, and this reflects my training from scholars who studied ethnic groups and their religion, and the "classical" readings from which I learned. We do need to fashion other intersections with the world, rather than retreat to the common reflex of sealing off ourselves in assumed modernity by refusing interested and open engagements with some pasts. I suggest that our idea of politics as variously oppressive or inherently antagonistic across certain frontiers is such a bad idea that it should be treated in the same way that Mien in my old field site responded to wild spirits (*hieh mienv*): They don't belong, and they only bring danger, misfortune, and harm. Some spirits belong in a Mien household, though only on a temporary basis; others do not, ever. If we can only tell things from the consequences, then we should examine how certain notions of the state, or of ethnicity and race, influence our ability to comprehend fields of relations, and then take some constructive follow-up steps.

Only a spirit medium (*sipv-mienv mienh*) can handle wild spirits in a Mien setting. So far this has only been possible for men, though many things can change. The medium draws on power derived from his lineage of teachers with whom he must maintain respectful relations. The chant he does mostly from memory, though he may consult his handbook, and he needs to know the genealogy of the ancestors of household members to ensure that all is as safe as possible. The act, like ethnography or other representation among realms, is always a risk. As he chants, he lures in the spirit with good things, such as rice grains and spirit-money bills. His big spirit-medium knife has many coins on it, and he makes them rattle to lure the spirit toward him. Wild spirits don't take simple orders to leave a certain location because they are feeding off what they can. As the medium attracts the wild spirit, he slowly traps it by folding the money bill around the rice grains upon which it had come to feed.

Meanwhile, the spirit medium's assistant has been fashioning a little boat, perhaps two or three feet long, out of banana leaves. He has made a house on the boat, and he has made little human-like effigies of spirits that surround it. The house and the human figurines are made of straw. Then the medium places the trapped spirit inside that house structure; it is a prison cell surrounded by guards. Now the spirit medium has abandoned all sweet talk and the temptations of riches and instead chants a string of threats describing the torture this spirit would meet if it were ever to return. The assistant carries the boat with its contents carefully to the edge of the village, where he puts it down. The spirit medium is still instilling fear in the wild spirit when they light a match and burn the thing badly enough to harm the spirit while not badly enough so destroy it, so that wounded spirit acts as a reminder of the encounter for other spirits and as a warning to them. The medium had set up the objects necessary for the ritual partly outside the house, where he now burns spirit money that flames convert from this world to the other one, to thank his unseen benefactors and assistants. He has certain relationships to maintain, and he works to preclude some others. That, I think, is politics.

The harm done in the Mien ritual of expelling a wild spirit was strategic and premeditated, and it did not spill elsewhere. The whole thing was devoted to protecting human well-being on a local scale, and it was a success. Being just an ethnographer, it has taken me twenty years to use this ritual for a perspective on anthropology, area studies, and theory. Ethnography is risky; it is about the same things as Mien rituals and politics—human contact, relations across difference, possible futures, and things that we may consciously or inadvertently burn.

Once, at a Mien New Year in northern Thailand in the early 1990s, many of us had been up for hours by the time day broke. We were having tea and chatting when, suddenly, *bang-bang-bang-bang-bang!* It felt like that loud sound would go on forever. Someone had lit firecrackers outside—this was the thing to do at New Year. The noise was for both humans and spirits, but it translates differently in each realm. One of my old sources and companions, a spirit medium, was explaining to me, when I was coming to understand some basics, why, in each chant, a medium has to invite the spirits three times in order for them to come: "Spirits are stupid, they don't pay much attention to people." When the firecrackers exploded, this explanation came up again as the reason for why things were suddenly so loud that we couldn't talk: That level of noise is needed to reach the spirit world.

In reference to academic study, I think that my old friend might be suggesting that the relationship between knowledge and power is arbitrary and that it has to be established through experience and observation for each case or setting.[33] Spirits, like the Mien and myself, are not a thing, but each can become one component in a field of relations. This is where new things can happen, in contrast to the scientific pin-ups of social types with already known characteristics or fate. If we can learn to see our selves in the social and academic picture, then we may wish to learn how the components interact. From that point, we may come into relations with particular selves and others, and then decide where we would like to take the effort.

---

[33] Here I am thinking with some old friends about the extended academic fascination in the United States with the works of Michel Foucault, *Power/Knowledge: Selected Interviews and Other Writings, 1972–1977*, ed. Colin Gordon (New York, NY: Pantheon Books, 1980).

AFTERWORD

COMING HOME, SLOWLY

For a good part of the twentieth century, anthropologists went to Southeast Asia to find and describe ethnic groups. Looking for pure samples, they tended to seek out-of-the-way communities that showed little sign of interaction with national societies. Not only did the scholars find what they were looking for, they did so in ways that normalized the outcomes in Burma, Laos, Vietnam, and Thailand. The recent analytical and theoretical shift from focusing on autonomous ethnic groups and concentrating instead on the various dynamics of marginalization, governmentality, and the like has, in some ways, simply changed the premise of how anthropologists keep finding what they seek, in ways that never insist on the ordinariness and urgency of negotiating diversity. Scholars conducting research in Southeast Asia have long provided an interested audience with a sense of a world wherein they cannot expect difference to be an opportunity for creative engagements for mutual benefit.

The case for Zomia is one logical conclusion to all this work. Had that case not implicated my own writing, I might never have sought a different sense of the Southeast Asian past and present and their relevance for anthropology and social life. My sense of the place relies on the essence of play, of call and response, rhythm and repetition, of playing out a premise in terms of some mutual agreement and then making a deliberate move to influence the way certain complex interactions can materialize once there are some accumulated outcomes from which to base an assessment. I respond with an alternative take on the same two thousand years others have studied and allude to patterns shaped for much longer and more generally as a feature of human sociality involving intersubjectivity and negotiation.

There is no undisputed scientific way of establishing origins or other boundaries of humanity in the past or present: questions of where the lines should be drawn can only be settled in moral and mythical terms.[1] A promising alternative would be to draw a distinction between objective facts—which can boost a researcher's claims to scientific authority and, in the process, dismiss ordinary people's knowledge except as "data" for science—and significant facts, those that enfold and express negotiations of reality with the peoples whom our work concerns in one or another way.[2]

---

[1] Robert Proctor, "Temporality as an Artifact: How New Ideas of Race, Brutality, Molecular Drift, and the Powers of Time have Affected Conceptions of Human Origins," in *A New History of Anthropology*, ed. Henrika Kuklick (Malden, MA: Blackwell, 2008), p. 273; and Lee Drummond, *American Dreamtime: A Cultural Analysis of Popular Movies and Their Implications for a Science of Humanity* (Lanham, MD: Littlefield Adams Books, 1996).

[2] I take this distinction between kinds of facts from archaeologist Alison Wylie, "The Promise and Perils of an Ethic of Stewardship," in *Embedding Ethics*, ed. Lynn Meskell and Peter Pels (New York, NY: Berg, 2005), pp. 59–60.

If we seek "significant facts," this implies that we will attend to diversity and the need for negotiation, and also a sense of purpose. Once a purpose has been decided, then people can come into particular roles and relationships. That is the essence of myth, play, and human intersubjectivity. By telling some stories involving the Mien past and present that counter the inevitability of assumed cultural or political loss and instead show the foundational value of negotiating difference, I suggest that we can benefit from a regional perspective and an evolutionary orientation in (perhaps) new ways.

Negotiations toward equivalences that respected, required, and occasionally made up difference were foundational to the shaping of social life and diversity in Mainland Southeast Asia. This matters not because such activities established a past to be revered, but because they suggest futures to be shaped—at home, away, and between them through representations anchored to mutual agreements and accountability. Political negotiation in the Asian hinterland is as old as social life in these hills, going back perhaps ten thousand years. Academic understandings of the modern nation state as a fundamental break with the past contribute to the silencing of certain social possibilities by making them unthinkable as relevant responses to contemporary worlds.[3]

It would be authoritarian to try to police what representations are trafficked between Southeast Asia or any other site of ethnological extraction and the Western audiences of academic books. But this sort of approach is useful when it makes people perhaps more aware of this extraction and traffic, how they work, and what may be at stake at home, away, and between those different locations. I saw my shadow and footprints in the case for Zomia and viewed the case as spelling out certain trouble. From that understanding, I tried—by reexamining the ethnographic and historical sources—to make things come out differently for the people I write about, those I write for, and for myself.

Both the traditional–ethnic–culture notion and the Zomia–notion take for granted that Asian highlanders were culturally shaped in isolation from lowland states and that their misfit societies would expire with modernity; these two notions simply offered different understandings of the process by which these cultures would fade. The characters and the outcome inhere in the premise. I don't accept the implications of either notion. In part, my response is that of an ethnographer; I work with contemporary peoples, Mien and others, and to me nothing is gained and much is lost by accepting that the real Mien were highlanders and that the real highland peoples thrived in isolation from modernity and from the negotiation of difference. As an ethnographer, my response can only go so far. But as an anthropologist of Mainland Southeast Asia, I can suggest an areal and historical image or representation that complements, and challenges, the above two myths with a different myth. This alternative myth asserts that sociality, representation, and the negotiation of difference for mutual benefit are foundational to humanity past and present.

Southeast Asia has always been diverse, ethnically, linguistically, and otherwise. More often than not, people have both made and taken difference as an opportunity for exchanges and other interactions of mutual benefit. From a combination of archaeology and linguistics, we may come to know patterns of ongoing negotiations

---

[3] This assertion is central to Benedict Anderson's *Imagined Communities: Reflections on the Origins and Spread of Nationalism* (London: Verso, 1983).

across difference, and I have striven to extend and apply these insights to the issues within the reach of cultural anthropology. Nothing (beyond racial ideologies that are endorsed by some contemporary national elites) supports the conventional models that define certain ethnolinguistic families and/or ethnically distinct tool traditions and social organizations, and propose that these distinctions are key to the region's diversity. Instead, we need to examine each case of interactions as singular and try to work from that to a sense of patterns, wielding some deep familiarity and indiscriminate curiosity.

Episodes of discrimination, conflict, warfare, and social collapse can be made to fit a general story about inherent antagonisms at ethnic frontiers. I took several such examples to tell a different story. I refuse to accept the upland–lowland divide as an ethnological premise. There have been periods when this particular social boundary has been both actual and consequential. My refusal concerns the politics inherent in particular ethnologies. I can no longer participate in producing the sense that there is an inherent conflict of interest between such highland and lowland groups as those labeled "Mien" and "Thai," nor do I assume that there is any inherent uniformity, homogeneity, or harmony of interests within any such highland group labeled "the Mien." Difference and diversity are analytical and social starting points that need not imply antagonism, but rather negotiation, experimentation, and an examination of the outcomes.

If I am to speculate on Mien origins, then I would propose that those origins draw on a cluster of ideas and practices that combine rice (or another grain) farming, rituals to spirits, and the domestication of chickens and pigs that are offered to the spirits in exchange for the soul-stuff that animates crops, domestic animals, and people's health. This farming-ritual-exchange complex brings about social units—households, kin-groups, and villages. Social life then reinforces the "agro-cultural complex,"[4] such as through the negotiation of marriages. People are experimental and observant in the production of food-crops, and this experimentation does not simply involve plants. Laura Rival, writing on the domestication of plants in the Amazon region, comments:

> The humans who first domesticated plants [perhaps fifteen thousand years ago] were capable of cognitive fluidity and creative imagination; they had religious beliefs and expressed their emotions through art forms. Domestication was, and still is, a conscious process. The actions of observing and experimenting, like those of selecting and propagating, are guided by cultural representations. The motivations underlying the actions involved in reproducing plants—or any form of life for that matter—are neither purely pragmatic nor simply aesthetic. Intellectual and scientific curiosity plays a role as well.[5]

My reason for speculating about Mien origins in an agro–cultural complex is, in part, due to the challenge posed by Zomia; what were people trying to achieve with their hinterland adaptations? The practical aspects of Mien farming, rituals, and

---

[4] The term is from Richard A. O'Connor, "Agricultural Change and Ethnic Succession in Southeast Asian States: A Case for Regional Anthropology," *Journal of Asian Studies* 54,4 (1995): 968–96.

[5] Laura Rival, "Domesticating the Landscape: Producing Crops and Reproducing Society in Amazonia," in *Holistic Anthropology: Emergence and Convergence*," ed. David Parkin and Stanley Ulijaszek (New York, NY: Berg, 2007), p. 88.

householding are all intertwined. But Mien as a people of the greater Mainland Southeast Asian region were also shaped by their interactions with traders, lowland leaders, and various others. Such adaptations helped create a differentiation between Mien chiefs and commoners. Without chiefs, who might receive an official title, there could be no interactions with certain lowland authorities. The designation of such Mien leaders made possible mutual accommodations between chiefs and commoners, and chiefs and lowland traders or authorities. And, of course, such relationships might also, at one or another time, fail.

In my historical understanding of the Mien, they have the same experimental and pragmatic approach to lowland authorities as they do to spirits—either and both can be made to avail certain benefits on the basis of contracts and particular exchanges. Power works similarly in the political world and in the spirit world; contracts and exchanges are necessary to keep things going and some benefits flowing. On the basis of this understanding, I could gradually assemble a response to the challenge of the Zomia analysis; nothing I know about the Mien would support the notion that they, as a highland people, were aiming to achieve freedom through some disconnection from regional exchanges, interactions, and even taxation or tribute. If a chief, a settlement, or a multi-village unit has paid its dues as part of a particular relationship, then they can call for some appropriate recompense, and this possibility was generally seen as an asset and not an act of extraction. If people have a relationship with a spirit or a lowland ruler, they can abandon the relationship when things don't turn out well, but, from the cases I know, Mien people have only reacted harshly against spirits or rulers when relations have either been absent or been denied.[6]

Here I use the term "Mien" to make a general point, but, of course, any particular Mien population has taken specific shape in terms of what relations are available to the group in any particular locality, and there has also been considerable variety in Mien ritual practice according to lineage and sublineage distinctions. Acting through a household offers the participants one set of relations to spirits (ancestors, spirit government, soldier spirits), while people may, as members of a village, have additional and separate relations to a village owner spirit (in most cases, the spirit of a valley ruler), and multi-village units may, through a chief, have yet other links. Households, villages, and multi-village units (through a chief) are each a "container" with a particular ritual- and social orientation that may be at odds with the others. People without the agricultural means to sustain a relationship with ancestors could not engage in the exchange of blessings that were standard at feasts following certain rituals. The unmarried children of a household did not have their own links to spirits, so they, too, did not participate in exchanging blessings. Thus, a married person's household link into the spirit world was a prerequisite for certain forms of sociality and identity that were premised on the proceeds of rice fields and domestic animals.

From the historical case that I made for Mien in Laos and Thailand during 1880–1940, it is clear that the agendas and options of small households and super-households were quite distinct and, in some ways, at odds. Further, for Mien in Laos during 1960–1975, households and the ethnic militia were separate "containers" for social and other orientations and were, at times, clearly at odds. In the public life of

---

[6] Hjorleifur Jonsson, *Mien Relations: Mountain People and State Control in Thailand* (Ithaca, NY: Cornell University Press, 2005), pp. 78–85.

Thailand's Mien during 1960–2012, there has been a fundamental shift from households to villages as the site of action and identity, while the action itself reveals tensions among village leaders and headmasters, farming couples, NGO workers, and teenagers, and these tensions may also fall along gender lines. Mien society has never been singular; the same holds for highland and lowland societies more generally.[7]

Mien negotiations of difference during 1860–1940 emphasized chiefs as links to lowland worlds, but recognized households, kin groups, villages, and chiefs as links to the spirit world. Most chiefs lost their lowland connections and, thus, also lost their local relevance in the early years of the twentieth century, but some Mien leaders in Laos and Thailand played a part in new connections related to the opium monopoly trade, national integration, and, in Laos, a civil war that had international sponsors. Since the 1980s in Thailand, the negotiation of difference has increasingly involved village festivals manifesting village-, subdistrict-, and ethnic identity. Village festivals are the predominant contemporary "container" for ritual- and social orientations, and the focus of such a festival is primarily on the nation—the social relevance of households and kin groups has largely been eclipsed by other "containers."

Many factors have surely motivated the Mien people's action in recent decades or previous centuries, but there is no evidence of a widespread concern with standing outside social, ritual, economic, and other obligations. Instead, the only people who stood outside such networks were the destitute. My observations have taught me that this—destitution—has not been a social position anyone aspires to. For this reason, I do not believe in the quest for freedom as a premise of highlander identities. But I recognize how that analysis might derive from settings of social collapse, where there is fundamental mistrust and hostility between some settlements or even whole social categories, categories that might include anything from certain highland villages to all of Thailand's Hmong at one time, or many of Burma's ethnic minority populations for the last decades—and lowland authorities.

By becoming familiar with the whole range of highland people's experiences of the ethnic frontier, or the "full house," to use a term zoologist Stephen Jay Gould

---

[7] For this approach to society in the Southeast Asian uplands and lowlands, see A. Thomas Kirsch, *Feasting and Social Oscillation: Religion and Society in Upland Southeast Asia* (Ithaca, NY: Cornell Southeast Asia Program Publications, 1973); and A. Thomas Kirsch, "Loose Structure: Theory or Description?" in *Loosely Structured Social Systems: Thailand in Comparative Perspective*, ed. Hans-Dieter Evers (New Haven, CT: Yale University Southeast Asia Studies, 1969), pp. 39–60. For the notion of "containers," I draw on Richard A. O'Connor, "Max, Tom, and Regions: Finding Southeast Asia among 'Meaning,' 'Power,' and 'In-group Displays,'" paper presented at "Religion, Society, and Popular Culture: An Interdisciplinary Symposium Honoring A. Thomas Kirsch," Cornell University Department of Anthropology, Ithaca, NY, February 19–20, 1999.

For case studies that highlight diversity, specificity, contradictions, and conflict of interest within highland ethnic labels and situate this in interethnic relations (including upland–lowland and state–minority), see Yoko Hayami, "Internal and External Discourse of Communality, Tradition, and Environment: Minority Claims on Forest in the Northern Hills of Thailand," *Southeast Asian Studies* 35,3 (1997): 558–79; Yoko Hayami, "Negotiating Ethnic Representation between Self and Other: The Case of Karen and Eco-tourism in Thailand," *Southeast Asian Studies* 44,3 (2006): 385–409; and Pierre Petit, "Ethnic Performance and the State in Laos: The *Boun Greh* Annual Festival of the Khmou," *Asian Studies Review* 37,4 (2013): 471–90.

advocates regarding studies of evolution,[8] one may come to recognize whether any one position or orientation is general or specific, and then to specify the situations where it appears. In recognizing how some particular experiences on Burma's ethnic frontier helped inform the image of a forever-escaping-highlander identity, I am not suggesting that it is invalid to draw on that situation of extended civil war and study the results. But we must be aware that this situation did not determine the shape of certain Asian ethnic frontiers over the last one or two thousand years, though it certainly influenced a particular situation for the last sixty years, a situation dominated socially and otherwise by antagonistic militias.

To supply the means for a different journey through Southeast Asian history, it is not enough to revise notions of what highlanders may be and have been; I have to offer a different characterization of the state. For this end, I draw on Greek philosopher Aristotle, who, in his *Politics,* suggests that a state (*polis*) is whatever community people establish for a collective purpose that can balance their different needs; any such community draws on "a social instinct [that] is implanted in all men by nature."[9] In order to make his case, Aristotle assembled the histories and noted the compositions of more than 150 states in the Mediterranean region. He distinguished among forms of government on a range from democracy to aristocracy to tyranny and explored how each of these played out.

That is, Aristotle held no categorical conviction about the state or about which form of political community would fit all conditions. Instead, he recognized that conditions having to do with population, resources, trade, and warfare were varied and important, but his aim was to find the arrangements that would best serve the diverse interests of its many stakeholders. He did not see the value in a uniform population, such as that one finds axiomatic in so many contemporary nationalisms: "[If a nation seeks any kind of self-sufficiency then] the lesser degree of unity is more desirable than the greater."[10] Difference can challenge people to arrive at some creative solutions that bridge groups in ways that are of mutual benefit, if they are so inclined. Aristotle's *Politics* is packed with examples of failure and political collapse. Any one of society's factions can turn against the interests of another, or families or the members of a faction or a city can fall apart because of internal conflict. This is not a naïvely optimistic image of politics or of community, and it seems rather realistic:

> A certain amount of social conflict and distrust is unavoidable among individuals who share an agreement about political justice. This distrust and conflict is part of the price, Aristotle would suggest, that we pay for political community. Hobbes is unwilling to pay that price and seeks to eliminate these sources of social conflict and distrust by suppressing our tendency to argue about substantive standards of justice. Aristotle is willing to pay that price not only because of the great value that he places on the capacities that Hobbes

---

[8] Stephen Jay Gould, *Full House: The Spread of Excellence from Plato to Darwin* (New York, NY: Harmony Books, 1996).

[9] Aristotle, *The Politics and the Constitution of Athens,* ed. Stephen Everson (Cambridge: Cambridge University Press, 1996), p. 14 (*Politics,* book 1, section 2).

[10] Ibid., p. 32 (*Politics,* Book 2, Section 2).

wants to suppress but also because he believes that any attempt to suppress these capacities will ultimately be self-defeating.[11]

Human sociality brings about a political community, and when it works well, then it is because the challenges of negotiating for mutual benefit and against exclusive self-interest bring out arrangements that can be sustained across difference. The aim of the political community is justice, but this is something that must be worked out in practice in each particular case. Morality cannot be legislated; the law can guard against certain harm and abuses, but the rest has to be worked out among the people who are party to a specific network of relations. If people can hold one another accountable, across difference, then justice can be brought about and sustained. Justice can be achieved when people have acquired a degree of friendship among themselves and their respective groups, suggests Aristotle in the *Nicomachean Ethics*, and he suggests that friendships are made and maintained through exchanges that combine "utility and pleasure."[12]

In three of Aristotle's works, *The Poetics*, *The Politics*, and the *Nicomachean Ethics*, he calls attention to human nature in ways that I find productive and stimulating for anthropology. Humans are, by nature, social, and they can harness this trait in ways that produce beneficial political community or may destroy it. While the aim of a political community is justice, and to shape a community that thrives on the negotiation of mutual benefit across various difference, the effort to create such a state cannot solely be a utilitarian pursuit because people also need distractions and pleasure. And humans are dependent on representation; this is how any of us learns, and both the apprehension of a representation and the act of understanding are sources of pleasure.

This view of human nature is perhaps not mainstream in anthropology or elsewhere, but some recent work has called attention to human uniqueness in terms of sociality that rests on both the capacity and the need for representation, intersubjectivity, common ground, and the ability to trade perspectives.[13] Michael Tomasello's research suggests several dimensions of this approach, in innovative comparative studies involving infants and chimpanzees.[14] Apes don't point, he shows, because they do not have the ability or the need for intersubjectivity and the trading of identities and perspectives. This characteristic, this sort of exchange, is what made humans what we are. Among the features that define human cognition and action are the capacity for joint attention and an inclination toward arrangements of mutual benefit. Whatever the cause, Tomasello suggests that these traits arose in conditions of security and trust, which are then maintained whenever and wherever humans can continue to arrive at arrangements that reinforce collaborative activities through joint attention and mutual benefit.

---

[11] Bernard Yack, *The Problems of a Political Animal: Community, Justice, and Conflict in Aristotelian Political Thought* (Berkeley, CA: University of California Press, 1993), p. 71.

[12] Aristotle, *The Ethics of Aristotle: The Nicomachean Ethics*, J. A. K. Thomson, transl. (New York, NY: Penguin, 1976), p. 296 (*Ethics*, book 9, section 5).

[13] N. J. Enfield, *Relationship-Thinking: Agency, Enchrony, and Human Sociality* (New York, NY: Oxford University Press, 2013).

[14] Michael Tomasello, "Why Don't Apes Point?" in *Roots of Human Sociality*, ed. N. J. Enfield and Stephen C. Levinson (New York, NY: Berg, 2006), pp. 506–24; Michael Tomasello, *Why We Cooperate* (Boston, MA: MIT Press, 2009); and Michael Tomasello, *A Natural History of Human Thinking* (Cambridge, MA: Harvard University Press, 2014).

The patterns that archaeologist Joyce White and linguist N. J. Enfield found for Mainland Southeast Asia—patterns that showed pervasive diversity being harnessed for local projects that made and maintained social boundaries as these boundaries were crossed through interactions—point to some regional specificities and, at the same time, to some aspects of human nature. People are social beings; they come up with differences at the same time as they are capable of trading perspectives and inventing complementary roles that can generate various combinations of utility and pleasure.

Southeast Asia can serve as an example of long-term diversity at local and regional levels being sustained for various collaborative ends. So long as these arrangements are of mutual benefit, conditions of security and trust are maintained, and people grow up with a recognition of ethnic and other difference as a boundary marker and as an invitation to create something that exceeds whatever is available locally. The region has various historical and recent examples of things falling apart, and I have resisted any temptation to arrive at convictions regarding "the Thai" or "the state" as inherently hostile to the interests of Mien or any other ethnic minority in the hinterlands. Instead, I suggested that the "hinterland minority" position is a product of how certain modern nation states were fashioned on exclusive grounds and in ways that were socially rather damaging. Some of the cases suggest decades of political collapse; while I may write with some optimism, it does not come from ignorance of how societies may fall apart in conflict.

The tendencies of anthropologists and other scholars to focus on the cultures of ethnic groups led to an inflated notion of ethnic homogeneity and a tendency to view negotiation (across difference, as much as within a group) as somewhere between irrelevant and dangerous. Historian Joan W. Scott suggests that it is important to "[insist on] equality that rests on differences—differences that confound, disrupt, and render ambiguous the meaning of any fixed binary opposition. To do anything else is to buy into the political argument that sameness is a requirement for equality."[15]

The negotiation of ethnic frontiers in Southeast Asia past and present has produced workable arrangements that can and should be situated in an areal and historical perspective, along with cases of failure and political collapse. The similarities among the ways the Mien peoples have responded to spirits and to political overlords is one sign of a regional pattern, one that falls completely from view as long as what anthropologists study comes to be interpreted as expressions of ethnicity and culture (or the search for freedom in isolation), instead of manifesting cases of the political and other negotiation of difference more generally. One reason that this pattern was reproduced was that valley kings and other lowland rulers were interested in cultivating such relations, because of the benefits they promised. If that sounds utilitarian, then I suggest that among the benefits of such relations were conditions of familiarity, trust, and security that were the precondition for a trade in goods as much as in favors.

Mutual accountability in terms of agreed-upon expectations is foundational to play, cognition, political justice, and more. Finding creative and rewarding ways to come to terms with others, across difference, is a political matter. Insisting that equality does not come down to sameness but, in contrast, thrives on difference as a

---

[15] Joan W. Scott, *Gender and the Politics of History* (New York, NY: Columbia University Press, 1988), p. 177.

key factor motivating people to arrive at mutually beneficial solutions, is a critique of any ideology that insists on the priorities of any one nationality, ethnicity, or another social category at the cost of others. Any anthropological representation constitutes a potential intervention regarding what world people can imagine and experience. By calling attention to precolonial equivalences and to long-standing practices of negotiating difference in the Asian hinterlands, I am not out to lament the loss of a golden age. Instead, I insist that such equivalences are an everyday possibility that has often been made unthinkable by particular structures of knowledge, representation, and inequality.

Whereas certain predominant evolutionary narratives are anchored to antagonistic win-or-lose situations, the examples I selected show a different picture of mutual agreement, intersubjectivity, and the negotiation of difference. Using some Mien materials for a discussion of evolution, I called attention to their specificity as much as their general implications. My point is to deny evolutionary speculation that assumes that some groups will inevitably achieve more than others or that some people are more advanced than certain others. If the measure of evolution is, instead, equality, justice, and the harnessing of difference for creative projects of mutual benefit, then my Mien examples may enable another sense of self, other, and world, one that also insists that anthropologists be accountable for their representations beyond the narrow and self-serving confines of academia.

The case for Zomia—the fundamental tension between Southeast Asian states and the people who became highlanders—is, in my view, an oracle through which the readers can arrive at a sense of the world and themselves. Academic books can, when successful, serve a "status function," similar to what Tomasello described regarding how play-agreement among children sets certain identities and interaction in motion:

> Children form with another person a joint commitment to treat this stick as a horse. There they have created a status function. Such status functions, socially created in pretense, are precursors ontogenetically and perhaps phylogenetically to collective agreement that this piece of paper is money, or that person is president, with all the rights and obligations those agreements entail.[16]

Academic books may offer imaginary journeys across time and space, such as over thousands of years of Asian history, from which readers can derive their sense of the world, self, and more. I have aimed for something of the sort in this book. Insisting on the importance of diversity and negotiation, I have tried to influence with stories—historical tales, ethnographic reports, and other episodes at several frontiers of difference in China, Laos, Burma, Thailand, and the United States—what a reader can imagine and experience at the intersections of Southeast Asia, Western academia, society, and fantasy.

> [Vincent Crapanzano argues] that the "self" is an arrested development in the ongoing dialectical movement between self and other; that this arrest depends upon the typification of self and other through language; that the typification of

---

[16] Michael Tomasello, *Why We Cooperate*, p. 97.

other depends on a Third—a guarantor of meaning that permits the play of desire.[17]

In the Zomia-narrative, the best that highlanders could do was to run away and hide in their abodes of egalitarianism and freedom. To place now-marginal peoples inside history in any other way, it is necessary to undermine the logic and inevitability of this marginalization and separation. I have suggested that difference did not imply inequality but negotiation, and based my assertion on cases from China, Laos, Thailand, and the United States.

If knowledge is not about objective facts but significant facts—matters that must be negotiated with particular stakeholders and purposes in mind—then the premise and the questions shift. The "margins" do not describe or account for the position of Mien or any other hinterland peoples of Southeast Asia historically. Instead, Mien can be as central and as diverse as any other component in the region. The attraction of the term "highlanders" (or "hill tribes," Montagnards, and so forth) for anthropologists was that it provided an object of study and analysis—the means of establishing one's scholarly expertise. This expertise was anchored to a modernist perspective that assumed highland cultures to be ethnic, bounded, and traditional, suggesting that they would inevitably erode when confronted with modernity and national integration. I have instead alleged that the perspective obliterated various diversity, negotiation, and historically specific regional aspects of social life. This is not narrowly a point about Southeast Asia past or present, but about what kinds of knowledge and social imagination are possible at the intersections of Southeast Asia, academia, and the readers of academic books, in North America, in Europe, in Asia, and elsewhere.

In general, ethnographers did not focus on the contingency of twentieth-century separatist policies in Thailand, Burma, Vietnam, or Laos because their quest for a topic (ethnic groups) benefited from such divides; it produced what looked like pure samples. Shifting the attention to the normalcy and need for negotiations across difference brings out several issues. Among them are a) the pervasiveness of such engagements; b) the various reasons such accomplishments have seldom been included in the annals of lowland courts or have otherwise received public recognition; and c) the twentieth-century undoing of localized interethnic networks, a pattern of disintegration related to particular separatist policies of nation-building. On this front, the study of anthropological (and historical) practice has to be part of our field of inquiry. Like the people they write about and the people they write for, scholars can and perhaps should be historically situated.

Objectivism is no solution because it sidesteps questions regarding for whom knowledge is produced, on what grounds, and with what purpose. I try to write at an intersection of the interests of various Southeast Asian entities and peoples, including states and lowlanders, potential readers in the United States—which include Mien individuals, and also many who may have never heard of the Mien— and academics in anthropology, history, and political science. What there is to find in the anthropological or historical record in Mainland Southeast Asia depends on what one seeks, and this quest will necessarily be influenced by whom one aims to serve with the knowledge.

---

[17] Vincent Crapanzano, *Hermes' Dilemma and Hamlet's Desire: On the Epistemology of Interpretation* (Cambridge, MA: Harvard University Press, 1992), p. 72.

Regional anthropology may become more plausible and rewarding if we do not take an ethnic category as an object of study, but instead insist on recognizing any encounter as an individual case of what has happened in mainland Southeast Asia as a region. If one takes an area like Southeast Asia for a field, with no preconceived notions of what is "Southeast Asian," then there are several possible benefits to be gained. One is that this exposes questions of accountability and bias. For whom do we write, and what worlds become imaginable through the categories we use and the interactions we draw on as telling incidents of a pattern?

Do we respond to situations of political or social collapse by ignoring them, by describing pure ethnic groups and natural ethnic divides, say, or by offering our readers the opportunity to take sides, as tends to happen when we define Zomians in opposition to the state, or noble Hmong freedom fighters in opposition to the ignoble Hmong mercenaries? It seems to me more democratic and responsible—in the sense of balancing the interests of the peoples and places we write about, the potential interest of our outside readers, and those of academic practice—to assume some equivalence among these worlds and a potential slippage among them.

Any social formation involves the negotiation of difference and diversity; clear binaries may make readers blind to the possibility and urgency of such negotiations, whose results may be similar at home and away. Similarity is not sameness, but, rather, potential equivalence. Mien people are for me a "significant other" with whom I must try to trade places and perspectives to guard against appropriation.

Michael Tomasello draws on the work of George Herbert Mead to suggest that an evolutionary shift in human cognition took place: "whereas early humans internalized and referenced the perspective of what Mead calls the 'significant other,' modern humans internalized and referenced the perspective of the group as a whole, or any group member, Mead's 'generalized other.'"[18] I do not refute this assertion by insisting that, in my account, an awareness of different perspectives is of fundamental importance at the intersection of several partly distinct domains—those of academia, general readers within Western society, Southeast Asia past and present, and Mien peoples in various positions in China, Laos, Thailand, and the United States. But perhaps this "generalized other" is composed of the colleagues and readers for whom objective scientific facts are made, and that possibility makes me further insist that my others are specific, diverse, and significant.

It is human nature to depend on and derive both pleasure and utility from representation as well as from political negotiation, suggested Aristotle. As I understand the matter, human nature is not fate, limitations, or unequal advantage, but a social and everyday matter of representation, deliberation, purpose, negotiation, and interaction. In their versions of the ethnological record from the Asian hinterlands, academics and national governments suggest, for the most part, a natural setting inhabited by separate ethnic groups and marked by fundamental social divides. I call attention to such representation as something to contemplate and learn from regarding the relations of academics to their peoples—those they write about and those they write for. Where can we go, with whom, and for what? Any negotiation of difference and diversity may invite tension. From this angle, anthropological representation involves similar risks, as do politics and play; there may be no neutral or objective way to tell the three apart:

---

[18] Michael Tomasello, *A Natural History of Human Thinking*, pp. 122–23, citing G. H. Mead's *Mind, Self, and Society* (Chicago, IL: University of Chicago Press, 1934).

Among the general characteristics of play [are] tension and uncertainty. There is always the question: "will it come off?" Tension and uncertainty as to the outcome increase enormously when the antithetical element becomes really antagonistic in the play of groups. The passion to win sometimes threatens to obliterate the levity proper to a game.[19]

---

[19] Johan Huizinga, *Homo Ludens: A Study of the Play Element in Culture* (Boston, MA: Beacon Press, 1950), p. 47.

INDEX

SOUTHEAST ASIA PROGRAM PUBLICATIONS
Cornell University

Studies on Southeast Asia

Number 64   *Slow Anthropology: Negotiating Difference with the Iu Mien*, Hjorleifur Jonsson. 2014. ISBN 978-0-87727-764-4 (pb.)

Number 63   *Exploration and Irony in Studies of Siam over Forty Years*, Benedict R. O'G. Anderson. 2014. ISBN 978-0-87727-763-7 (pb.)

Number 62   *Ties that Bind: Cultural Identity, Class, and Law in Vietnam's Labor Resistance*, Trần Ngọc Angie. 2013. ISBN 978-0-87727-762-0 (pb.)

Number 61   *A Mountain of Difference: The Lumad in Early Colonial Mindanao*, Oona Paredes. 2013. ISBN 978-0-87727-761-3 (pb.)

Number 60   *The* Kim Vân Kieu *of Nguyen Du (1765–1820)*, trans. Vladislav Zhukov. 2013. ISBN 978-0-87727-760-6 (pb.)

Number 59   *The Politics of Timor-Leste: Democratic Consolidation after Intervention*, ed. Michael Leach and Damien Kingsbury. 2013. ISBN 978-0-87727-759-0 (pb.)

Number 58   *The Spirit of Things: Materiality and Religious Diversity in Southeast Asia*, ed. Julius Bautista. 2012. ISBN 970-0-87727-758-3 (pb.)

Number 57   *Demographic Change in Southeast Asia: Recent Histories and Future Directions*, ed. Lindy Williams and Michael Philip Guest. 2012. ISBN 978-0-87727-757-6 (pb.)

Number 56   *Modern and Contemporary Southeast Asian Art: An Anthology*, ed. Nora A. Taylor and Boreth Ly. 2012. ISBN 978-0-87727-756-9 (pb.)

Number 55   *Glimpses of Freedom: Independent Cinema in Southeast Asia*, ed. May Adadol Ingawanij and Benjamin McKay. 2012. ISBN 978-0-87727-755-2 (pb.)

Number 54   *Student Activism in Malaysia: Crucible, Mirror, Sideshow*, Meredith L. Weiss. 2011. ISBN 978-0-87727-754-5 (pb.)

Number 53   *Political Authority and Provincial Identity in Thailand: The Making of Banharn-buri*, Yoshinori Nishizaki. 2011. ISBN 978-0-87727-753-8 (pb.)

Number 52   *Vietnam and the West: New Approaches*, ed. Wynn Wilcox. 2010. ISBN 978-0-87727-752-1 (pb.)

Number 51   *Cultures at War: The Cold War and Cultural Expression in Southeast Asia*, ed. Tony Day and Maya H. T. Liem. 2010. ISBN 978-0-87727-751-4 (pb.)

Number 50   *State of Authority: The State in Society in Indonesia*, ed. Gerry van Klinken and Joshua Barker. 2009. ISBN 978-0-87727-750-7 (pb.)

Number 49   *Phan Châu Trinh and His Political Writings*, Phan Châu Trinh, ed. and trans. Vinh Sinh. 2009. ISBN 978-0-87727-749-1 (pb.)

Number 48   *Dependent Communities: Aid and Politics in Cambodia and East Timor*, Caroline Hughes. 2009. ISBN 978-0-87727-748-4 (pb.)

Number 47   *A Man Like Him: Portrait of the Burmese Journalist, Journal Kyaw U Chit Maung*, Journal Kyaw Ma Ma Lay, trans. Ma Thanegi, 2008. ISBN 978-0-87727-747-7 (pb.)

Number 46   *At the Edge of the Forest: Essays on Cambodia, History, and Narrative in Honor of David Chandler*, ed. Anne Ruth Hansen and Judy Ledgerwood. 2008. ISBN 978-0-87727-746-0 (pb).

Number 45   *Conflict, Violence, and Displacement in Indonesia*, ed. Eva-Lotta E. Hedman. 2008. ISBN 978-0-87727-745-3 (pb).

Number 44   *Friends and Exiles: A Memoir of the Nutmeg Isles and the Indonesian Nationalist Movement*, Des Alwi, ed. Barbara S. Harvey. 2008. ISBN 978-0-877277-44-6 (pb).

Number 43   *Early Southeast Asia: Selected Essays*, O. W. Wolters, ed. Craig J. Reynolds. 2008. 255 pp. ISBN 978-0-877277-43-9 (pb).

Number 42   *Thailand: The Politics of Despotic Paternalism* (revised edition), Thak Chaloemtiarana. 2007. 284 pp. ISBN 0-8772-7742-7 (pb).

Number 41   *Views of Seventeenth-Century Vietnam: Christoforo Borri on Cochinchina and Samuel Baron on Tonkin*, ed. Olga Dror and K. W. Taylor. 2006. 290 pp. ISBN 0-8772-7741-9 (pb).

Number 40   *Laskar Jihad: Islam, Militancy, and the Quest for Identity in Post-New Order Indonesia*, Noorhaidi Hasan. 2006. 266 pp. ISBN 0-877277-40-0 (pb).

Number 39   *The Indonesian Supreme Court: A Study of Institutional Collapse*, Sebastiaan Pompe. 2005. 494 pp. ISBN 0-877277-38-9 (pb).

Number 38   *Spirited Politics: Religion and Public Life in Contemporary Southeast Asia*, ed. Andrew C. Willford and Kenneth M. George. 2005. 210 pp. ISBN 0-87727-737-0.

Number 37   *Sumatran Sultanate and Colonial State: Jambi and the Rise of Dutch Imperialism, 1830-1907*, Elsbeth Locher-Scholten, trans. Beverley Jackson. 2004. 332 pp. ISBN 0-87727-736-2.

Number 36   *Southeast Asia over Three Generations: Essays Presented to Benedict R. O'G. Anderson*, ed. James T. Siegel and Audrey R. Kahin. 2003. 398 pp. ISBN 0-87727-735-4.

Number 35   *Nationalism and Revolution in Indonesia*, George McTurnan Kahin, intro. Benedict R. O'G. Anderson (reprinted from 1952 edition, Cornell University Press, with permission). 2003. 530 pp. ISBN 0-87727-734-6.

Number 34   *Golddiggers, Farmers, and Traders in the "Chinese Districts" of West Kalimantan, Indonesia*, Mary Somers Heidhues. 2003. 316 pp. ISBN 0-87727-733-8.

Number 33   *Opusculum de Sectis apud Sinenses et Tunkinenses (A Small Treatise on the Sects among the Chinese and Tonkinese): A Study of Religion in China and North Vietnam in the Eighteenth Century*, Father Adriano de St. Thecla, trans. Olga Dror, with Mariya Berezovska. 2002. 363 pp. ISBN 0-87727-732-X.

Number 32   *Fear and Sanctuary: Burmese Refugees in Thailand*, Hazel J. Lang. 2002. 204 pp. ISBN 0-87727-731-1.

Number 31   *Modern Dreams: An Inquiry into Power, Cultural Production, and the Cityscape in Contemporary Urban Penang, Malaysia*, Beng-Lan Goh. 2002. 225 pp. ISBN 0-87727-730-3.

Number 30   *Violence and the State in Suharto's Indonesia*, ed. Benedict R. O'G. Anderson. 2001. Second printing, 2002. 247 pp. ISBN 0-87727-729-X.

Number 9   *Southeast Asian Capitalists,* ed. Ruth McVey. 1992. 2nd printing 1993.
               220 pp. ISBN 0-87727-708-7.

Number 8   *The Politics of Colonial Exploitation: Java, the Dutch, and the Cultivation
               System,* Cornelis Fasseur, ed. R. E. Elson, trans. R. E. Elson, Ary Kraal.
               1992. 2nd printing 1994. 266 pp. ISBN 0-87727-707-9.

Number 7   *A Malay Frontier: Unity and Duality in a Sumatran Kingdom,* Jane
               Drakard. 1990. 2nd printing 2003. 215 pp. ISBN 0-87727-706-0.

Number 6   *Trends in Khmer Art,* Jean Boisselier, ed. Natasha Eilenberg, trans.
               Natasha Eilenberg, Melvin Elliott. 1989. 124 pp., 24 plates.
               ISBN 0-87727-705-2.

Number 5   *Southeast Asian Ephemeris: Solar and Planetary Positions, A.D. 638–2000,*
               J. C. Eade. 1989. 175 pp. ISBN 0-87727-704-4.

Number 3   *Thai Radical Discourse: The Real Face of Thai Feudalism Today,* Craig J.
               Reynolds. 1987. 2nd printing 1994. 186 pp. ISBN 0-87727-702-8.

Number 1   *The Symbolism of the Stupa,* Adrian Snodgrass. 1985. Revised with
               index, 1988. 3rd printing 1998. 469 pp. ISBN 0-87727-700-1.

SEAP Series

Number 23   *Possessed by the Spirits: Mediumship in Contemporary Vietnamese
               Communities.* 2006. 186 pp. ISBN 0-877271-41-0 (pb).

Number 22   *The Industry of Marrying Europeans,* Vũ Trọng Phụng, trans. Thúy
               Tranviet. 2006. 66 pp. ISBN 0-877271-40-2 (pb).

Number 21   *Securing a Place: Small-Scale Artisans in Modern Indonesia,* Elizabeth
               Morrell. 2005. 220 pp. ISBN 0-877271-39-9.

Number 20   *Southern Vietnam under the Reign of Minh Mạng (1820-1841): Central
               Policies and Local Response,* Choi Byung Wook. 2004. 226pp. ISBN 0-0-
               877271-40-2.

Number 19   *Gender, Household, State: Đổi Mới in Việt Nam,* ed. Jayne Werner and
               Danièle Bélanger. 2002. 151 pp. ISBN 0-87727-137-2.

Number 18   *Culture and Power in Traditional Siamese Government,* Neil A. Englehart.
               2001. 130 pp. ISBN 0-87727-135-6.

Number 17   *Gangsters, Democracy, and the State,* ed. Carl A. Trocki. 1998. Second
               printing, 2002. 94 pp. ISBN 0-87727-134-8.

Number 16   *Cutting across the Lands: An Annotated Bibliography on Natural Resource
               Management and Community Development in Indonesia, the Philippines,
               and Malaysia,* ed. Eveline Ferretti. 1997. 329 pp. ISBN 0-87727-133-X.

Number 15   *The Revolution Falters: The Left in Philippine Politics after 1986,* ed.
               Patricio N. Abinales. 1996. Second printing, 2002. 182 pp. ISBN 0-
               87727-132-1.

Number 14   *Being Kammu: My Village, My Life,* Damrong Tayanin. 1994. 138 pp., 22
               tables, illus., maps. ISBN 0-87727-130-5.

Number 13   *The American War in Vietnam,* ed. Jayne Werner, David Hunt. 1993.
               132 pp. ISBN 0-87727-131-3.

Number 12   *The Voice of Young Burma,* Aye Kyaw. 1993. 92 pp. ISBN 0-87727-129-1.

Number 11   *The Political Legacy of Aung San*, ed. Josef Silverstein. Revised edition 1993. 169 pp. ISBN 0-87727-128-3.

Number 10   *Studies on Vietnamese Language and Literature: A Preliminary Bibliography*, Nguyen Dinh Tham. 1992. 227 pp. ISBN 0-87727-127-5.

Number 8   *From PKI to the Comintern, 1924–1941: The Apprenticeship of the Malayan Communist Party*, Cheah Boon Kheng. 1992. 147 pp. ISBN 0-87727-125-9.

Number 7   *Intellectual Property and US Relations with Indonesia, Malaysia, Singapore, and Thailand*, Elisabeth Uphoff. 1991. 67 pp. ISBN 0-87727-124-0.

Number 6   *The Rise and Fall of the Communist Party of Burma (CPB)*, Bertil Lintner. 1990. 124 pp. 26 illus., 14 maps. ISBN 0-87727-123-2.

Number 5   *Japanese Relations with Vietnam: 1951–1987*, Masaya Shiraishi. 1990. 174 pp. ISBN 0-87727-122-4.

Number 3   *Postwar Vietnam: Dilemmas in Socialist Development*, ed. Christine White, David Marr. 1988. 2nd printing 1993. 260 pp. ISBN 0-87727-120-8.

Number 2   *The Dobama Movement in Burma (1930–1938)*, Khin Yi. 1988. 160 pp. ISBN 0-87727-118-6.

Cornell Modern Indonesia Project Publications

Number 76   *Producing Indonesia: The State of the Field of Indonesian Studies*, ed. Eric Tagliacozzo. 2014. ISBN 978-0-87727-302-8 (pb.)

All Following CMIP titles available at http://cmip.library.cornell.edu

Number 75   *A Tour of Duty: Changing Patterns of Military Politics in Indonesia in the 1990s.* Douglas Kammen and Siddharth Chandra. 1999. 99 pp. ISBN 0-87763-049-6.

Number 74   *The Roots of Acehnese Rebellion 1989–1992*, Tim Kell. 1995. 103 pp. ISBN 0-87763-040-2.

Number 72   *Popular Indonesian Literature of the Qur'an*, Howard M. Federspiel. 1994. 170 pp. ISBN 0-87763-038-0.

Number 71   *A Javanese Memoir of Sumatra, 1945–1946: Love and Hatred in the Liberation War*, Takao Fusayama. 1993. 150 pp. ISBN 0-87763-037-2.

Number 69   *The Road to Madiun: The Indonesian Communist Uprising of 1948*, Elizabeth Ann Swift. 1989. 120 pp. ISBN 0-87763-035-6.

Number 68   *Intellectuals and Nationalism in Indonesia: A Study of the Following Recruited by Sutan Sjahrir in Occupation Jakarta*, J. D. Legge. 1988. 159 pp. ISBN 0-87763-034-8.

Number 67   *Indonesia Free: A Biography of Mohammad Hatta*, Mavis Rose. 1987. 252 pp. ISBN 0-87763-033-X.

Number 66   *Prisoners at Kota Cane*, Leon Salim, trans. Audrey Kahin. 1986. 112 pp. ISBN 0-87763-032-1.

Number 64   *Suharto and His Generals: Indonesia's Military Politics, 1975–1983*, David Jenkins. 1984. 4th printing 1997. 300 pp. ISBN 0-87763-030-5.

Number 62	*Interpreting Indonesian Politics: Thirteen Contributions to the Debate, 1964–1981,* ed. Benedict Anderson, Audrey Kahin, intro. Daniel S. Lev. 1982. 3rd printing 1991. 172 pp. ISBN 0-87763-028-3.
Number 60	*The Minangkabau Response to Dutch Colonial Rule in the Nineteenth Century,* Elizabeth E. Graves. 1981. 157 pp. ISBN 0-87763-000-3.
Number 57	*Permesta: Half a Rebellion,* Barbara S. Harvey. 1977. 174 pp. ISBN 0-87763-003-8.
Number 52	*A Preliminary Analysis of the October 1 1965, Coup in Indonesia (Prepared in January 1966),* Benedict R. Anderson, Ruth T. McVey, assist. Frederick P. Bunnell. 1971. 3rd printing 1990. 174 pp. ISBN 0-87763-008-9.
Number 48	*Nationalism, Islam and Marxism,* Soekarno, intro. Ruth T. McVey. 1970.
Number 37	*Mythology and the Tolerance of the Javanese,* Benedict R. O'G. Anderson. 2nd edition, 1996. Reprinted 2004. 104 pp., 65 illus. ISBN 0-87763-041-0.

Copublished Titles

The Ambiguous Allure of the West: Traces of the Colonial in Thailand, ed. Rachel V. Harrison and Peter A. Jackson. Copublished with Hong Kong University Press. 2010. ISBN 978-0-87727-608-1 (pb.)

The Many Ways of Being Muslim: Fiction by Muslim Filipinos, ed. Coeli Barry. Copublished with Anvil Publishing, Inc., the Philippines. 2008. ISBN 978-0-87727-605-0 (pb.)

Language Texts

INDONESIAN

Beginning Indonesian through Self-Instruction, John U. Wolff, Dédé Oetomo, Daniel Fietkiewicz. 3rd revised edition 1992. Vol. 1. 115 pp. ISBN 0-87727-529-7. Vol. 2. 434 pp. ISBN 0-87727-530-0. Vol. 3. 473 pp. ISBN 0-87727-531-9.

Indonesian Readings, John U. Wolff. 1978. 4th printing 1992. 480 pp. ISBN 0-87727-517-3

Indonesian Conversations, John U. Wolff. 1978. 3rd printing 1991. 297 pp. ISBN 0-87727-516-5

Formal Indonesian, John U. Wolff. 2nd revised edition 1986. 446 pp. ISBN 0-87727-515-7

TAGALOG

Pilipino through Self-Instruction, John U. Wolff, Maria Theresa C. Centeno, Der-Hwa V. Rau. 1991. Vol. 1. 342 pp. ISBN 0-87727—525-4. Vol. 2., revised 2005, 378 pp. ISBN 0-87727-526-2. Vol 3., revised 2005, 431 pp. ISBN 0-87727-527-0. Vol. 4. 306 pp. ISBN 0-87727-528-9.

THAI

A. U. A. Language Center Thai Course, J. Marvin Brown. Originally published by the American University Alumni Association Language Center, 1974. Reissued by Cornell Southeast Asia Program, 1991, 1992. Book 1. 267 pp. ISBN 0-87727-506-8. Book 2. 288 pp. ISBN 0-87727-507-6. Book 3. 247 pp. ISBN 0-87727-508-4.

A. U. A. Language Center Thai Course, Reading and Writing Text (mostly reading), 1979. Reissued 1997. 164 pp. ISBN 0-87727-511-4.

A. U. A. Language Center Thai Course, Reading and Writing Workbook (mostly writing), 1979. Reissued 1997. 99 pp. ISBN 0-87727-512-2.

KHMER

Cambodian System of Writing and Beginning Reader, Franklin E. Huffman. Originally published by Yale University Press, 1970. Reissued by Cornell Southeast Asia Program, 4th printing 2002. 365 pp. ISBN 0-300-01314-0.

Modern Spoken Cambodian, Franklin E. Huffman, assist. Charan Promchan, Chhom-Rak Thong Lambert. Originally published by Yale University Press, 1970. Reissued by Cornell Southeast Asia Program, 3rd printing 1991. 451 pp. ISBN 0-300-01316-7.

Intermediate Cambodian Reader, ed. Franklin E. Huffman, assist. Im Proum. Originally published by Yale University Press, 1972. Reissued by Cornell Southeast Asia Program, 1988. 499 pp. ISBN 0-300-01552-6.

Cambodian Literary Reader and Glossary, Franklin E. Huffman, Im Proum. Originally published by Yale University Press, 1977. Reissued by Cornell Southeast Asia Program, 1988. 494 pp. ISBN 0-300-02069-4.

HMONG

White Hmong-English Dictionary, Ernest E. Heimbach. 1969. 8th printing, 2002. 523 pp. ISBN 0-87727-075-9.

VIETNAMESE

Intermediate Spoken Vietnamese, Franklin E. Huffman, Tran Trong Hai. 1980. 3rd printing 1994. ISBN 0-87727-500-9.

Proto-Austronesian Phonology with Glossary, John U. Wolff, 2 volumes, 2011. ISBN vol. I, 978-0-87727-532-9. ISBN vol. II, 978-0-87727-533-6.

To order, please contact:
Mail:
Cornell University Press Services
750 Cascadilla Street
PO Box 6525
Ithaca, NY 14851 USA

E-mail: orderbook@cupserv.org

Phone/Fax, Monday–Friday, 8 am – 5 pm (Eastern US):
Phone: 607 277 2211 or 800 666 2211 (US, Canada)
Fax: 607 277 6292 or 800 688 2877 (US, Canada)

Order through our online bookstore at:
SEAP.einaudi.cornell.edu/publications